JEFF BUCKLEY

FROM HALLELUJAH
TO THE LAST GOODBYE

JEFF BUCKLEY

FROM HALLELUJAH TO THE LAST GOODBYE

DAVE LORY
WITH
JIM IRVIN

Post Hill Press

A POST HILL PRESS BOOK

Jeff Buckley:
From Hallelujah to the Last Goodbye

First Post Hill Press Hardcover Edition: May 2018

ISBN: 979-8-88845-834-1

Cover art by Ryan Truso
Cover photo by Merri Cyr
Interior Design and Composition by Greg Johnson, Textbook Perfect

Post Hill Press
New York • Nashville
posthillpress.com

Published in the United States of America

This book is dedicated to the memory of Jeff Buckley,
who gave me the opportunity to witness—and contribute to,
in a small way—some of the greatest moments in music history.
I miss jumping off those cliffs with you, my friend.
Without you, I would never have met my wife,
nor had my two beautiful daughters.
Samantha and I miss you each and every day.
Here's to eternal life.

CONTENTS

INTRODUCTION

Sunday, October 10, 1993

The guy's late. I don't really need this. I don't care how much buzz there is about him. I'm fried from booking the New Music Seminar—the largest music conference in the world—which has just finished, and there are a whole lot of things I could be doing with my Sunday morning: watching football, doing my laundry. I hate having to wear my work suit on a Sunday. I don't really want to get into a management situation with an attorney, and I resent people jerking me around by being late.

But the sun is shining; St. Mark's Place is humming gently after the usual Saturday-night maelstrom. It's quiet in here; the brunch crowd hasn't come out yet. This coffee's pretty good, and George Stein, my ex-lawyer, who has been acting as this kid's manager, is taking care of the conversation. I'll smoke another cigarette and then I'll leave.

George has seen him. He's standing up to welcome him.

"Hey, Jeff!"

He's cute. Not tall, only about five foot eight. Hair cropped short, stuffed under a fedora. Rumpled looking. Like he was asleep ten minutes ago. Black jeans and a white V-neck T-shirt, scuffed Doc Marten boots and a keychain tucked into his pocket. Good-looking kid, but forty-five fucking minutes late. That's just rude.

George isn't a hugger. He shakes the guy's hand and introduces us. "Good to see you. This is Dave Lory. Dave, Jeff Buckley."

We shake hands. He says hello in the softest voice and apologizes for being late. He orders a cappuccino.

George is doing all the talking. He's into his sales pitch:

"Dave, you have to understand that if you're involved, Jeff is a huge priority for Columbia. All the labels were bidding on him. Jeff came to me to get him off the Imago deal and I'm his manager, but I need someone to take the touring role and you have that experience."

I'm biting my lip. George is implying I'm just a tour manager. I've just come off managing Gregg Allman and Ronnie Spector. I brought the Allman Brothers Band back after ten years away and co-managed them for five years, with Danny Goldberg, who's managing Nirvana at this moment. I know my way around.

George continues. "Jeff's first release is an EP, *Live at Sin-é*, that's coming out next month. Recorded at that Irish café down the street. It's great. He does two of his own songs and covers Van Morrison and Edith Piaf. It's very eclectic, very Jeff. We wanted something that showcased his voice, showed how he is in front of a crowd."

"Crowd" is a stretch. Sin-é holds about forty people.[1] He starts telling me about how all these other managers wanted to work with him, but I know they all turned George down. I'm feeling like some kind of last resort. And he's talking like he's the boss, but I know that Columbia insisted George get a partner and that's why he's taking these meetings.

I'm a fan of planning. It sounds as if all the planning's coming from the record company. Columbia is a good label, but that's not okay. It should be the artist and his management calling the shots.

Meanwhile, this kid's saying nothing. Just nodding his head occasionally. He drinks his coffee, and when he does speak it's in this soft, almost feminine voice. George rambles on about how great Jeff is and how much great stuff he's done for him, for about half an hour. Then he announces he is leaving so we can visit alone. Decent of him. He pays the check, shakes our hands again, and goes.

"I have a pet peeve," I say once George has gone.

"Oh yeah?" says Jeff.

"Lateness." I hand him a piece of paper with my bio, a list of the things I've done in the business, and the acts I've managed.

Why am I so upset with him just for being late? Perhaps because I really don't want to co-manage an artist with George Stein. Managing

[1] Sin-é (pronounced "shin-AY") is Gaelic for "That's it."

Photo by Jim Irvin

122 St. Mark's Place, New York City. The site of Sin-é in 2017.

the Allmans with Danny Goldberg was okay; he was experienced and we complemented each other. With George, a lawyer who's never managed a rock act before, I figure I'll be doing all the work and making half the money, so I don't care about blowing this kid off. I agreed to take a meeting on my precious Sunday, and he couldn't be bothered to show up on time. He is already behaving like a wild horse that needs someone to jerk the reins. There's a lack of structure to this whole deal.

"Look, I don't care what George says," I say, as he looks at my bio. "I'm not a tour manager. I have other options. If you want to work with me, I'll put together a plan for you—it'll take a few weeks to get to know you and what you want—and then we'll follow that plan together. Piss-poor planning equals piss-poor results. The record company doesn't dictate what's to be done. That has to come from you and your team. Anyway, I've got somewhere else I'd rather be right now. The football ain't gonna watch itself."

I get up and leave.

I've gone about thirty feet down St. Mark's Place when Jeff catches up with me.

"You're the first person that hasn't kissed my ass," he says.

"Listen, man," I say. "If I were you, I'd be scared, because with all the hype I'm hearing about you, the industry could very easily chew you up and spit you out."

His head tilts almost imperceptibly to one side.

"Can we start over? Come back inside and let's talk about that."

"Okay," I say. I'm no use until I've had at least two coffees anyway.

We start talking about music. Jeff says he's a fan of the Allmans; he asks about my time managing them. He's delighted I toured with Savatage, Megadeth, and Dio in the 1980s.

"I love all that '80s metal shit," he says, laughing. "Did you ever work with Van Halen?" I tell him about the time I worked with Harriet Vidal on Prince's *Purple Rain* tour; she was Van Halen's first publicist, so I went out with Roth one night in New York. We went to the Limelight, had a bunch of fun.

Jeff laughs gleefully, suddenly getting excited as he describes seeing a Van Halen show in LA. He recalls Roth's prowling the stage and doing the most clichéd leap off the drum riser. "It was so bad it was badass," he says. "But Eddie was the don."

"Eddie's incredible," I say.

"I spent three days straight learning how to play the solo in 'Hot For Teacher,'" Jeff says, almost bashfully. He looks up at me from beneath his eyelashes. He's working me.

"You should try playing those drums at the start," I say. "I spent weeks perfecting those!" I tell him about my time drumming in cover bands in my twenties.

He knows so much music. He's talking about metal and jazz and Pakistani singers, all kinds of music. I wasn't expecting this. I don't really know much about Tim Buckley, but I assumed his son would be some kind of folk singer. I didn't expect someone who was keeping up with Eddie Van Halen, Sun Ra, and Nina Simone.

What the hell is this guy's music like? I suppose I'd better listen to some of it.

Sunday, May 28, 2017

I went through every emotion on my ride with Jeff Buckley, one of the defining rock voices of his generation—perhaps of all time. At the launch of his career, his impact was subtle. Great buzz, great reviews, and a gentle uptake as far as the spreadsheets were concerned, but on the ground it was like nothing I'd ever seen. Jeff was so good that people wouldn't just tell their friends; they'd radiate like they'd had a religious experience. Gradually, clubs, theaters, festivals, and cities—the fans in Paris, London, Sydney, and others—fell under the spell of this artist, and I was managing his career. Forty-four unforgettable months of triumph, failure, hysterical laughter, blazing rows, schemes, dreams, and deepening friendship. And then it was tragically cut short.

I'd come from a world where rock music functioned like a traveling circus. Jeff didn't come out of the same mold, and he didn't want to do things the old-school way. I had to adjust my sense of what a rock star was, adapt my methods of managing an artist. Jeff and I grew together as we flew together, and kept together when the engines began to sputter. We felt fearless, so when it was suddenly over, and all that promise was snuffed out, it hurt more than you can imagine, more than anything I've ever known.

One weekend, a couple of years ago, something drew me into the storage room where I kept boxes marked "Jeff Buckley" that had sat there, taped shut, since a lawsuit between myself, his estate, and Sony Entertainment. As I went through that archive of photos and paperwork, fading faxes and weighty contracts, I was overwhelmed by emotion. I realized almost twenty years had passed since that awful day, and I was still dealing with it. (I'm writing these words a day before the twentieth anniversary.) Apart from occasions with close family and friends who had joined me on this ride, I hadn't been able to really discuss what I felt

Photo by Merri Cyr

Official publicity shot for the EP and tour for Live at Sin-é.

about Jeff. The facts behind his death and its aftermath were so bizarre and unexpected, it's no wonder I couldn't process them. I have mostly refused to talk about my time with this unique artist. I found it too painful to revisit, but now I'm ready to tell my side of his story.

He was effectively taken away from me twice, once when he died and again when his mother, Mary Guibert, who took control of his estate, sacked the people who'd been closest to his career. For a long time, I knew that anything I said or wrote in public would come from a place of anger and resentment, injustice, just being pissed at fate, at death, at the music business, at lawyers, and at mothers with their own agendas. Luckily, I was self-aware enough to know that my anger wouldn't do me—or Jeff—any favors. I've always wanted to do whatever was best for his memory and the things we achieved together.

We worked on raw instinct. Sometimes we did things in a screwy way, did the opposite of what people expected. We weren't always right, but we made those decisions together and knew they were right for us, for him, for the good of his sanity, his career, and his personal integrity. We had a catchphrase for whenever we made one of those crazy leaps into the unknown: "You did pack a parachute, right?" And we'd laugh, knowing that neither of us knew how hard the landing was going to be this time.

I couldn't bear to listen to his music again until recently. I went through all the stages of bereavement with the added weight of responsibility. I should have actually packed that parachute. I've worked with plenty of party animals, drug-and-booze-addled musical geniuses who somehow couldn't rustle up a brain cell to work out what a hash they were making of their lives with a needle or a bottle or a groupie—or all three. But that wasn't Jeff; though he was no stranger to the clichés of a rocker's life, that wasn't what defined him. He was driven by something purer than that. We had another saying we would repeat to each other, our code of honor, that summed up what drove Jeff: "It's about the music, stupid!" We used this phrase throughout the time we worked together. It was our way of answering the question, "Should we do this or not?" Music made everything make sense.

When Jeff was on form, was flying, you could feel your life altering while you listened. I've seen fan mail from school kids, international statesmen, and prisoners on death row. All of them encountered something in Jeff's music, in his sole completed album, *Grace*, which spoke to them in a way no other music could, which transported them somewhere. Many fans describe a similar experience: discovering that album and listening to it over and over, at first with curiosity, then in awe or disbelief, and then, after dozens of plays, finding that it functioned as some sort of musical guru, confidant, or healer. The music Jeff most admired did the same for him.

During my first encounter with him, in that café on St. Mark's Place, I knew Jeff Buckley was a star. And he had a vulnerability that I recognized; I saw my own damaged innocence in him, and I wanted to protect him. Sensing his fears of being buried or controlled by a record label, I reassured him he would not be harmed with me involved.

The only time I felt Jeff was truly happy was when he was onstage, where he felt free, where he said, "I can forget my own name." Offstage he was restless. He had to face cold reality, deal with the sometimes self-exerted pressures he was under, and with his "family situation," as he would call it. He hated the spotlight and never wanted to be a celebrity, but he wanted to sell records; he wanted his music to be heard.

You think of the manager as the guy with the baseball bat who runs off with all the money, right? Perhaps my story can enlighten you, show you the day-to-day reality of managing a genius. I didn't always get it right. The hardest part about being a manager is accepting that you cannot simply fix an artist and that, despite whatever comfort you can offer, there are certain times artists will naturally struggle with the job, and with themselves. If you're a songwriter, you need to draw from the well of your experience for material; therefore, the act of writing inevitably stirs up memories you find painful.

I stirred up some memories myself, going through those boxes. In this book I'm going to share them with you, recall some key episodes in our time together, show you how the relationship between an artist and a manager works, and bring together the stories of people who witnessed other sides of Jeff under different circumstances, hopefully to provide you with an understanding of the charismatic, complicated grace of Jeff Buckley and what it was like for those who walked or worked at his side.

CHAPTER 1

Hallelujah

BEFORE I TELL YOU about my time with Jeff Buckley, I'd like to bring in some people who knew him before I did, to tell the story up to my arrival in December 1993. Let's begin with Jeff himself.

Jeff Buckley[2]

I was born in Martin Luther King Hospital in Los Angeles, California, on November 17, 1966, at 6:49 in the morning. I think I'm Scorpio with Scorpio rising. Your place or mine?

My mom was 18 at the time, and we lived in a lot of places pretty much from then on. It was a big struggle for her to take care of me and be a mom at the same time, like she'd have to take care of me by going to work in other cities, and I'd be raised by my grandmother and my uncle and my aunt Peggy.

My mom was the most musical of the three kids. Uncle George sings and he had a big influence—he was the first guy I ever saw sleep late, have a band in the garage and the killer girlfriend and the killer car.

My grandmother and my mother came over from Panama in 1950. My grandmother raised me first, and she sang me little Spanish songs.

When I was about five or six I found my grandmother had an acoustic guitar that she got in the hope that one of her children would start to

[2] Interview for *Grace* electronic press kit, February 1993.

play it, but it sat there until they became adults, and then I found it and I strummed on it but mostly I just put my marbles on it.

I met my father, Tim, for the first time when I was about eight. I met him for a week, Easter vacation. Lost contact with him in between his visit and his death. No calls were returned. Saw an obituary. The end.

I had my first band when I was 13. I moved up to Willits, California, to spend the year with my stepfather, Ronald, and that was the same year I got my first electric guitar, a black Memphis Les Paul copy, and that was cool. Anyway, I went up there and fell in with the wrong crowd and got a band together.

At that time in Los Angeles, I was about 18, 19, I was in a few bands at once, trying to make money. I would shy away from filling out job applications, because you always had to fill out your high school, your elementary, and there were so many it was just too embarrassing. If I wanted to earn my salt as a musician, I just had to play music all the time. So I did. And as usual, whether you're a musician, a writer, or a catamaran sailor, you pretty much start out by doing the most demeaning work you'll ever do in your life.

I first came to New York in 1990. I just sold everything and split Los Angeles. I had been living in Southern California most of my life. Never fit in. I walked, talked, ate, drank, fell in love and out of love faster than anybody I ever knew. I just never fitted. I moved in February 1990. Lived with my friend Brooke. Spent a year starving on Ninth Street. And then I went back to LA to record a four-song demo, ran out of money, and couldn't get back for a while. Then I came back, fell in love, and moved back for good last year. I'm never leaving; I'm done with going away. It's the greatest place in the world, New York.

Steve Berkowitz

Vice president of marketing and A&R, at Columbia Records

I joined Columbia in 1987. I'd started out as a musician in Boston, a kid in the mid-1960s playing guitar in British invasion cover bands and blues-rock bands. I studied jazz with the great drummer Max Roach. I worked on college radio, in record stores, and booked various clubs. I started tour managing in 1977. A guy I worked with told me about The Cars. I knew Elliot Easton a little—I'd played guitar with him—and I went out as their tour manager around the first album, and by the second album I was their acting manager and joined Lookout Management, Elliot Roberts and David Geffen's company, where I also worked with Ministry and Devo, Joni Mitchell and Neil Young.

In 1986, I managed a Boston band called Push Push and signed a demo deal with them at Columbia, who became more interested in me than the band. [They asked me] to work there in a marketing role, right at the end of the Walter Yetnikof and Al Teller era, when the record business was the largest it ever was. When I arrived, in June 1987, I spent a great week hanging out at a no-holds-barred Sony convention in Vancouver with a guy called Gary Lucas, who was writing copy for the CBS ad department. We became friends.

I started working on re-issues, the Robert Johnson boxed set and Bob Dylan's *Biograph*. Pretty soon I was doing A&R [artists and repertoire]. Because I'd worked on a number of projects that were out of left field and had made money, I had the ear of all parts, like the sales department or the international department. So by the time I met Jeff Buckley, I had really started to understand what this organism of corporation could do.

I first heard about him through Chris Dowd of Fishbone. I was Fishbone's new A&R man, and Jeff was Chris's roommate. Chris said, "You gotta hear my roommate sing." This would be about 1991. And he played me a tape of him and Jeff in their living room doing Led Zeppelin songs. I said, "Whoa, this guy can sing his ass off."

He said, "Yeah, that's Tim Buckley's son."

Now, I'd been a Tim Buckley fan. In 1966 when the first album came out, he played at the Unicorn Coffee House in Boston for a week by himself, and I went three nights in a row. But that didn't affect my judgment regarding Jeff. I think I said, "Whoa, that guy can sing his ass off, but I'm not looking for a Led Zeppelin covers band."

Chris Dowd[3]

Founding member of Fishbone

Fishbone started in 1979. We were South Central kids in Hollywood, seniors at high school. I met Fish, the drummer, when he was in sixth

[3] Chris wrote "What Will You Say," a song contributed to and frequently performed live by Jeff.

grade. We were always the odd black kids. We grew up listening to Jaco Pastorious, Weather Report, Parliament, Stanley Clarke, and everything that was coming out of England: The Clash, The Specials, Gang of Four; all of that informed our music. We were these black musicians saying, "Hey, rock is our shit too. There's as much James Baldwin and Langston Hughes all up in this..." I could have been in an NWA, but when we heard Bad Brains for the first time, we thought, "That's our lane!" I suppose we were the birth of alternative: us, Jane's Addiction, and the Chili Peppers. But, you know, the pioneers get the arrows and the settlers get the land.

I wrote "What Will You Say" in the summer of 1989. I was 24. I'd been touring consistently since I was 17 or something. I needed some time off from the band, and so I went down to Arkansas, where my parents are from, and saw my grandmother and that was a very cathartic experience. I'd had a shitty relationship with my father, and my grandmother showed me these pictures: "This was your father when he had his singing group." Oh, so my dad was a frustrated musician and had this whole other thing. And I started to write "What Will You Say" about this visit.

I had moved into a loft downtown on Melrose, back when Melrose was the place to be. By then, Fishbone could play a week of shows at the Roxy or fill the Palladium. We were punk rock kids, and nothing we related to was on the charts, like Mike Watt or Soundgarden. Bands in England were telling society to kiss their ass and getting on the chart, trying to further a social conscience. And so I'm feeling this duality happening. Am I an artist? Am I trying to do this shit for the money? Also, when are we going to break through? We're playing and Rage Against The Machine is opening up for us, and that became my joke: "Come open for Fishbone and a week later your record will go platinum." We had the Midas touch for everybody but us!

So I was going through a very rough period, exhausted and depressed. And then I met Carla Azar, who was this amazing person who made everything magical. She was playing drums with Wendy & Lisa, right after they had left Prince's band and signed to Columbia. They were proper pop stars. And one night, to cheer me up, Carla shows up with Jeff Buckley. We're in the Jeep, I'm wasted on tequila, I have the window down, we're riding, and it starts raining and I realize there's someone sitting behind me, and it was Jeff.

He was very quiet and unassuming then. He had a reverence for Fishbone; he'd just came along to meet me. I'm like, "Who's this dude?!" Carla says, "This is my great friend Jeff." They'd met at the Musician's Institute in Hollywood, back when it was GIT, the Guitar Institute of Technology. Jeff felt embarrassed to have gone to that school; it didn't carry the prestige it has now. Anyone who was a musician kind of looked down on GIT as, "Oh, that's where rich kids' parents send them when they don't know what to do with them." I got that, but Jeff wasn't a rich kid.

When you have a certain level of musicianship in a band, everybody wants to be Joey Solo. My thing was trying to write a song that'd get us on the radio. Jeff was trying to figure his shit out too. Ever seen that movie about Chaplin with Robert Downey Jr. where he doesn't know what the tramp is going to be until he finds the hat? It's the same thing when you're playing an instrument. All these different players, from Sonny Rollins to Hendrix or whoever, have a character to the way they play, and that's as important as being a virtuoso. I wasn't interested in trying to masturbate and play ten thousand notes. Jeff was the same; he *had* been interested in that at one point, because that was the vibe at GIT, but then he started to ask, "What's my own original voice as an artist?" So when we met, we were having that conversation with each other. We were looking for our hats.

Jeff is working at the Magic Castle up on Sunset as a waiter. He was like the lyric to "Walk This Way" about the high school loser who couldn't get the girl, and he used to joke about it, like there was something wrong with him. But he had a huge crush on Carla—which I found out later, about six months after we met.

Carla was frustrated playing with Wendy & Lisa, I was frustrated playing with Fishbone—tired of arguing about creative shit or being musically invalidated—and Jeff was frustrated working at the Magic Castle and hadn't found his hat. So we started hanging out and playing. All three of us became kinda inseparable. At one point I was gonna make a record with me, Jeff, Carla, and my friend Todd, who was playing bass in The Cult at the time; we were going to put a band together. Jeff started showing me stuff on guitar. Jeff could hear something once and play it back to you. He could really play, but the way he felt music at that point was very generic. If you hear his demos from that time, it's kind of shocking.

That's because GIT was mostly about being a session musician. That shit is hard. If you're an artist, it's very hard to play someone else's music. Jeff had to be somebody's sideman, and that wasn't what he wanted to do. At that point he was just a guitar player who could play his ass off. Then when we started hanging out and started writing together, the stuff that we wrote, even though it was only a couple of songs, Jeff defined his style off of that. It changed the way he heard music. That's the story of our relationship.

Fishbone had just finished *Reality Of My Surroundings*, and Jeff was telling me he's going to be homeless. I was about to go out on tour for ten months; I'm never in the apartment, so I say to Jeff, "Sure, stay there and make sure nobody robs the place." I didn't give a fuck about him paying rent or any of that.

We're doing the tour and he asked me to pick up a guitar and amp that had wound up in Harlem. I picked up this stuff from this guy who's like a rock star and I'm thinking, 'What is this shit doing up in Harlem?' Then Jeff tells me he'd been playing with some weird reggae band and he lived there for a while. He was always funny like that. He would do some super-secret sauce and never tell anybody what was going on. He really compartmentalized people. Which probably made him feel safe.

By 1991 I was touring so much and Carla was doing so many gigs, playing with Mick Jagger and Doug Wimbish and whoever, and Jeff started to feel like a third wheel, partly because of his romantic interest in Carla. By that time, a lot of the musical ideas I was coming up with for Fishbone, they were basically just shitting on them, and Jeff and Carla became this other outlet and validation. Carla was playing with this guitarist called Jimmy Rip, and he had a recording studio in the Hollywood Hills, and Jeff and Carla and I went up there to record "What Will You Say," and they added to the song, wrote the bridge. It was me singing, Jeff playing guitar.

Steve Berkowitz

Early in 1991, a friend of mine, Hal Willner, said, "I'm organizing a tribute to Tim Buckley at St. Ann's. Do you have any of his records?"

"Yeah, I have them all."

He needed them to check out which songs to give to people, so I lent him my records. I'm not sure he even mentioned that Jeff was going to be there. But I couldn't go to the show anyway because of other commitments, so I didn't see Jeff play at St. Ann's. I heard about it, though. Gary Lucas—who, by the way, wrote some of the greatest Fishbone poster copy—tells me all about it. He was also a guitarist and was putting a band together, and he says: "This kid is really good. I might even do something with him."

Hal Willner[4]

Music director for Saturday Night Live and curator of Greetings from Tim Buckley, the tribute show at St. Ann's

Through one of Tim's managers, we were told he had a son. He was talking to Janine Nichols [program director at St. Ann's], and the conversation went something like, "He had a son who is a singer and a guitarist." "Is he any good?" and the guy went, "Much better than Tim!" That was what we heard. We didn't know whether to invite him, but he took it upon himself to call St. Ann's. He just called and said, "Hi. This is Jeff."

It did become his concert. We even sent him out there to do an encore by himself.

Jeff Buckley

Introducing "Once I Was" at Greetings From Tim Buckley, April 26, 1991

Long time ago, when I was a little kid, my mom sat on a bed and put this record on. It was the first song where I ever heard my father's voice. I must have been six years old.

Hal Willner

All these people were giving him business cards afterwards. He was in tears after the show. He had fallen in love with Rebecca [Moore]. This is

[4] Interviewed in the documentary *Jeff Buckley Remembered.*

where he was gonna live. In the course of that one show, he was accepted by almost every musical grouping in New York. Everyone just adopted him, and it became a natural thing for him to come to New York. He'd walked into a new life.

Chris Dowd

He went to New York to play the Tim Buckley tribute, and Rebecca was working on the show. She came back to LA with him. I was happy that he had met someone. "I've found someone who loves me for me." He'd been carrying this torch around for Carla for so long, it was retarded.

He's telling us all about this show, and I'm like, "Well, what did you sing?" And he says, "'I Never Asked To Be Your Mountain,'" and I'm like, "Okay, what's that?" I didn't really know Tim's stuff. The only time I'd ever heard Jeff use his voice was when he was mimicking things. He could do Robert Plant and all that. We knew his voice was high. Carla and I wondered if he could do Prince stuff. But he used to say he couldn't really sing; he was always being weird about his voice. Then he busted out "I Never Asked To Be Your Mountain," and I'm like, "The fuck you mean you can't sing? News flash, motherfucker, you can sing! It's gonna be okay! I think you might have a grasp on this singing shit."

My friend Paul Bushnell did the music for the movie *The Commitments*, about an Irish soul band. So I helped him put a band together for the promo tour for the movie, as none of the actors could really play, and Carla's on drums and Jeff is playing guitar, traveling around the States playing all these promo junkets with the Irish guy [Andrew Strong] singing out front. One of the guys in *The Commitments* is the guy who ends up writing *Once*, Glen Hansard. He and Jeff become friends, Jeff has this Irish connection, and Glen introduces Jeff to this Irish bar in New York and that's Sin-é. So, see how it all fits together? He's here in LA, he does the *Commitments* thing, he's kinda frustrated, he goes to New York, he gets all this attention at the tribute show, he meets Rebecca, he starts singing at Sin-é, and he probably thinks, "Chris is never gonna leave Fishbone; Carla will be playing with Jagger and whoever forever; I gotta take this chance for myself."

Gary Lucas[5]

Co-composer of "Grace" and "Mojo Pin" and founder of Gods & Monsters

I'd got the name from *The Bride of Frankenstein*, where the scientist toasts to a "new world of gods and monsters!"

It seemed like a good vehicle for Jeff, who was talking about staying in New York. I booked time in a demo studio in August 1991 and we worked on "Grace" and "Mojo Pin." Jeff arrived for the rehearsal but kinda hung back, which is something he would do. He would step up to the mic but turn his back to everybody, like he was shy and didn't want to reveal what he was ultimately going to do. He didn't even sing all that clearly. We cut the band tracks and Jeff wasn't there; he came in early evening, and that's where I saw magic happen. He sang all these vocal parts with intricate Eastern influences, a sinuous vocal arrangement. He surpassed my wildest expectations. He came out of the booth with a "Did I do good?" look on his face.

The engineer was playing through these tunes as we were packing up to leave, and some jazz musicians were coming in for the nine o'clock session and I saw the look on their faces: "What is *this*? Never heard anything like this." Over the next few days, I listened to the rough mixes and thought, "This is the coolest, most stunning music I've worked on to date." I felt it could shake the world.

I took Jeff as a guest to the CMJ festival in October of 1991. I brought him onstage to do three numbers in the middle of the show, "Grace," "Mojo Pin," and "Bluebird Blues." John Cale was there; Nick Cave and some of the Bad Seeds were there, checking us out. We went to do "Bluebird Blues." The first line of the song on the version we'd done in rehearsal was: "I have an angel, her eyes are the ocean blue." When he came out, the first thing he sang was, "I am a stone-cold loner." I heard this onstage and a thing went off in my head: Jeff's first statement of principles appearing with my group!

Jeff Buckley

I met Gary Lucas at the gig at St. Ann's, and we got together and he had all these raw, instrumental song ideas on guitar. Gary was formerly of

[5] Interviewed by Jim Irvin in 1997.

Captain Beefheart's Magic Band, he was on *Shiny Beast* and *Ice Cream For Crow,* and he's miraculous, eccentric, and really sweet, and we got together and did a few things, and started a little side project. I thought that would be cool.

We got about twelve or thirteen numbers together. Played [our own] show at St. Ann's, which is a fantastic place. Then we did a gig at the Knitting Factory. It was me, Gary, Tony Maimone, and Anton Fier. We hit it off. There was a great friendliness and a great tension; both came equally at once. It was a project.

Gary wanted it to be a band and go all over the place, be like Led Zeppelin, and that was a cool idea, but it was moving too fast and I had something else in mind. So after the second gig, I told Gary that I wasn't going any further with the project.

It was like a baby was coming and I had to prepare and get things out of the way and be still. I also had to earn some money. So I decided to find little places all over the Lower East Side and wherever in New York, and just start playing, playing whatever. It was an old-fashioned idea. I wanted to be a singer, a chanteuse[6], an idea that I had been obsessing about even back in Los Angeles. I guess I wanted to dash myself on the rocks. I wanted to burn away a film that I thought was settling on me. I just wanted to work.

What I'd wanted to do before I left LA for the second time was get to a place where it was impossibly intimate, where everybody was really up close, and Sin-é is like that, you're right in front of the people. Some come there to talk to each other, not to listen; sometimes there's a lot of noise. It's a strength I wanted to get into as a natural force in my playing and singing. If I couldn't move people close up, there wasn't any point in going any farther.

Sin-é felt most comfortable because of the way Shane [Doyle] has it set up. He doesn't want to make a bunch of money at it; he just wants it to be a very solid place. He doesn't advertise and anything can happen. If you're prime time, you play from 9 p.m. until after midnight. It's like long-distance running; you totally run out of steam but then after that, because you're totally unself-conscious, you're not even thinking about

[6] This is the French word for a *female* singer. Jeff knew that.

the mechanics anymore. The moves you make then are incredible. So I guess I wanted to be disoriented at least twice a week. I played there; I played at Cornelia Street Café, at Tramps, at First Street Café, CB's Gallery. But none more than at Sin-é. I would just come in and say to Shane, "Give me as much as you can. Give me all of February; give me all of May; give me all of August." And he'd say, "Right."

Steve Berkowitz

A few months after the St. Ann's show, I worked with Hal Willner on a record called *Weird Nightmares: Meditations On Mingus.* One day, as we were walking to Hal's place along St. Mark's, we passed by this little club and Hal said, "Tim Buckley's kid sings in there now." And that was Sin-é. So we go in—it's just Hal and me in the place, as far as I recall—and the barista was Sinead O'Connor! I turn to Hal and say, "What the hell is Sinead doing here serving coffee?" This is like a year or so after "Nothing Compares 2 U." She just hung out there all the time. And Buckley is there with Janine Nichols's Telecaster. Janine was the promoter at St. Ann's. When Jeff came to New York to do the Tim Buckley show, he didn't have a guitar and she lent her Telecaster to him, and he kept it for the next six years...

Anyway, there's Buckley, me and Hal, and Sinead, and I'm quite taken by what Jeff's doing. I grab Hal by the arm after a song or two and say, "Do you hear what I'm hearing? It's all in there, isn't it?" And Hal is just smiling like a Cheshire Cat. I was obviously impressed by the voice and how it was soaring around, but I'm *really* taken by all these chordal inversions and passing tones on the guitar. He can *really* play the guitar and he understands orchestration, but also had his reggae and blues and Jimmy Page and Jim Hall and prog rock in there all at the same time. I'm just stunned. How does this kid know all this?

Michael Murphy[7]

A&R at Imago Records

When I encountered Jeff, I was a talent scout for Imago. He was the guy you went to see anytime that you were free. Every night that Jeff was playing, we went down. And there were times when the audience was

[7] Interviewed by Steve Cummins for the RTÉ documentary *Jeff Buckley's Irish Odyssey.*

five or six people. So, you're seeing somebody very early in their career. They're not playing to an audience, because there is no audience. You're seeing a naked form of self-expression.

Eventually, I said to Jeff, "My old school in Dublin is four hundred years old and they're having a big dance. Would you like to play there?" and he said, "Yeah, that would be great." (It was May 1992.)

Most people when they come for a short period of time would bring at least a rucksack with some clothes, but Jeff was standing at Dublin Airport in his Sex Pistols T-shirt and a red-and-white check jacket—almost like a vaudeville comedian would wear—and he had with him this big, New York–style ghetto blaster that he had brought for two and a half days in Dublin, like he didn't want to go anywhere without music.

I had organized a dinner in town with some music industry people that had flown in, and I invited Jeff along, but he said, "No, is it okay if I stay here with your mum and dad?" So, instead of going out for this showbiz dinner, he elected to stay here, sitting at the kitchen table, eating biscuits, to watch *The Late Late Show* with Mum and Dad. He didn't sit with my parents saying, "This'll be good for my career; they'll introduce me to Bono!"

I can't remember what he played at the Trinity Ball, but I filmed it.[8] He was a fun guy to be around. He was as nice a person as his music.

George Stein[9]

Lawyer and co-manager

It's funny, he just kinda wandered in the door one day, through a referral, with a little development deal [for Imago music] that he asked me to look at. I just rubber-stamped it for this kid, another client among hundreds, but it wasn't a good deal and I had to tell him that. And then I went down to see him play, because I always like to see what new clients are up to, and I was blown away.

---

[8] In the RTÉ documentary, you can hear Murphy and journalist Steve Cummins watching the VHS footage Murphy shot that night. Coming on at midnight in front of over a thousand inebriated students in ballgowns and dinner jackets, Jeff starts off with Sister Rosetta Tharp's "Didn't It Rain." Murphy couldn't persuade Imago boss Terry Ellis to sign Buckley. "My exact recollection of Terry's statement was, 'We don't need a spaced-out poet who doesn't write his own songs on the label.'" Murphy left Imago soon afterward.

[9] Interviewed by Jim Irvin in 1997.

It was at a club called Tramps in New York, where he was playing with Gods & Monsters. I only saw one show before they split up, and then he said he wanted to do his own thing.

He'd play Sin-é every Monday night, all night, start at 9 p.m. and go until 2 a.m. with breaks. So people knew that summer—the summer of '92—to come down on a Monday night to this little hole in the wall on St. Mark's Place. Anybody could come, literally; there was a guy called Tree Man who was a fixture in the East Village, who had branches coming out of his hair like antlers, and Jeff loved him.

And I said to Jeff, "Let me make a couple of calls for you." And he said, "Sure." I did, but there were no takers, because basically he was only doing covers at the time. People said to me, "There's gotta be more than that," and I said, "You'll see way more than that. You've just gotta see him; trust me, you'll get it." I made a few more calls and a couple of people started coming down, and slowly it was one of those things that took on a life of its own and I ended up fielding calls.[10]

Martin Aston

British music journalist

I used to write a column for *College Music Journal* called "Overseas," about British music, and I'd often visit New York for CMJ or the New Music Seminar. My friend Rachel Felder was very involved in that New York scene, and for a while, whenever I went there I would stay with her, and she told me about Jeff Buckley.

Tim Buckley is pretty much my all-time-favorite singer. And I didn't know anything about Jeff. This was pre-Internet, and nobody in Britain knew about the St. Ann's show, which Jeff had appeared at. Tim had been resuscitated somewhat in the UK via This Mortal Coil covering "Song To The Siren," and his *Dream Letter* live album. I had every Tim Buckley record going, so I was very, very curious to hear Jeff. Rachel told me he was playing at Sin-é.

Back in those days you were mistrustful of "sons or daughters of." You never thought that they were going to be any good, but you could

[10] Among the labels I know that approached Jeff (apart from Sony) were Imago, Big Cat, Sire, Arista, A&M, Ensign, Mute, Elektra, and London Records.

instantly hear how strong and charismatic his voice was. And he was being an entertainer. He's singing, playing brilliantly, and joking, doing improvisations and little impersonations of people. It was very unusual that someone might do a Van Morrison cover and then an old blues, an Elvis ballad, a Smiths song, and a Bad Brains song. In those days, I'd make mixtapes of my favorite artists, and Jeff was singing songs by half of them! In terms of the breadth of what he was tapping into, there was nobody else at that time. It was very hyperactive, but all one continuous performance, fully formed and yet raw.

I asked for an interview. I just did it on spec, because I thought this was incredible, what I'd just seen. I'm told that it was his very first interview, and I got it probably because Rachel vouched for me. And no one else had ever asked, I suppose. We met at the Yaffa Cafe down the road from Sin-é. I said to him when I got there, "Your show was incredible—Nina Simone, The Smiths, Cocteau Twins, Edith Piaf, all my people..." He assumed I was there just because I was a huge fan of Tim's. There was no point in saying to him, "I've never heard your dad's music," coming on as if I knew nothing about him. Honesty is the best policy, so I had to say to him, "I love your dad's music—I always have—but that has nothing to do with how much I've loved seeing you play." He immediately fired back: "I have nothing to do with my dad; I didn't inherit anything; this is me." It was awkward but I totally got it. There's this idol being dangled in front of him, if you like, a man who hugely influenced the path of his life and didn't make it at all easy. He obviously knew the music, though. He'd sung "I Never Asked To Be Your Mountain" and "Once I Was" at the St. Ann's tribute, and how could you not be curious about what your dad had done?

He was quite restless during the interview, very articulate, but it was quite stream of consciousness.

I did the piece for *OOR* magazine in Holland. It was still really early; he hadn't signed a record deal yet. They just took it as read that he was an interesting new artist because I'd said how great he was.

• • • • •

This is that first press interview, conducted on August 12, 1992:

Martin Aston: When did music first hit you?
Jeff Buckley: *As a child. There was my mother's breasts and then there was music. It felt like another person in the house that floated with me everywhere. All my life I've sung along to the radio, stuff like "I Love You More Today Than Yesterday."*

My mom would drive me to school, playing mellow Californian radio: Chicago; Crosby, Stills & Nash; Blood, Sweat & Tears; Sly & The Family Stone; James Brown; The Temptations, every day! She married a car mechanic, who couldn't carry a tune, but he had amazing taste, and he turned me on to Booker T., Led Zeppelin and Joni Mitchell, Hoyt Axton and Willie Nelson. My mom sang to me—she's a classically trained pianist and cellist. So it was mainly me and my mom, because my parents split before I was born. I hung around my grandmother too—she'd play me stuff like The Chambers Brothers.

It's rare to hear someone equally smitten with traditional blues as well as modern forms. I'm thinking of your cover of "Fare Thee Well"...
That's "Dink's Song." It was originally written by a washerwoman. That's where the best music came from, from old European-American criminals bringing Africans to America. My favorites are Robert Johnson and Bukka White, The Staple Singers, Billie Holiday. I cover "Strange Fruit" too. The thing I figured is, I wouldn't be able to meet these people, so I learn from them by hearing them sing.

I guess what I want to do is be an archetypal entertainer, an archetypal bard, a minstrel. I guess I have a romantic vision. Even though punk happened to me, and Robert Johnson, I want to be a really good storyteller, and those songs have great stories.

What do you love about "Twelfth of Never"?
I cover the Nina Simone version. It's just the way she does it. I can't get into Elvis's version; it doesn't capture my imagination, though he had a beautiful voice. Every time I hear "Can't Help Falling In Love," I cry. I can't separate Charles Manson from The Beatles or the Clam Bake movie from Elvis, though. But I love all music. I'm the Cocteau Twins' biggest fan. They allow their deepest eccentricities to be the music itself, and not just something they want to project. Liz Fraser is one of the only originals. They're just regular people too. I got to meet her once. She was very shy, which puts a weird curve on that

music as well. Imagine that sound coming out of her mouth when she's in the kitchen scrambling eggs. I lose my mind when I'm washing the dishes.

Was music your first true love?
Besides sex? One surrounds the other. I can remember being obsessed with my stepfather's stereo, getting into trouble for using it. He was really possessive of control over it, like a car. It was really expensive equipment, so I was really careful, then one day, I wanted to listen to a live bootleg of Jimi Hendrix, and he went mad. I had a tape player in my room, which I shared with another kid in the family. You had to stick a coat hanger in it for it to work.

How do you feel when you open your mouth and sing?
Like it's real. I feel like crying...I feel like I am crying! It's the middle point between laughing and immense joy and crying. I feel the best when I'm singing.

When did you start?
In front of an audience, at a family get-together. My stepfather got drunk and fell asleep in front of everyone, and my grandmother got really embarrassed, so to direct attention away from him, I sung every Elton John song I knew. I was a huge fan then. They gave me some silver dollars for it. I was thirteen (laughs). My friend and I started playing electric guitars, you know, "Stairway To Heaven," for a talent show at junior high school. We lost...We were living in Southern California then. I later had a band in Northern California, in Willits, called Axxis. It wasn't my idea. It's one of the nineteen cities I've lived in. I attended four high schools. One I spent two weeks in. My mom was quite a gypsy.

What did you make of your own voice?
I hated it, but I got over it. I'm horribly self-critical. I think that the first time I heard it, I thought no way that I could ever keep anything from anyone; it was all there in the voice. Some ways that people sing, they put it across in language, and it's almost impossible, because they have a wall between them and the expression. I'm trying to get deeper in the hole, trying to learn things when I heard voices.

Did singing on a stage come easily to you?

It was totally natural; I just did it. It was like going to the beach, like, I'm going into the ocean, the water! I never thought about it. I first sang at a dance in Northern California [at a] Methodist church, to high school kids. When I was thirteen, I already knew what I wanted to do. My all-time favorite was Led Zeppelin, and I knew that I wanted to belong to that. I spent hours listening to Magical Mystery Tour.

I left home when I was seventeen, because I was tired of moving around. I played in lots of LA bands, just to make money. There was a reggae band for a while, The AKB Band, a ragtag motley crew, with one Rasta guy. I played guitar. We ended up backing up U-Roy, Shinehead, and Judy Mowatt, and playing at the Bob Marley day at Long Beach. We did cheesy session work for demos too.

What did the experience teach you?

The simplicity. I guess it didn't teach me much at the time. It's like your parents telling you what not to do. But Pablo Black, the Rasta, everything he said about playing makes sense now.

I then decided not to spread myself that thin. I didn't like Southern California, LA especially. Hollywood isn't a real town, but that's the reality of it. I'd wanted to see New York since I saw it on TV when I was twelve, to experience the energy, so I took off in 1990. I got a couple of jobs and went hungry for a long while before I got an offer to record songs in LA, so I flew back and recorded four songs. I went back and forth a bit, before I met Gary Lucas at a show in New York, at a tribute show to my father. I thought playing with Gary would be interesting, but it turned out to be a disaster. We had two completely different paths; the cart was before the horse. But I learned to go out and sing in impossibly intimate settings, when guys are right up against you. You learn how to move a room. The biggest challenge is to put a song across live. The audience shouldn't see your face or your body; they should just hear you. People really like it.

Do you enjoy the New York scene?

I dig it. If I was in LA, I wouldn't be doing anything, but here, there's a real respect. There are a lot of other emotions too, but there's a respect for anything original. Maybe I'm over-romanticizing New York, but so many amazing things happen here—like, Lou Reed lives here, wow! I first heard him in '76 but he got into my soul...That song "Heroin" is so beautiful, like a big black kiss, the way it builds....I couldn't get enough of that song, and it led to everything else. He sounds like a punk who knows absolutely everything. He's got such erudition, but he's not too smart.

What stage do you see yourself at?
Always at the beginning. I'd love to make a record. The night you came down to see me, record company people were coming down. Clive Davis at Arista wanted to sign me but he hadn't heard me; it was just on the basis of what his head of A&R had said, but he has to hear me himself. I plan to start from what matters. I wanna find people to play with. Yeah, a band, just because of the certain feeling I need. An energy.

Can I raise the delicate matter of your dad, Tim?
Sometimes, with people who knew him, they've come see me for a nice night out, but they see me; they don't think about him. They don't really know him. Those who do, I don't hang around them. We're different. The people who knew him, they have apparently a very magic memory, but it's been a claustrophobic thing all my life; I knew him for a total of nine days. He never wrote, never called.

Do you listen to his records?
Yeah, mostly to learn about him as a person. It's there for anybody to take from, pretty much. He wrote a couple of songs about me and Mother, which is sometimes tough, sometimes not. His style had nothing to do with what I do. It's funny that we were born with the same parts, but when I sing, it's me. Technically, I can do what he did, but our expression is not the same; it's a completely different sphere. His was a different time, influenced by Dylan and the folkies. I don't even talk like him. But I can do a good impersonation of him, knitting up my eyebrows, which makes people laugh.

I'll leave the conclusion up to you.
I want to make something completely new. I want to work so hard that everything of me burns away, like the chemical in the match. Which leaves what really is me, or what I think is me. There's something about music that hits the cavemen in us, even more than a speech or painting. I just want to achieve my own vibe. I want to go someplace else. There's more, so much more. More ways of saying, "I love you," more ways of saying, "Where the hell do I fit in?" [and] more ways of saying, "Why doesn't anyone love me?" And it's nothing

arty, nothing lofty; it's just fucking different, and I want to leave this world behind a little so that maybe I will see that it's bigger and I haven't left it at all. I'm just trying to do my thing."[11]

• • • • •

Steve Berkowitz

By the third or fourth time I saw him, it was clear we could hang and talk about stuff, about reggae or Led Zeppelin, Nusrat, Stravinsky, Billie Holliday or Sun Ra. We did not talk business. How could I talk business with a guy who didn't know what he wanted to do? He didn't know what he wanted to do, and I found that attractive. He had almost no songs, "Lover" maybe, the beginnings of another, plus "Mojo Pin" and "Grace," which he'd written with Gary Lucas.

Jeff was like a jazz musician; he could go anywhere. He didn't know what he wanted to do, except that he wanted to make "badass" music. He had this hand gesture that he did when he said it, like his was gripping a wad of notes: "It has to be badass!"—not some cookie-cutter thing.

Four or five months into Sin-é gigs and Jeff has made himself the It guy of the Lower East Side. Clive Davis from Arista had been there, and many others. Jeff called me up one day and said, "Clive has offered me a million dollars." I said, "Fantastic, congratulations. You're buying lunch." He said, "Why shouldn't I sign with Clive?" I said, "Well, he's an amazingly successful music executive. I don't have bad things to say about him. And when you sign for a million dollars to an executive like Clive, that means he knows what he wants you to do. Which I find amazing, because you don't even know what you want to do! Why would you take that money? He clearly must have an idea of what you can become if he's willing to throw down a million dollars before you even have a demo tape."

---

[11] During the summer that he gave this interview, Jeff's primary source of income was busking in the subway, which he would do for up to six hours a day, before moving on to Sin-é or other gigs in the evening. In between he would undertake his "James Brown Prison Workout" of push-ups, sit-ups, and crunches, then after shows would work on new songs or learn covers until early morning. Also that summer, he was well received playing the lead role in a Fluxus production of Georg Buchner's *Woyzeck*, the story of a mentally ill soldier who murders his girlfriend during a fit of rage, then walks into a lake to wash away her blood and drowns.

George Stein

When we were in the middle of record company frenzy and everybody wanted to sign him, sometimes he and I would go out to City Island, a little boating community [in the Bronx]...and just drive out there and cool out by the water and talk. I'd drive, and I'd try and start the conversation because I thought it was important to talk about his future, his goals and his thoughts, the deep stuff, but all he wanted to do was hunch over the radio and jump from station to station like he was a primitive man who'd just discovered a new device that was making magic. And he would jump from pop to reggae to rock to classical, humming along and so fucking involved, like he had never had a chance to listen to music before and if he didn't listen to it now, in this half hour, he was going to miss something. He was just so wrapped up in it.

At the first showcase for the Columbia brass at Sin-é, Jeff yelled out to the audience, "What do you want to hear?" And someone shouted out, "Nusrat," and Jeff proceeded to play—not a riff, not a minute, not two, but about fifteen minutes of Nusrat Fateh Ali Khan! I thought I was having an acid trip from the '60s. I couldn't believe that my artist, just signed, was singing a fifteen-minute Pakistani cover song. That was so Jeff; he didn't care that the company guys were there. It was just about the music he loved.

Leah Reid

Product manager at Columbia

I was hired as a product manager for Columbia in late 1991. A product manager guides an album through the record company system. An old boss of mine used to say they are "the guardian of the vibe." You create awareness of an act within the company, working with the art department to come up with the packaging, the copy department to sort the credits and lyrics; you talk about photographers, and advertising—discuss what posters are going to get made; you bring it all together, making sure all the deadlines are being met.

I was still pretty new to the job when Steve Berkowitz wrote a note to certain people at Columbia saying he wanted us to see him play. "Hey, Leah, this guy I'm trying to sign, Jeff Buckley, is playing at Sin-é Monday night..."

Jeff Buckley and Leah Reid (Columbia Records product manager).

I was surprised how small Sin-é was. As you walked in, it felt like you could immediately touch the counter where they're serving coffee. There were four tables on the right, some longer tables on the left, and an aisle down the middle. Hanging on the left, there was a metal sign saying "Sin-é," and a piano in the corner. Comfortably, forty people would fill it, but on the nights Jeff played, there'd be eighty people and they'd spill out onto the street. There was a sound system but nothing huge; you could still hear people talking and coffee grinding throughout the night.

When he came out, he was just wearing some dark green or gray pants with black suspenders and a white V-neck T-shirt, and I was like, "This is it? This kid? What's this about?" When he started, it was like a calm came over the whole room, and when he opened his mouth and sang, I thought, "What in the world is this?" I was transfixed for the whole two hours. I'd never heard anything like this, never seen anything like this. It was immediate and real.

You'd routinely describe somebody as the next Soundgarden or the next Beatles or whatever, but there was literally nothing you could compare Jeff to at that point. He was the first him. If anyone was doing the chanteuse thing, it was in a nightclub or theatre, a cabaret thing. No one was doing that in rock.

I went back to Berkowitz and said, "That was amazing," and he said, "Well, he's going to be in here today. I want you to come in and meet with him." It was me, Paul Rappaport, head of promotion, Howard Wuelfing, press, and Berkowitz, a small bunch of us in Paul's office, and Jeff sat there on the couch eating a sandwich from Le Pain Quotidien. Everyone said what department they were in and described their job. Then I said, "What I saw the other night, I've never seen or heard anything like it, and it left me speechless." At that point Jeff just put down his sandwich and looked at me. It was the first time I got that stare where he makes you feel like you're the only one in the room. He wasn't used to people talking about him and his music yet.

Steve Berkowitz

The first night I took Donnie Ienner [president of Columbia Records] to see Jeff at Sin-é, he fell asleep! He had poison ivy and was taking Benadryl, and it was downing him out. Donnie says, "If I start to get droopy, give me the elbow, because I took this stuff." Anyway, Jeff sings "Lover, You Should Have Come Over." Donnie is sitting next to me and he leans over and whispers, "He's a fucking star," and then he falls asleep. And then he left before the set was over, which was an interesting thing for an executive to do, a powerful, disruptive thing. But he was clearly interested, and a number of other people from the label had come on board with me and shown great support. Jeff and George Stein liked that it wasn't just one guy at the company; it was a whole staff of people who got it.

George Stein

He was a little fearful of the record industry, afraid of being chewed up and spit out as a commodity. He had to work out whether it was possible to work with a major label and keep his integrity and keep his music. In a sense it was a leap of faith he made in going with Columbia, that they would honor his vision, and he had to get that confirmation that he could follow his own path musically. But he really connected with Steve Berkowitz on a musical level.

Steve Berkowitz

George Stein did a very good job of getting the right kind of contract. Someone recently wrote I ensured this gigantic contract for Jeff, which is inaccurate. In fact, I suggested he not take a lot of money from Columbia: be as prepared as possible to record, get the smallest amount possible, do not use the record company as a bank. That's very expensive money with a lot of strings attached; the less money you take from the record company, the more sway you have over your own stuff. Keep control of yourself; that was my advice. It was not a huge deal, way less than others had offered.

Leah Reid

Steve Berkowitz never positioned himself as someone who was going to sign hit bands, so there was no pressure on him to produce the next hit record. Steve did the deals that were more esoteric and kept the legacy of Columbia, the weirdness and the depth: Hal Willner, Branford Marsalis, and Buckethead. Which appealed to Jeff because it meant he wasn't going to be manufactured as a pop star and pushed out the other end.

The good thing for Jeff was, the way the deal was made, he had more say than anybody in that day and age. There were cases where the artists didn't even have a say in what their album cover was. Jeff had pretty much whatever Jeff wanted. He saw he would have to participate, but it wouldn't be in the "hit single, pop video, bam bam bam" way. He realized that as long as the correct people were involved, the vibe would be maintained and he wouldn't be put in a position to do anything he'd feel uncomfortable doing.

George Stein

He signed in October of 1992, and the understanding with Columbia was, sign with us and then we'll just leave Jeff alone to write for a year. Record companies don't usually do this. Donnie Ienner, when he signed him, said, "I don't know what this kid is, and I don't know what he'll come up with, but I know he's a great artist and he'll put out something that Columbia will be proud to put out. If he wants to put out just cover versions, we'll do it."

Leah Reid

There were projects that we informally called "DWI projects," which meant "Donnie wants it." Donnie Ienner would say something at upper-level meetings, and it would come down as a DWI. Donnie felt Jeff was a priority, but I don't think everybody knew what to do with Jeff Buckley. We were handling this differently from other acts at the time. It was some time after we signed him that they worked out what kind of record he wanted to make.

Merri Cyr

Photographer

The first time I met Jeff was on assignment for *Paper Magazine* in New York in the fall of 1992, around October. They didn't really pay anything, but I was able to photograph a lot of directors, musicians, and actors. The editor gave me a choice between some musician and some actor to shoot, and I chose the musician. There was a buzz about him playing at Sin-é, I was told. I didn't know anything about him. We went to his apartment for the shoot. It was a walk-up, four stories, somewhere on Elizabeth Street.

The first thing we did was set up my small strobe and take some shots of Jeff in a top hat and a flannel shirt. He told me later that the top hat was one of the few possessions he had from his dad. We did those, then some on the roof.

Right from the beginning, he was fun to shoot. I could tell he was smart, and he liked being photographed, but he also had something else going on. It made me curious about the work that he did. When we were on the roof, there was this one point when he squeezed in really close and gingerly plucked this dust bunny off my sweater. It was this weird thing where he was really getting in my face, a bit invasive, an intimate gesture. He lured me in; it was very seductive. He was good-looking, but I'd photographed a lot of good-looking people. That wasn't the main thing. I was sure after that session that he was very unusual. I could tell that he was good, even though I hadn't seen him play yet.

Some of the pictures turned out well, and I was curious to see him play, so I went to see him at Sin-é a week later, and brought some prints with me.

I don't think anybody's music had really hit me with that immediacy before. He played a version of "Hallelujah" that made me feel totally bereft. I didn't know it was a Cohen song, but his voice just struck a chord that broke my heart, and I just wanted to sob. I was so embarrassed, sitting there sobbing to myself.

After the show, he was hanging around and all the cool kids were talking to him. The girls were going crazy. When I first walked up to him, he looked like he didn't recognize me, so I say, "Jeff, it's Merri. I photographed you last week," and he just kept looking at me in a suspicious way, and I said, "I made you a couple of prints."

He opened the box and looked at the pictures, and then he jumped on me and gave me a big hug and a big, sloppy kiss. He was very excited about the pictures. And then we started talking, and he started working me a little bit, getting into his seduction routine.

I had a book with me, a book of poems by Rumi, the Sufi poet. Jeff took the book out of my hand and started talking about how he wanted to read me a bunch of this poetry. He was really working me at that point, and I was like, "Yeah, sure." And he gave me his number and said, "Call me anytime. We'll get together, and I want to read you this poetry."

So about a week after that, I called him and I left a message on his answering machine, something like, "Hey, I'd like to hear some of that poetry. Let's get together." I didn't know he was living with Rebecca at that time, the little shit; I didn't know he had a girlfriend. That's on him. I left a message and, like, two days later he called back and left me some really shitty message: "No I don't want to get together, thanks." He was being, like, a total dick, and I said to my roommate, "What an asshole! I'm never talking to that dick again. Fuck that guy."

After that I didn't see him for seven months.

Steve Berkowitz

A number of months go by; the company wants a record, and Jeff still doesn't know what he wants to play. We talk about bands and solo acoustic records, strings, big-band swing records, cabaret records, reggae, and he's not making any decisions—a direction is not clear. He could sing on Broadway; he could play string bass in a jazz band. His talent seemed limitless.

I suggest we go into a studio and record whatever he wants—create a table of contents—and there might be something there that lets him pick a direction. We book two or three days at Shelter Island Studio, with Steve Addabbo the engineer, and after about six or seven songs, it's obvious Jeff's tight as a tick, uncomfortable, uneasy, because this is his first time recording on the record company's dime. He couldn't elevate his voice to get to those parts I called "the flying Buckleys," where he's like Plant, Nusrat, or Freddie Mercury. He's wound up really tight. I say to Steve, "This isn't going to work." So I get up and play the fool a little bit, get some coffee and some beer and sing along with him, use pencils as drumsticks on the table next to him, and after a while he says, "Nah, I'm done." I say, "You're kidding. You know every song out there. How about some Isley Brothers?" He says, "No." "Impressions?" "No." "Sly?" "Hmm. Sly, huh?" And he starts playing "Everyday People" on the guitar, but he doesn't know the words. I think I called my wife and asked her to transcribe the lyrics or something—couldn't look it up online back then. The tape stops and then you hear him saying, "Hand me those lyrics," and he starts to play the shit out of it. Having broken his own ice, he really started to sing. That's the version on that *You And I* record.

We stayed there for two more days, and he recorded about fifty songs. That's when he started to feel like himself in a recording studio, started feeling comfortable and opening up.[12]

One of the reasons we did *Live at Sin-é* was to diffuse the big bang of Columbia Records, which could spoil an artist before they were ready, like Chris Whitley or James McMurtry. I had seen this mighty machine pushing too hard, too fast. Since Jeff wasn't sure what he wanted to do yet, we had to take it easy.

You have to remember that Jeff's community at that time on the Lower East Side was Rebecca and her family, Hal Willner, and the Fluxus

[12] Shortly after signing to Columbia, Jeff asked Andrew Goodsight, a bass player he'd met at Sin-é, to join him in some experimental sessions and bring a drummer. Goodsight invited his friend John McNally. The trio rehearsed for a week at Context Studios and then recorded everything onto sixteen-track tape the following week at the Knitting Factory. Only one song from those sessions has surfaced publicly. "Strawberry Street"—a song Jeff had also demoed in LA—appeared on the Legacy edition of *Grace* released in 2004. If nothing else, these sessions appear to have pointed Jeff toward the band format he wanted to use.

organization. It was all way left-of-center counterculture; those were his people. So there's this fight going on in his head: "Am I small and arty at PS 122, or am I headlining Madison Square Garden? Which am I doing?" My thing with him was, "Come into this place [Columbia] and see that Michael Jackson, The Clash, Marvin Gaye, and Miles Davis are here too, and they don't suck. Bob Dylan is playing big places. Springsteen. You have a problem with that? You could do that." He wasn't opposed to becoming big; he just didn't want to be part of the star-making machinery.

Merri Cyr

One day—on Friday, July 9, 1993, to be exact—he called me out of the blue and left numerous messages. He kept saying, "I want you to shoot my album cover. I'm doing this EP, *Live at Sin-é.* I'm gonna do it Monday! We have to go up to the record company right now and show them your work. I want you to show those people up there [at Sony] what you can do." He left about ten messages. I'm like, "Fuck that guy, no way." My roommate at that time was fielding a lot of his calls too, and I told her, "I'm not interested. That guy's a dick." But he didn't stop calling. It was relentless. He'd just decided I was going to do it, but it didn't really make sense. But then finally, to stop him calling, I picked up: "What!? What do you want?"

"Come and do this with me right now!!" He wouldn't take no for an answer.

I was totally noncommittal because I thought he was a jerk, but my roommate was like, "It's for Sony Music, you dummy. Take it." So I gave in. I ended up meeting Jeff at Sony and took my portfolio up there. We went in to see the art director, Chris Austopchuk. Chris had already hired another woman, Patricia Macdonald, who I also knew. She is a really good photographer. Jeff's saying to Chris, "Merri has to do this!" Chris goes to Jeff, "Okay, but I'm not firing Patricia. You have to do it."

Jeff never apologized for being a dick the previous time I'd met him. His technique, as shitty as he had acted, was to overwhelm you with affection. He would act so sorry. It was part of his *modus operandi.* If you knew him long enough, you were going to be subject to him being a little shit to you and then him feeling dramatically awful and having to make it up to you. It was a pattern that would repeat a lot. That's how he was with me, anyway. I don't know how he was with other people.

I went to his apartment and watched him call Patricia and fire her, and that was very uncomfortable. He was very nice to her, though.

On the Monday of the performance, the idea was, he was going to rehearse all day and then play a set at night. He was really nervous—it was his first big thing—so he engaged my sympathies. Everything was at stake that day, it seemed. I was really an outsider; I wasn't someone who hung out with him at that time. I was taking pictures and the only one not from Sony who was interacting with him for many hours. That was when I first discovered how, when you were with him, he had this ability to totally encapsulate you in his personal bubble.

He stood in the corner next to the piano. Sin-é was a weird room—tiny, and the sound was horrible. The coffee machine was always going off, hissing really loud. Because the space was very small, I wanted something that made it feel a little bigger, so that shot was done on a Widelux 35mm panoramic camera, which creates a longer negative. I found a ladder, and by getting up there I could see Jeff and the coffee machine and all the staff at the back, get an overview of the room. There was a guy with a newspaper smoking away—not giving a shit about Jeff—who ended up on the album cover with him.

I love that Jeff chose that shot for the cover. He had some great big balls to choose that for his debut. An almost empty room with no one looking at him.

We went to the park for some fresh air, and I took some shots. He looks so totally by himself, so alone in those pictures. It made me feel so close to him. Afterwards, we went back to Anseo and I was sitting down changing some film in the Widelux, and Jeff just walks in, takes off his jacket, then shirt, and looks like he was about to collapse. Jeff could sleep on anything. If he needed a catnap, he would just pass out—floor, bar, wherever. I was sitting next to a row of chairs, and he draped himself across them and put his head in my lap and fell asleep. I couldn't really move, so for more than an hour I sat there as he dozed. I didn't know him at all, and I felt like he was putting all this trust in me; it crushed my heart. Then it was showtime; all these people he knew started showing up. Jeff was still nervous, but it was like we came out of this weird fog we had been in for eight hours. The place was so crowded; some of his friends couldn't get in. I have this great picture of Hal Willner with his nose pressed up against the window.

Steve Berkowitz

We recorded *Live at Sin-é* twice. The first night, we set up the microphones and put the recording equipment in the corner of the club and, once again, Jeff sensed the pressure of commitment. I could tell by the second song that this night was shot, that he wasn't going to loosen up. He wasn't regular amazing Jeff. But at the end of the night, I went over to him and said, "You nailed it; it's fantastic. We got it. You're done." But I didn't let him hear the tapes. Then I suggested, "You know, that went so well, let's do it again." And I got Shane Doyle to give me the club a month later, and this time we decided we're not gonna be in the room to record; we're gonna be somewhere else. Shane had another bar next door, called Anseo, and we ran a snake through the air conditioning duct and down the street and set up our equipment there so Jeff's not gonna notice any recording. Plus he thinks it's already done, so he's gonna play the audience and be relaxed. And it worked. Almost everything from the *Live at Sin-é* full album comes from that second night.

Chris Dowd

When Jeff left for New York, Carla and I were pissed off. "Fuck you for leaving, breaking up the band"—that kind of attitude. But I was torn between feelings like that and feeling, "Jeff's my friend. I gotta be happy for him." Carla wasn't talking to him. So by virtue of me being with her at the time, I wasn't talking to him either. But at a certain point I started sneaking off and calling him. I missed him too much: "I'm not doing this shit. This is dumb; that's my boy!"

So I'd call him, but he's not really telling me what is going on in New York. I didn't hear anything about Sin-é until Steve Berkowitz is like, "Oh yeah. I've been working on these demos with Jeff, and he didn't really want you to know..."

I'm okay with that. I get it. Jeff was trying to find himself and figure out his own shit and take all the millions of discussions we'd had about what makes an artist and have his own self-realization. But he's being super Captain Vague. I'm like, "Are you making a record now?" And he's going, "Yeah, mumble mumble."

I was sitting on a tour bus somewhere when I got a copy of *Live at Sin-é.* When I heard it, I was freaking out and was really happy for him.

Leah Reid

In that summer of 1993, before he started recording *Grace*, Jeff would literally get out of bed, get something to eat, come up to 550 Madison, and just sit in my office for hours and hours until it was time to leave. I always had the alternative radio station on; I always had MTV on the TV with the sound off. He would read all the music magazines—*Spin* and *Rolling Stone*—and hear conversations that I had; he would meet people that way. He just came and went as he pleased. People started expecting him. He'd be walking up the hallway; people could hear his keys jangling on his chain: "Oh, Buckley's here."

That was pretty unusual; not many artists just hung around the office. He went from this thing that no one understood, an enigma, to this guy that they all knew, who sat in the office all day. Howard's office for a while too. So, Monday, Wednesday, and Friday in mine, Steve's on Tuesday, Howard's on Thursday. It was literally him wanting to see how a record company worked, getting a vibe for how people interacted with each other. If you don't want to be afraid of bears, go and hang out at a bear cage, I guess.

If he connected with somebody, Jeff had the ability to make them feel like they were the only person in the world. He made every single conversation feel like something special and like it meant something special to him—even in line at a record signing at Tower Records, even for a split second, he could connect with people. But he was like a cat. You have to just take what they give you; don't ask for anything more. Ever tried to grab a cat when it doesn't want to be held? Yet if you're sick, the cat will curl up to you because it knows that you need something. You could never ask for more than he could give, and a lot of people started to expect things from him that he couldn't give.

Steve Berkowitz

We had done *Live at Sin-é*, though it hadn't come out yet, and the label is starting to put some pressure on us. It's around August 1993 and he's been signed almost a year, and I say, "You've got six or seven songs. Let's agree to put down a date in October to start making a record."

But we needed a producer. Andy Wallace was the idea of a guy named Mark Beavan, a manager of producers and engineers. I had worked with Andy previously with a band called The Front, who were somewhere between The Doors and INXS, and a band he produced called WILD, [on] a very interesting, before-its-time, funk-metal record. Andy knows how to make everything sound good; he has an excellent sense of dynamics and he can work forever. At that time I didn't think of him as a producer or editor, just an excellent, tireless engineer and mixer who could make the moment of recording transparent, and then, with Jeff's improvisational, musical way, there'd be no barrier between the creation and getting it to tape... "You're right, Mark. Andy would be a good choice!" So I arranged for Jeff and Andy to meet in my office.

Andy Wallace

Producer and mixer, Grace

We talked and Jeff was his charming, jocular, scattered self. I felt in tune with a lot of what he was saying. Steve is highly musical as well, so the three of us had a nice chat centered on music. And I imagine Nirvana would have come up somewhere, because almost everyone who talked to me around that time wanted to talk about that record.[13] At that point I was working around the clock, producing two records a year and the rest of the time I was mixing.

I came away thinking he was an incredibly intelligent, effervescent, and talented guy and felt there was a good connection, a good chemistry between us.

The first time I actually heard him play was at one of the Sin-é shows. That was the first time I heard the song "Grace," and [I] remember asking Steve, "Did he write that?!"

There was some conversation about whether the album should be cast in the single-guitar-and-voice mold of *Live at Sin-é*. Jeff expressed a strong desire to make a band album, but not with studio session players, and I totally agreed with that. So we hit on the idea of having a little bit

[13] Wallace mixed Nirvana's *Nevermind*.

of the solo thing, with some original songs being more produced and having a band involved. It would be transitional, a logical step on from *Live at Sin-é*, some band material and covers like "Hallelujah" and "Lilac Wine" that he had been doing in the solo shows.

Steve Berkowitz

Jeff had met Mick Grondahl in the Village—a very unusual bass player, almost like McCartney in his use of counter melody. He listened very intently to what Jeff was singing and was able to stop on a dime with Jeff's dynamics, which were so diverse and precise and delicate.

I had no idea how Jeff was going to find a drummer his own age who could hang in all those diverse musical idioms that Jeff was capable of, so Jeff finding Matt Johnson was kind of a miracle. Matt's a spectacular drummer, able to steer and follow and feel.

Matt Johnson

Drummer

I moved to New York from Texas when I was 18 to go to music school, a double major on a five-year program at the New School for Social Research. I dropped out in the last year because I wanted to tour and work and because opportunities started to present themselves, and I didn't want to spend any more time in academia. I was fed up with it.

I was 22, playing in some bands around town, trying to be a drummer. There was a guy called John Moran, involved in theater and arts music; he wrote *The Manson Family: An Opera*. He was a friend of Rebecca Moore, Jeff's girlfriend, and I met them on the street and said hi to John. I was interning at the Looking Glass, which was Philip Glass's studio on Broadway, and he'd been recording there. He introduced me to Rebecca as a drummer, and she said, "My buddy Jeff is looking for a drummer." I'd never heard of him but I scrawled my number on a napkin for her, and within a day I had Jeff's raspy voice on my answering machine. I called him back and he was pretty up-front: "I have a record deal and I need to move fast because we're going to be recording, and I'm holding auditions." We set something up within a couple of days at Context Studios on Avenue A, where so many bands from that area rehearsed, and he seemed committed straight away. Mickey was already playing with him.

Jeff could play all the instruments. He could play the drums well; he could play bass very well; he could play guitar exceptionally well and sing extraordinarily well. He knew that, economically, he didn't need to have ten people onstage. He needed a core band that was dynamic and intelligent, solid and flexible, capable of being supportive players but with interesting personalities too.

Though I was a rock drummer, I tuned more for Motown and jazz. I idolized Philadelphia jazz drummers from the 1950s. I didn't play like that, but that was how my ear worked. I loved hard rock drumming too, heavy metal, hair metal; we thought that stuff was kinda cool. But I understood Jeff didn't want a stock LA rock guy for his sound. He wanted some musicians who were thinking a little differently.

He was a bit of a mystery man to me. I didn't have an archetype to ascribe to him; he was a different kind of musical animal. There were points of reference we had in common, in terms of musical taste, but it was my first time getting inside the heart and mind of someone who was a singer and lyricist and musician. He came off as being intense. I was ultimately very impressed by him.

Initially we were just free-associating, limbering up and getting to know each other, and then there was a period where we specifically got down to the songs. He was very reticent in the beginning about getting onto the microphone. It seemed like he didn't have much interest in singing; he wanted to establish on some other level.

It was some weeks before I heard him sing, and when he started, that was a bit of a surprise. To this day, I don't know of any singers who used so much of the potential of the human voice as Jeff did, from incredible serrated screaming and punishing scowls to very ribbon-like, serene, very pure, clear passages of melody, to almost talking. He just used so much of the potential of the human voice to communicate and bring an emotional catharsis from himself and the people who were present with him.

I once told him, "If you weren't a singer, you could be a great actor," and he was offended. He would not let that pass. Maybe it was something to do with being from LA. He really didn't look at himself that way.

Andy Wallace

Jeff went and found the band and I went to a couple of those early—I wouldn't even call them practices, they were jams, after he found Matt and Mick. I wanted to let them develop a bit before I started interjecting too much. I didn't want to push it in a direction where it might not have gone naturally.

During that time he started to introduce some of the material. He had about half of the album written. I don't remember being stressed about there being a shortage of original material. Jeff may have been, but I was flying by the seat of my pants and just trusting that given the people involved, and Jeff's ability, we would come up with a good record.

Julie Borchard

Director of international at Columbia Records

I arrived at Columbia in October 1993, after about six and a half years in the record business in California, working at Capitol Records. I got recruited as the number-two person in international, and within about three weeks the vice president was chucked out and I was made the head of the department, aged twenty-eight. I was taking all the US acts out to the rest of the world. I had to coordinate their schedules, make sure the territories had the marketing materials, tell the story, whatever it was. It's a balancing act between the music and the corporate structure.

Donnie Ienner was my direct boss, and he really understood where I was coming from and empowered me to right the department, which he felt had been mismanaged in the past. He called me Boutros Boutros Ghali. I had to be that UN ambassador-type of person. I couldn't ruffle any feathers, couldn't tell people what to do. It was always about carrot and no stick.

Coming from California, I had no sense of the New York club scene. That wasn't my focus—I worked in the international realm—so I was more attuned to what was going on in the UK than New York. I hit the ground running with a visit to the UK in my second week in the job. I took *Live at Sin-é* to the UK marketing department, and they went, "We don't get it; we don't understand it." Kip Krones was the UK head, but the words came from David Bower on the marketing team.

Photo by Meredith Zinner Photography

Julie Borchard
Vice-President, Columbia International

So I started helping with the live side. I went to [the agency] Helter Skelter and met with Emma Banks to play her the music, and she took Jeff on right away. She was such an important part of Jeff's success, a smart, savvy, really credible booking agent who got it immediately.

Steve Berkowitz was very pushy in a good way about the global nature of what Jeff had. We had some great knockdown fights about it: "What makes you think this is going to work for *me*, Berko?!" But he was right, and I gave him credit for that, at least I hope I did, along the way, because he understood that Jeff was an artist that should not just remain in our borders. Berkowitz knew I had my hackles up about his pushing into my territory, so he invited me to come to the studio while they were doing some mixes for *Grace*, and that's where I met Jeff.

He was so like a kid brother, a little bit put off by having to meet this person, "Who is she? Why do I have to care?" A little embarrassed by someone having to listen to him for the first time, a little awkward. I was awkward too, because I sat there listening to this music thinking, "What the hell is *this*?" I heard "Eternal Life" and one or two others.

It was sonically like a blow to the head wrapped in a warm hug, and I may have told him something to that effect. I was thinking, "Shit, this is really moving." I felt really privileged to be one of the few people who had heard it so far.

From then on, I was able to do my job better, to really believe in him, take these songs that they entrusted to me. I took "Hallelujah" to conferences and played it for the Brits and the Australians, and people got it, with a little bit of encouragement, and those people in the various territories really did their job.

Leah Reid

We'd gotten up to the recording of *Grace* and were discussing what we were going to do, and decided that the best way for people to experience Jeff was the way we had experienced him: live, on his own, and that we had to put him out on the road. But we all realized George Stein had his limitations when it came to certain things that management would normally handle—specifically, how to put a band on the road, how a tour worked, all that stuff. Naturally, George didn't know how to do that because he was an attorney, so that's when Steve said, "We need a real road dog to work with Jeff, a guy who knows touring inside and out," and he may have even said, "Someone like David Lory." That's how that happened; we'd hit a watershed: "Jeff's going to need some help to do what we need him to do." And that's when Dave was brought in.

CHAPTER 2

Tour Party Member #1

BEING BORN IN LEAVENWORTH, Kansas, sticks to you. The assumption is that you're either from a military background—there's a huge base there—or related to someone residing in Leavenworth state penitentiary, home to the nation's most hardened criminals. Either way, you're a person of interest to people in airports who think they're smart.

My dad, Robert Lory, wasn't a soldier or a convict. He was a shoe salesman, forever on the road. Every few years he'd get some kind of promotion that meant uprooting his family and starting over in another part of the country. I was born in Leavenworth in April 1959 and was nine years old when we went to Lincoln, Nebraska, then a year later to Omaha, where we stayed for six years. Then, in the summer between my junior and senior year of high school, my mother put her foot down at the prospect of moving to Minneapolis. She couldn't face the winters there. So Dad switched to a different firm, and we moved halfway across the US to Charlotte, North Carolina, which effectively eliminated every friendship I had made.

I attended mostly Catholic schools until I begged my parents to let me go to public school in the seventh grade in Omaha. I hated wearing uniforms and being beaten on by nuns and priests whose sadistic behavior was taken for granted.

Dave Lory performing at Worrell Bros., circa 1984, in Virginia Beach, Virginia.

I started playing percussion in the seventh grade and got my first drum set when I was twelve. My mother, Emerita, known to everyone as Ree, was a music teacher who taught after school every weekday from our home, and I assume that any musical talent I have was inherited from her. She was also busy bringing up four kids. I was the eldest, followed by Michael, Jennifer, and Christopher.

It wasn't until high school that I knew music was what I wanted to do with my life. In my junior year, I was playing drums in bars most nights or seeing other bands play, and I didn't want to show up at 6 a.m. to lift weights per my coach's instructions, so I quit playing quarterback for the football team. My parents and I were called to the school guidance counselor's office. She looked over at me with her most condescending smile, and even though I had great grades at the time, said: "Do you want to be a ditch digger the rest of your life?" I leaned across her desk and said, "No, I know exactly what I want to do. I am going to cut the soles off my shoes, climb a tree, and learn to play the flute. I'm going to be a musician!" Mom, bless her, just laughed at the counselor. The look on the woman's face was priceless.

For the next few years, I'd play my drums for up to six hours a day until I had blisters on blisters, playing along with Led Zeppelin, Rush, and all the metal bands who used double-kick drums. After several thunderous hours (which we later discovered had loosened many of the drywall studs in the house), Mom would walk into my room to announce that enough was enough and to point out that there was a crowd of girls out in our yard, listening. I couldn't get a date in high school; now I literally had females hanging around outside my window. The heavy, musky aroma wafting from my bedroom, a blend of drummer's sweat and marijuana, might well have attracted them.

After high school, instead of going to college I got a day job as a roofer and started playing in bands, doing summer seasons. By 1984, I knew I had to get to New York City to be successful in the music business. I was playing in a metal band called Buster Cherry, but no bar owner would put that on a marquee, so we changed our name to A.K.A., which stood, naturally, for Always Kicking Ass. We were doing good business on the East Coast, and I was managing as well as performing, beginning to enjoy the business end more than playing music. So I decided to attend NYU that fall to major in music business.[14]

While at college I got an internship at the Howard Bloom Agency, and learned about PR the hard way by assisting on Prince's *Purple Rain* tour while working seven nights a week at Colony Records, on Broadway, running the cash register until 2 a.m., to make my rent money. I was also managing a singer, Nick Seeger, son of the legendary Pete Seeger, working his album with two singles on the independent country charts.

After college, I spent the rest of my twenties tour-managing bands around the world, until I hit a psychic limit after a stint with Savatage, an unhinged metal band on Atlantic Records. When we were out with Dio and Megadeth, performing in arenas, it became a mobile riot of drugs, partying, and lawlessness—heavy metal at its most debauched. After months of dodging law enforcement, inter-band vendettas, and chemically assisted chaos, with gigs so rough there'd be barbed wire stretched across the front of the stage in some places, it all ended for me when our

[14] I got a local drummer, Scott Travis, to replace me in the band. He later became the drummer in Judas Priest and is with them to this day.

tour bus caught fire just outside Charlotte and I limped home, close to a nervous breakdown. This all happened just after Dad had died suddenly of a heart attack while dropping my brother off at college. It was a time to take stock. I was almost thirty and burnt out.

In 1989, I started booking guests for the panels at the New Music Seminar, a five-day and five-night event, the largest music conference in the world at that point. Jonny Podell from William Morris, the agent for The Allman Brothers Band, asked me to step in to tour-manage guitarist Dickey Betts's solo tour for two weeks, as his regular guy was unavailable. The Allman Brothers Band were preparing to announce that they were getting back together after a ten-year hiatus. They were the first huge rock band I ever saw, when I was fifteen. I got backstage and Dickey came up to me and said, "How're ya doing, hippie?" I asked him if he had anything against hippies, and he said, "No, I don't mind beating up a few every now and then." Now, fifteen years on, I was going to be this charmer's tour manager.

I managed to impress Dickey by standing up to him, and wound up tour-managing the reunion tour and subsequently co-managing the band with the brilliant Danny Goldberg. I also had former Ronette, Ronnie Spector on my roster. From 1990 through 1993, I booked the music at the New Music Seminar too. It was thirty-five venues with several artists in each venue nightly. It was an exciting time, as hip-hop was exploding along with the Seattle sound—Pearl Jam, Soundgarden, and Alice in Chains were among the new acts that I was booking.

But in 1993, I had to stop working with both Gregg and Ronnie; the chaos due to drugs, alcohol, and other distractions was becoming too much to handle. It just wasn't worthwhile for me anymore, dealing with stuff other than the music.

And that's where I was in my life when George Stein, my former lawyer, inquired if I'd consider co-managing Jeff Buckley. Several weeks after our café date, I agreed to start work just before Christmas 1993. Despite knowing I was going to be doing the bulk of the heavy lifting for half the commission, there was enough that interested me about Jeff to make me want to get involved. When I came on board, Jeff had been with Columbia Records for about a year. His debut EP had just been released, but it looked like it would be some time before his recordings generated any money. By any financial reasoning, I was crazy to take this gig. But I wasn't in it for the green. I was, like many others, fascinated by Jeff's approach to music, amazed by his talent and drawn to his personality. I was intrigued to see where it might lead. But I was also ready to bail if I didn't like the setup. I wanted to gauge how Columbia operated—and what Jeff was capable of onstage—before committing to signing on as a partner to George.

• • • • •

Step out your door in New York City on a January morning and you're stepping into a giant refrigerator. And if your door was in Hell's Kitchen in the mid-1990s, that would be a giant refrigerator full of prostitutes and drug paraphernalia. My neighborhood, 49th Street between Eighth and Ninth Avenue, wasn't the most desirable back then. It was lousy with people you wouldn't invite in for spaghetti. Plus all their garbage. Actually, when you got to know them, most of them were fine and left you alone and it was really pretty safe, but no one would call it picturesque. There was always construction work going on—clanging and drilling and jackhammering—and always bodies curled up beneath the scaffolding, living bodies mostly, the homeless and the unfortunates who'd nodded out after scoring. I got to like it though. Years into the future, Disney would buy up a lot of the surrounding buildings and the area would become chic and "family-oriented." The junkies and I weren't consulted. As an annex of the magical kingdom, Hell's Kitchen kind of lost its flavor.

On one particular Friday morning, January 14, 1994, the refrigerator was chugging away nicely but nothing too extreme. The streets were wet; there was some old snow clinging to the sidewalks. Angel, the doorman at The Worldwide Plaza, a modern development of apartments built around its own courtyard and mall, greeted me as I came out to my car. Angel acted like a concierge for my business, DE-EL Entertainment, which I ran out of my rented studio apartment. Although he wasn't actually an employee, he organized everything we needed at street level. He was great.

"Good morning, Mr. Lory. Going anywhere nice?"

"I wish," I said. "I'm going north, like an idiot."

Rule number one about touring is that you play the south in the winter and head north in the summer, but the whole Jeff Buckley project seemed to have thrown out the rulebook. I hadn't been in charge of the planning for this trip. It was booked before I came on board by Jeff's agent, Don Muller, and Missy Worth, the Senior Vice President in charge of marketing and promotion at Columbia. They were good people, but they weren't the ones facing hours driving through a North American winter to play tiny clubs with God knows who in them.

We were going to start in Canada, colder than a gravedigger's ass in the winter, but a great place to try out before having to play in front of anyone with an opinion. I'd checked on the weather in Vancouver, and it was due to be in the high forties Fahrenheit. Could have been a lot worse. So I allowed myself a little jolt of optimism. If I'm being honest, I was relishing going out on the road again. Just Jeff and I winding our way toward Los Angeles from the chilly northwest.

Angel hauled my Samsonite into the trunk of the waiting car.

"How far north, Mr. Lory?"

"Vancouver," I said.

"Bring me back a moose," he said, and gave a little wave like a low-level salute.

"East 12th Street," I said to the driver.

Jeff's apartment was number 2D at 233 East 12th Street, off Third Avenue, right around the corner from the recently opened Village East cinema and a few blocks away from St. Mark's Place, where he'd cut the record this trip was promoting. He lived modestly considering he'd signed a healthy record deal. His home was a little two-story walk-up with hardly any furniture. The bedroom was in the bottom half, a futon on the floor, the sparse decoration just some giant purple candles that had melted onto the bedside shelf. It had a wall of exposed brick, and there were a bunch of odd-looking Indian instruments and piles of cassettes next to his stereo. Off that was a tiny kitchen area, its sink always crammed with dirty dishes. The bathroom was on the little floor above, up a spiral staircase.

The Lower East Side at that time was a hip neighborhood, teeming with artists and poets and creative types. There were still a lot of squats

Photo by Jim Irvin

Jeff's apartment block on East 12th Street.

where artists lived rent-free, and plenty of weird places to hang out and hear Dadaist poetry and off-the-radar music and see improvised theater. Jeff fit right in. He lived like he could throw all his belongings onto a stick and go where the hell he wanted, which is more or less what he did.

When the car pulled up, he was outside on the sidewalk, dressed in his uniform—the same clothes he was wearing when I'd first met him: white V-neck T-shirt, shapeless black jeans with his keychain in one pocket, Doc Marten boots, topped with a vintage furry long winter coat. He had a backpack instead of a suitcase and was carrying his guitar for the trip—the white Telecaster he'd borrowed from Janine Nichols—and his boombox, which went everywhere with him. He was also holding one of his ever-present notebooks. He was always writing down ideas and observations, keeping a journal and emptying his emotions onto paper. He had books of lyrics he'd copied out for the Sin-é shows and one, he told me, that noted all the dreams that he thought were interesting. Most of his songs began in those books. He carried around several at a time, and they all had a skull-and-crossbones design on the front that he'd drawn himself.

I had a bunch of DE-EL Entertainment luggage tags. They had my contact information and a big black "#1" written on them. I put one on each of his modest pieces of luggage.

"What are those for?" he asked softly.

"Well, if you lose anything, someone can call the office, and they're easier to spot coming off the baggage belt at airports. Everybody joining the tour will have their own number, so the tour manager knows that, for instance, tour party member number one has five items of luggage to account for at every stop."

"Cool," he said, smiling. I could see it sinking in that he was actually going on tour. He started bouncing around the street while I smoked a Marlboro before heading to the airport. It was something I got used to seeing, Jeff the impatient kid, dancing around, anxious to go somewhere.

"I've got something for you," I said as we got into the car, and I handed him the tour book. This was a bound itinerary with all the dates that had been booked so far. Jeff was going to play a lot of solo dates across the country and do promotion with just the local independent media outlets, fanzines, and college radio, none of the majors at this stage. It was all going to be grassroots stuff. People are so much more committed if they feel they've discovered something without being hyped about it. Old-school marketing but effective with the right act. I hoped Jeff was the right act. I'd heard *Live at Sin-é* and a few songs he was recording for his first album, but I still hadn't seen him play yet. I was going to accompany him on the first leg to get to know him and then a full-time tour manager would take over for the rest of the shows so I could get on with my management duties.

Jeff spent almost the whole ride out to JFK leafing through the tour book, checking the capacities, the stage times, the publicity he'd be doing. We expected that to pick up as we went along, for people to be inspired to talk to him on the spot. He was up for that. Every now and then he'd make a comment about the number of people a club held, or a place he was due to play that he liked the sound of. His eyes were excited, dancing around the pages. The book meant it was all real at last. Something was actually happening.

I kept quiet and let him take it in. He didn't need someone talking his ear off, discussing business. There'd be plenty of time for that.

When we got to the airport, I called over a porter to take our bags. Jeff looked a little surprised.

"From now on I don't want you to hurt yourself picking up something the wrong way or carrying too much," I explained. "That's what we get tour support money from Sony for. There's a category for tips, tour party member number one."

He laughed. "Wow, you really do have this covered."

Remember, back then, air travel was pretty relaxed, especially domestic flights. It's hard now to recall how easy things were at airports before we started waging a war on terror. I could check in a whole band with just a list of passenger names. Jeff gave me his passport and took off to mooch around the bookstore, and I checked in all the bags, except his guitar, which I carried to the gate.

Jeff met me at the gate looking relaxed. I asked if he was okay about flying.

"Sure, I'm used to it," he said. "You didn't check in my guitar?"

"No, I try to avoid putting guitars in the hold. They always get bent out of shape."

As we boarded the plane, I told the stewardess that the guitar was a valuable vintage model, worth a lot of money, and asked if she could store it in the first-class closet. Jeff nodded at her and she smiled and took the guitar.

It was a six-hour flight to Vancouver. Jeff must have stared out of the window for the whole first hour and then he started writing in his journal, which he did for most of the flight. I looked over and saw the tight, tiny writing in black ink. He had a lot of thoughts to get out. I had some paperwork to do and some trade papers to read. I watched a movie and slept a little.

When we stepped off the plane at about 8 p.m., a stiff wind was coming in off the sea. We picked up our hire car, a white Ford Contour, perhaps the least sexy vehicle ever produced—but cheap. Jeff checked out the view on the way to our motel with anticipation. I'd told him how much I loved Vancouver, its ocean views, dramatic cliffs, and mountain scenery—one of the most beautiful coastal cities in the world, an underrated beauty, but right now just a streetlamp-lit highway in the winter darkness.

I'd been here many times with The Allman Brothers Band, so I'd gotten to know the city's less beautiful spots too; the Allmans liked to tickle the underbelly of every city they visited. I'd become well-acquainted with the Penthouse Club, a strip joint that all the rock bands would stumble into while in Vancouver. After Jeff and I had dinner, he said he wanted to get to bed. I decided to go over to the Penthouse and have a few drinks before turning in.

It wasn't quite the same, sitting there on my own nursing a Jack Daniel's without Gregg, Dickey, and the guys. I thought back to one time when I was tour-managing them in 1989 and we were approaching the Canadian border—always a ball ache at the best of times, but notoriously tricky with a band of the Allmans' dubious reputation—and one of the band yelled out, "Lory, I've lost my acid!" Acid came in tiny tabs on sheets of paper in those days, so that could have been anywhere. We searched as hard as we could but couldn't find his stupid sheet of dreams.

We arrived at the border, and I got off the bus with all the passports. When they worked out that Gregg Allman and co. were on board, the border goons went to town. They threw us off the bus and demanded that everyone be searched, including all our luggage, so we had to empty the baggage bins beneath the bus, while eight agents and two German shepherds went over it nose-first for contraband. I was smiling like everything's cool, but cussing the band member under my breath, because if the agents turned up this freaking acid, we were all going to jail for a few decades.

Thankfully, the Mounties and their hounds didn't uncover a thing on the bus or in our luggage. They looked kind of upset about it too. We got back on the bus and got the hell out of there. About an hour later, a cry went up: "Lory! I found my acid!" I didn't ask where.

I calculated that looking after Jeff Buckley wasn't going to be the same kind of gig, a circus of excess and slightly faded glory, all herding cats and damage control. I finished a second Jack Daniel's and figured that a lap dance for old times' sake wouldn't get me anywhere, so I made it an early night.

Saturday, January 15, 1994
The Railway Club, Vancouver

The Railway Club was a cute place with a long history. It began as a joint for railway workers in the early 1930s, the private club being a way to get around the tight drinking laws in British Columbia, which even after Prohibition didn't allow beer parlors to serve hard liquor. In the '80s, a local politician bought it and gave it to his kids to run; they turned it into a funky dive with pictures of the railway on the walls and a real toy train running around the ceiling, which was a bizarre touch. It was two rooms on the second floor of a commercial building, with windows onto the street, so the acoustics were a little wild.

I'd arranged for a Fender Twin amp to be delivered for the show, the perfect amp for small rooms. Jeff was going to plug straight in and sing through the PA. There was no need for a sound check, so we just showed up. Janet Forsyth, one of the sibling managers, was really cool. She'd booked acts like k.d. lang and Los Lobos for their first local shows and had grown a nice reputation for the club as a vibey spot to hang out and hear good music. Unfortunately, the hanging out seemed to take precedence. The place couldn't have held more than one hundred fifty people and was less than half full, but they were all drinking and talking loudly, clinking glasses, laughing and smoking. It wasn't the ideal place for a solo artist to make himself heard, but Jeff had done the Sin-é thing, so he took the same tack: strolled on, plugged in, said hi shyly, and began singing.

Nobody stopped yelling. The crowd was acting weird, like they'd been drinking all day. It felt like they couldn't even see Jeff was there. No one was paying him any attention.

Jeff hadn't prepared a set list. He was just doing what he'd always done, singing whatever came into his head and hoping to connect with the crowd—in this case, a pissy crowd. One or two people started listening, and Jeff directed his whole act at them, trying banter between the songs. Feeling left out, the rest of the room acted oblivious. Jeff had become used to rapt attention at Sin-é, but he was laying an egg at The Railway Club.

He, and the audience, started to get a little restless. After about five songs had ended to coughs and pathetic applause, someone shouted out: "Hey, play one of Tim's songs!" Instead of brushing it off, Jeff lost it and snapped back: "Fuck that. I'm my own person. I didn't know him. I don't play any of his songs. Go home and listen to his albums, if you want."

Well, that was great, taking a swipe at the only people listening. I felt for Jeff, but here he was insulting the audience, barking at someone who'd obviously bothered to come and check him out.

Tim Buckley was a prickly subject. But Jeff knew it would come up. He'd chosen to use the name professionally, after all. He could have used his childhood name, Scott Moorhead, or Jeff Guibert, if he wanted, so part of him must have been proud of the legacy, and he knew there wasn't much else for a curious gig-goer to latch on to at this point, but boy did he bristle whenever his father's name came up.

The atmosphere tanked from then on and never recovered. After forty-five minutes, he walked off to the sound of nobody giving a shit. I stood at the bar and I beckoned him over and handed him a beer. He was reluctant. I knew he didn't want to stay.

"Are you okay?" I asked.

He sighed.

"Tough crowd," I said. "Look, we can ask the next place not to toss bottles around during your set, but there's a lesson learned here. We're not going to walk into Sin-é every night. We've got to be prepared for these situations."

"And," I thought, "you've got to get that wasp out of your ass about your dad," but it wasn't the time to bring it up. He also needed to quit telling lame jokes. That was okay at Sin-é, where half the audience was in love with him already, but he needed to command respect a little sooner. He'd been spoilt by Sin-é's standing ovations. We had a bunch to discuss. But not yet.

We went back to the motel, which was a dive a couple of blocks away whose name I can't remember. We had an 8 a.m. flight to Seattle the next morning, so we just called it and went to bed.

I lay there for a while wondering if I'd made a mistake taking on this guy. Sure, he was talented, but his stagecraft seemed way off. I'd heard he was brilliant at reading the room at Sin-é, but perhaps he only knew how to preach to the converted. We were further away than I had realized.

There was something else I hadn't told him. Before the show, I'd had word from Columbia that they were getting resistance from college radio. The DJs didn't like *Live at Sin-é.* This was deep in the time of grunge. The college stations, which should have been Jeff's lifeblood, were still hammering Nirvana, Soundgarden, Pearl Jam, and their raucous cousins; an androgynous guy singing Edith Piaf and Van Morrison covers wasn't really on their radar. I wondered if the label had made a major error putting out the record we were promoting. This wasn't good. I needed to use this week with Jeff to come up with a decent plan setting up *Grace.* Although Berkowitz, Leah Reid and all the team were good people who understood Jeff's requirements, it didn't feel right to be letting the label lead the way. I had to get our vision on the table first. I had to make sure we were all in sync and doing what Jeff felt capable of. And here I was, weeks into this new job, facing an artist who was making music no one wanted to play, flopping in front of his first non-partisan crowd and losing the reins of his career before he'd started. I fell asleep and dreamed of climbing a mountain with a Fender Twin on my back.

Jeff was quiet the next morning on the way to the airport. He looked deflated; the enthusiasm was missing from his eyes. Or perhaps he was just exhausted—a 6 a.m. start was an unwelcome novelty. I left him alone to his thoughts.

I was thrilled to discover that Vancouver airport had a smartass at passport control, some guy who thought it was funny to make me sweat because my passport said I was born in Leavenworth. Jeff also thought it was funny. "You might have mentioned you were a wanted man," he said.

I was annoyed. Pointless shows of authority always make me angry, but it broke the ice and we started talking about our backgrounds. I told him how I'd been moved around a lot as a kid and how I'd lost touch with all my school friends. He said his upbringing had been the same—he was always moving—and he didn't really have any friends from the past either. He told me about his mom, Mary Guibert, and stepdad, Ron Moorhead, and his half brother, Corey, and how they'd moved around Orange County. He told me Ron had been the biggest influence upon his taste in music. He remembered lying in the dark in the back of Ron's van listening to Led Zeppelin playing at high volume on the stereo, and how good he felt soaking up the music. Ron had bought him his first album, Led Zeppelin's *Physical Graffiti*, when he was nine years old. I didn't realize at the time that the building on the cover of that album is on St. Mark's Place, in fact it's on the same block as Sin-é, directly opposite the site of the Yaffa Cafe, where Jeff liked to meet people. I assume he knew that. If he didn't, it was a spooky coincidence that his career began right there.

I told him about my mother, Ree, the music teacher, how I'd been a drummer in metal bands but also played in the Charlotte Symphony Orchestra. He loved that I'd been in a band called Always Kicking Ass. He told me he'd studied at the Guitar Institute in LA, which, I realized later, he would almost never mention; he'd been unhappy there and didn't want it defining him. And we talked again about how we both loved Zeppelin and Van Halen, and when I reminded him I'd tour-managed metal bands in the '80s, he asked lots of questions about their live shows.

Inevitably, we got to the subject of guitar setups, a major obsession of all rock nerds. I told him about a guy I had worked with, Chris Oliva, the guitarist with Savatage, who everyone on the tour called "Captain Crunch" because of his biting guitar sound. He went onstage with one distortion pedal nailed to a piece of plywood and got such an incredible tone that Dio and Megadeth both fired their guitar techs, as Chris was getting a better sound. I told Jeff how Angus Young of AC/DC didn't use any pedals at all, just came straight out of his amp. It's a feel thing; more is not necessarily more. Jeff lapped up this stuff. I did too. We were a couple of music-crazed loners getting forensic about the sounds that had stirred us.

We discussed how the focus for these shows was for him to be seen by the grassroots press, find some fans, and meet people in retail. I explained how if those guys aren't on your side, you can kiss your career goodbye. There is fierce competition to be stocked by the best stores and to have your albums in the prime sites, the window displays, the

Photo by Jim Irvin

94–96 St. Mark's Place, New York City, 2017. This, the building that appeared on the cover of Led Zeppelin's "Physical Graffiti," Jeff's treasured first album, is on the same block as the site of Sin-é.

point-of-sale bins, the "Now Playing" disc on the counter—what went in those slots was all down to the store managers and distributors, and you only got them if they like you. Some of them need to be "sweetened" to like you. Some are happy with free records they can make a pure profit on; some play ball for a steak dinner and a few lines of coke to soften their snarky asses and remember you fondly. Some just like to mingle with musicians, bathe in their starlight and get to feel important for a while. The artists who realize this and are prepared to shake hands, exchange some small talk and plump up a few egos, always do much better than the rest. Jeff was happy to give it a try.

All the advance press—phone interviews and introductory pieces based around *Live at Sin-é*—had already run, and there had been considerable hype about Jeff's five-octave vocal range and his lineage, and what Columbia had spent on signing him. I've never understood why the amount of money someone throws at an act is news, but there you go. Those stories are always bullshit anyway. A "million-dollar record deal" is usually spread over several long contract periods that few artists ever see out. We had to dial back that hype. We needed to show people he was a regular guy—his own man, as he said, not some mystical throwback to his tragic dad. Also, we needed to show he was musically relevant, make it clear this was just a little acoustic hello before we returned with the full band and unveiled the extraordinary album they'd just recorded. Finally, it was vital that he developed his craft away from the make-'em/break-'em cities, New York and LA, so that when the big media players finally got to see what the fuss was about, there was actually something to see.

We didn't get into a postmortem of the Vancouver show. It felt like we'd bonded a little, and I could see Jeff's spirits had lifted; I didn't want to bring him down again. Besides, before we knew it we had landed in Seattle.

Sunday, January 16, 1994
Cafe Paradiso, Seattle

If there's such a thing as a connoisseur of rain, he or she is probably sitting pretty in Seattle. That city's weather is the worst, and January 16 was no exception; we stepped off the plane into a thick fog with torrential rain. I didn't know that was even possible. Somewhere under eight varieties of clouds was the hip district where Cafe Paradiso buzzed. If there's something a Seattleite appreciates even more than precipitation, it is caffeine. The coffeehouse boom was just heading into its upswing then, and places like Café Paradiso were leading the charge. The vibe in there was what it must have been like in Greenwich Village when Dylan was making a name for himself: hipsters enjoying their seat at the sharp end of a new culture, feeling sexy discussing art and politics over frothy java.

There weren't many of them there, but they had actually come to check Jeff out, not drown him out. They still talked during his set, still called out for Tim's songs, but Jeff handled it better. He could see they were interested in the sound he was making. He kept telling jokes and constructed his set list as he went along, alternating songs he'd cut for *Grace* with some of the zillion random covers he'd memorized, but it was a better show because the audience was on his side.

He went off to some genuine appreciation. There was a tight little group of people who wanted to talk to him afterward. Jeff was gracious to them, and I watched them walk away nodding, discussing how good he was, how cool or cute or whatever. "So here we go," I thought. "One person at a time."

I'm an early riser. By 8:30 the next morning, I was ready for breakfast. Figuring Jeff would marinate between the sheets until at least noon, like all night owl musicians, I slipped a note under his door. To my surprise, he opened it, standing in the doorway in his underwear.

"Hey, man, it's a little soon for love letters, don't you think?"

I laughed. "Just letting you know I was going out for breakfast, handsome."

"Let me powder my nose and I'll join you," he said.

Of course, once we ventured outside we were greeted by more freezing slops from heaven, so we made it only as far as a divey diner next to our divey motel.

Over questionable eggs and greasy home fries, we discussed what was coming up. He was clearly still down after the last couple of shows, a little confused by why he wasn't connecting with these people.

"I feel like background music," he said into his coffee.

"Look, for some people, you are," I said. "It's always like that in these places, but fuck 'em. You're really talented. In a year's time, they'll all be bragging about how they were at your first show."

Jeff sniffed a little laugh.

"This is what paying your dues feels like, man," I said. "It's not a sprint, it's a marathon. But, despite that, we've a lot to do before we hit LA in a few days. This is where you have to trust me." I caught his eyes like a hypnotist. "I mean, you have to trust someone in this whole process, and it should be your manager. I want you to feel, to *know* you can trust me.

If you don't, then I'm the wrong guy for you, and you should say so soon, before it all kicks off."

He didn't say anything at all, just nodded at me, like he wanted to hear more.

"Give me a shot. Let me show you that I can do what's right for you."

"I trust you," he said softly.

"All right. Here's what I'd like you to do. Tell me everything. I need you to open up with me personally, musically; tell me your fears, your dreams, what makes you run, what makes you mad. I need to know everything so I can protect you and your work. To represent you, I have to know what's driving you. Can you trust me with that responsibility? Can you give me that information?"

He nodded again.

I knew that Jeff trusted almost nobody. Fathers and homes and schoolmates had evaporated. He neither expected trust nor gave it away. I was asking a lot, but it was what I needed in order to do my job. I didn't want to scare him; I just needed him to think about it, to get used to the idea of letting someone in.

"Cool. We've got a long drive after Portland, and then you can start telling me what you want me to do for you. You know, I think we should do the whole drive in one hit rather than stop off in Reading."

"Really? That's a long way."

"Ten hours door to door," I said.

"Can you handle that?" he asked.

"Trust me," I said, laughing. We had two long drives coming up, from Portland to San Francisco and from there to Los Angeles, where we'd meet up with people from the label again, and I was aiming to use those hours alone on the road to construct our plan together, plot the future to his specifications, not simply follow a plan that was convenient for his record company. This next part's corny, but it's what I felt. "Do you know *Butch Cassidy and the Sundance Kid*?" I asked.

"Sure, I love that movie," Jeff said.

"Well, that's what we've got to be," I said. "Two guys blasting our way out of a corner. Us against the rest of the world, if necessary."

"Okay," he said, thinking about it.

"I'm Butch, by the way," I said.

"Guess I must be Sundance, then."

"You got it."

As we left the diner; I pulled out the sheet for that day's show.

"You're going to like this one," I said. "Who couldn't love a place called the Velvet Elvis theater? It's gotta be better than the last two nights. For a start, it's an actual theater. With seats in it. Facing the stage and everything."

Butch and Sundance stepped out into the rain.

Monday, January 17, 1994
Velvet Elvis Arts Lounge, Seattle

Yes, it was a real artsy place, low-fi, with torn seats and a nice vibe. And no bar in the auditorium! Also, we'd attracted a crowd that was twice the size of the previous night, so perhaps something was working already.

Backstage, Jeff seemed genuinely excited to play this time. Even a little nervous—which I'd not really sensed from him before—pacing around the tiny dressing room, making those shrill purrs that singers use to warm up their voice, and singing scales.

He came out to a hushed room, walked into the lone spotlight, plugged in his borrowed Telecaster, said hello, and checked he was in tune.

"It's an honor to be inside Velvet Elvis," he said. It wasn't a great line, but it summoned a murmur of amusement. "I hope I can live up to its name." He started singing the first line of "Heartbreak Hotel."

I was cringing offstage. "No, please don't start with an Elvis song," I thought. "That's not gonna get them." Luckily, he stopped after the first line. Somebody sniggered.

"Er, I think I just made an album," Jeff said in his typically self-deprecating way. "This is something from it. It might be the title song."

"Grace" sounded great. The applause was warm and real. But somehow the show slipped away from him after that. He talked too much, tried to be funny, and the set was different again from the previous nights. The crowd was receptive, willing him to be great, and they were enjoying what he was doing, but he kept dropping the ball with a false start, a lame comment, or a song he hadn't played enough. It was like watching someone lose to himself in a game of Snakes and Ladders.

A quick glance told me that some of the women were paying very close attention to what was in front of them, but otherwise this audience wasn't especially engaged. I wondered if here, in the capital of grunge, we were witnessing the problem that was hurting us at college radio: they weren't quite ready for what Jeff was offering. I didn't realize that in just a few months' time, grunge's leading light would put a gun in his mouth and blow the whole movement away. Things can turn on a dime in this business.

For now, I had to assume Jeff was ahead of his time. I'd been with ahead-of-their-time artists before. I once worked with Nick Seeger, talented nephew of folk legend Pete Seeger. Nick was trying to break into country music. He had some great songs. One in particular, "Where Are You Now," reduced me to tears. He made a demo of it, and we shopped it around Nashville. All the labels told us it was too much, too sad for country radio. Three years later, Kathy Mattea cut it and had a smash that was voted the Country Music Association's Song of the Year. Same song, different time. Like I said, things can turn on a dime in this business.

The applause was polite when Jeff finished, and there was an audible buzz of appreciation as the audience filed out of the room, but the overall mood was underwhelming.

"How was that for you, Sundance?" I asked as Jeff came backstage.

"Trash and vaudeville," he said. That was the name of a famous punk clothing store on St. Mark's Place. We laughed. Some people were gathering outside the dressing room to talk to him.

"Watch out for the girl with the ponytail," I said. "I saw her taking notes while you were on. She might be a journalist. Or a stalker. Either way..."

At least he'd enjoyed himself and blossomed a little. It was a start. I felt we were edging into a routine now: do the show, press the flesh, go back and get plenty of rest, and I was beginning to get an idea of how to fix this wonky cart.

• • • • •

Our next stop was Portland, Oregon. I was looking forward to it, because a very good friend, Michael Bazzanni, ran an Italian restaurant there. Michael and I went way back. I met him when he ran Le Bar Bat on West 57th Street in New York. I was a frequent customer in the '80s. We got talking and it turned out we shared a birthday, April 2. He was interested in bringing music into the bar; he knew I was in the business, and he got me to consult on attracting a crowd. The place was on the site of an old recording studio. He collected gold discs from all the artists who'd recorded there and put them on the walls, and then Pete Fogel, the music booker, hired great session players to come by and do some of the hits they'd appeared on. Naturally, they'd invite famous friends to sit in, and you never knew who'd show up. It became a permanent party. It also got a reputation as a great pickup spot for singles and, if you knew who to ask, a place to score coke. After several years, I had free rein of the place, with food and drink on the house, which was a nice perk. But all good things come to an end. I was mortified when Michael decided to move out and open a place in Portland, called Pinocchio's, and I'd not seen him since. It was going to be a sweet reunion.

It was a crisp, sunny morning when we left Seattle. It seemed a different city without the blanket of cloud. We needed some gas, so we pulled into a truck stop. Jeff went into the store and came out with a clutch of cheap cassettes: Emmylou Harris, Hank Williams, Anita Baker, and some random hair-metal bands. It seemed a bizarre selection, but he played through them on the journey and found something he loved about each one, singing along to them, mimicking the vocal styles in a way I'd never heard anybody do before. He was uncanny, like a mynah bird, able to pick up and replicate a vocal tone immediately.

He knew a lot about all the artists too, and he'd talk about their lives while he tried on their sound and had little conversations with them. I didn't say much, just listened to Jeff on his one-man ramble through music history. It was really entertaining. I was bowled over by how much he understood about so many different kinds of music, and I loved his non-judgmental attitude, so respectful toward the musicians and mindful of what it took to make any music that he didn't put any of it down. He was as moved by the shittiest one-hit hair-metal band as by the seasoned iconic country singer, but for different reasons. It all had value to him. Music made him weep, made him laugh, made him pine for someone or punch the air. He had obviously immersed himself in it completely to achieve this level of knowledge and maturity. It was staggering. Music was the love of his life.

We walked into Pinocchio's in the late afternoon, when it was nice and quiet. Michael welcomed us warmly and immediately started bringing out food: antipasto, pasta, oysters, mussels, veal, you name it. Jeff and I had been eating like shit for the previous few days, so this was an incredible treat. We fell on it like locusts. Michael brought wine for each course too. So we were pretty relaxed when he sat down and started reminiscing about our days together at Le Bar Bat. He told Jeff how I'd strut around supervising the music every night and how the place became like a club for fifteen hundred crazy people with all the wild stuff we got up to—the parties, the women, the hell we raised. Jeff peppered Michael with questions about me.

Michael started talking about Pam, a beautiful woman he had introduced me to. We'd hit it off immediately and borrowed Michael's keys to get to know each other better at his apartment. He recalled coming home with a bunch of friends early the next morning and walking in to find me and Pam butt-naked, doing lines of coke off his coffee table.

Jeff looked at me in a mock disapproving way.

"Hey, I wasn't always a manager, you know," I said. He burst out laughing and repeated it in a perfect imitation of me. 'I wasn't always a manager, you know!'

We had to leave for our sound check at 6 p.m. We staggered from Pinocchio's like we'd had Thanksgiving and Christmas dinners on one night.

"Do you wanna do a show tonight or go to sleep somewhere?" I said, only half joking.

"I feel like that guy from *Monty Python*," said Jeff. "I could just go onstage and eat a wafer-thin mint..."

Tuesday, January 18, 1994
La Luna, Portland

The booker at La Luna, Anthony Rhodes, was obviously a fan, very pleased to have Jeff at his club. Unfortunately, this show was the worst yet. Everyone in the sparse crowd seemed to be obsessed with Jeff's father, constantly calling out for Tim Buckley songs, even shouting out how much Jeff looked like him.

Jeff tried to be cool about it, but I could see it was his patience that was wafer-thin. He spent a long time talking to them, trying to make them see that he was about something else, but they wouldn't take the hint. At one point he tried singing one of the Hank Williams songs he'd been listening to on the journey down. He did a brief, beautiful version. When it was over, someone shouted out, "Buzzin' Fly," another Tim Buckley classic. For a second, I thought Jeff was going to smash his borrowed guitar. He breathed in and spoke with his jaw clenched.

"Listen, I'd appreciate it if you forgot about my father. He was never there for me. I didn't know him. I didn't even get to go to his funeral. Did anyone here see him play?"

Nobody spoke.

"Well, you listen to his records, obviously, which is more than I do. So you probably know my *dad* better than I do."

You could eat the silence with a spoon.

He closed the set with an angry version of "Last Goodbye," walked off, and came straight over to me at the bar. "Jesus, what's wrong with these people? Let's go. I hate this city."

"No, I'm finishing my drink."

He stood at the bar sulking until I was done.

• • • • •

It was a perfect night for our long ride to San Francisco—a balmy night, no wind, no rain, just Jeff and me on a deserted highway.

When we got into the car, it was my turn to hog the stereo. I put on a tape of the Allman Brothers, recorded directly off the sound board from the time I was managing them. It was perfect road music. Jeff listened carefully to the Allmans cooking up a storm. After one of Dickey Betts's pealing solos, he laughed out loud and thumped the dashboard:

"Mother...fucker!"

I knew what I needed to tell him. "You know, man, you got to learn something out here, on this trip, on that stage, something I can't teach you. When Dickey or Keith Richards or one of those dudes puts on their guitar, it's like a gunslinger putting on their holster. They've got to believe they're the best or they can't fight. It's all about attitude. You've got to own the stage and the audience every night. You're up there and they're out there. They deserve a show, and you can deliver it. You're the best in the West, and they gotta see it. They've gotta be a little in awe of you. Attitude."

"Okay."

"Why do you talk so much up there?"

"I'm connecting with them. Making them feel comfortable."

"You're making them feel uncomfortable, because you're not in charge. You're asking permission. You're hoping they like you, not demanding they listen. You can get up there and take their breath away. You know you can, so that's what you do. Not say, 'Thanks for coming out, folks,' like you're grateful, but say, 'Look what I can do with my pistol.' Attitude."

Jeff was thinking about this, gazing out of the window.

I was just warming up. "You've got to quit making jokes. Maybe once you fascinate them, fine, but first you've got to slay them with your music. Don't react to the shit about your father. Show them you're vulnerable and they'll turn on you or turn away. Show them what you do and they won't care about him anymore. They want to be taken by surprise; they didn't come to see a nice guy and his guitar. Or if they did, show them that you're more than that. They don't want a peck on the cheek; they want to be ridden."

Jeff smiled at that. "That's a whole other kind of show."

"You know what I mean," I went on. "You got to take them and take them with you. Your sets aren't flowing. They don't ebb and build; they don't climax. You just play some songs and say some dumb shit. With each song, you're starting from scratch. Structure your set to take them on a ride. It'll take a while to figure out, but that's what you got to work toward, starting from the next show." I knew Jeff already knew all this, but I didn't want him to take it for granted. I wanted him to see that you needed to think about it every day.

On the stereo, the Allmans' show was building.

"These guys are incredible," I said, jabbing the air for emphasis. "Check out how they go from 'One Way Out' into 'Melissa,' faster to slower, then building up again, taking their audience on a trip. They left them wrung out by the end."

"Spent."

"You got it."

Jeff listened to the music for a while.

"We'll be in LA soon," I said. "Those shows are sold out with a guest list of who's who in Tinseltown. That crowd's going to be tougher but also more open than anywhere else. You've got to take that crowd by the scruff of its neck and..."

"Attitude its brains out."

"Yes!"

We laughed out loud in unison.

"So, Sony called me the other night and said that college radio isn't picking up on *Sin-é*. It's not right for their formats," I said. "Sucks, but there it is. We need to do what R.E.M. used to do, take care of college radio first. We'll just show up, tell them we're in town, and get ourselves on air. We've got to build it from the ground up so that they're on your side by the time *Grace* comes out. We'll get Columbia to take you round those stations. You cool with that?"

"Yes, sure."

"Good. You're different, so you've got to work a bit harder to make people notice, to earn the right to be different. But different is best; once something original sticks, it's there forever. You kick a door down and no one can do it again."

We started to talk about where he saw himself musically, where he wanted to be in five years. He said he hated the hype and agreed he needed to let the music do the work. He wanted to win people over gradually, like he had at Sin-é—let it happen organically, not by performing on TV shows, having a hit single, or getting on film soundtracks, and definitely no advertisements. MTV was still massive at the time, and he said he didn't really want to do videos either.

"Okay, this is all going to get me a warm reception over at the label," I thought. "We might need to compromise a little here and there, but this is something to work with."

"Who do you see yourself as?" I said. "Whose career would you like yours to resemble?"

"Dylan," he shot back, without a thought. "He's the reason I signed to Columbia. Him and Springsteen."

"Good, I can work with that." That gave me the focus. I could instruct the label to think of how they grew two of their A-list acts.

I had to put together a marketing plan that built things city by city. We'd aim to make our money touring, make Jeff Buckley self-sufficient. If he didn't need to go cap in hand to Columbia, they couldn't tell him what to do. We'd aim to get him off tour support by the end of the first record.[15]

Jeff pulled one of his journals out of his backpack. It was a small, thick diary held together with duct tape, with what looked like a lock on it. He began to write in it—urgently. I got used to seeing him do this. Sometimes he would take scraps of paper from his pockets and copy them into one of his books. Just before this trip, he had been to England for a week over the new year, to visit Elizabeth Fraser, the singer with Cocteau Twins, whose voice, he told me, stopped him in his tracks. "It sounds like light," he said. They'd met briefly a couple of times and had been talking on the phone since just before we first met. He'd gone to stay with her in Twickenham. I don't know what happened there, but I knew later that they were lovers and saw that he went misty-eyed when he spoke about her. They'd been introduced when Cocteau Twins toured the US in 1991. In 1983, Liz and her fellow Cocteau Twin and partner, Robin Guthrie, had cut a cover of his dad's beautiful, desolate "Song To The Siren" with This Mortal Coil, a version so arresting that Jeff would have no choice but to be attracted to it. She in turn had gone to check Jeff out, and remarked later that she had "sweated like a June bride" when she first heard him sing. She had separated from Guthrie by this time and was having an unhappy time in the band. "To meet Jeffrey was like being given a set of paints," she said in a TV documentary. "I had all this color in my life again. I couldn't help falling in love with him; he was adorable." She noted that he had idolized her and she had fallen for the son of someone whose music she loved, and it felt a bit creepy. But they couldn't help themselves. She also remarked

[15] Tour support, a loan from the record company to cover touring costs.

that they had read each other's diaries. I wonder now if he was writing about her then on that long drive.[16]

After a while, Jeff put the little book away and brought out another sheet of paper. It was a letter to Bob Dylan.

"I've got to tell you what happened a few months ago," he said. "I met Dylan after a show one night. He was really great and told me to make a great record, and the next night I was playing at the Hole in the Wall, so I did 'I Want You,' and I was doing Dylan's voice, you know..."

He goes into a spookily accurate impression of Bob Dylan, all the cadences right on the money.

"And I was telling the crowd how I'd seen him play and he could still be brilliant on some songs and then others he just tramples over. Then I sang 'Grace' as if I was Bob. I love the guy so much, I sent him up. And the people got it. But then the next day Steve Berkowitz tells me that Dylan's management had been in the audience, and they didn't see the funny side and they were pissed off about it. They were gonna tell Dylan that Tim Buckley's son was doing impressions of him and being disrespectful."

"And that's the opposite of what you were doing?"

"Right! The guy's my hero. I thought it was obvious."

"Idiots being touchy on behalf of their meal ticket, telling tales out of school," I said.

"I felt awful that it got back to him. Couldn't shake it. Couldn't sleep. I thought, 'I have to write and tell him.' I want to know what you think of this," he said. We found somewhere off the highway to pull over so I could read by the roof light.

The letter was sweet, not too groveling, mature, really heartfelt:

> *It kills me to know that whatever they told you is what you think I think of you. Not that I love you, not that I've always listened to you and carried the music with me wherever I go, not that I believe in you. And also the show was great. It was only the supper club crowd I was cynical about, and that's what I was trying to get at. And I'm sorry that I'll never get to make another*

[16] I'd learned long before I met Jeff not to ask too many questions or make judgments about an artist's personal life, because if you're drawn into it or know too much about it, it's never good for the artist-manager relationship.

first impression. You were really gracious to let me backstage to meet you and I'll never forget what you said as long as I live...I'm very honored to have met you at all...Someday you will know exactly what I mean, man to man.

"Should I send it?"

"Sure, why not? It's obviously sincere. You write well. He'd dig that. And you're right; a letter is probably the best way to reach him. He doesn't answer the phone much, I hear. Do you want me to get his address?"

Jeff nodded. He carefully put the letter in his backpack.

"Dave?" said Jeff. "Do you ever, like, when you're on the highway and there's no one else around, take your hands off the wheel?"

"No," I said, wondering where this was leading. "I always keep my hands on the wheel."

"Okay," said Jeff, apparently satisfied with my answer.

We pulled into a 7-Eleven for some coffee around 3 a.m. It was a peaceful night. We walked around the parking lot to stretch our legs, and I lit a cigarette. Jeff grabbed it out of my hand and stole a hit.

"That's not too good for the voice," I said.

Jeff laughed and danced around like a kid, waving my Marlboro by his ear. He took another hit and sang some corny song, like Marlene Dietrich or someone. Then he just handed it back to me.

"I'm letting that go," I said. "Try it on Dylan and see where it gets you."

He burst out laughing, like it was a relief. I felt good that he'd taken me into his confidence about the letter. He knew I was on his side.

When we got back on the road, Jeff started telling me, without prompting, why he was sensitive about mentions of his father. He referred to it as his "entire family issue." His mom, Mary, was only eighteen when he was born, and Tim was already out of the picture. She took him to meet Tim in the early years. Jeff had a dream-like memory of being with both parents on Venice Beach, which must have happened before he was two. When he was three, little Scotty, as the family knew him—Scott was his middle name—was best man at his mom's wedding to Ron Moorhead. Ron was a mechanic, totally different than Tim, but he loved music and was always buying albums. Scotty really liked him. Tim sent money occasionally, and his management would forward his new releases, so his music was in the household, but it made Ron angry and he wouldn't play it. Scotty loved Ron's stuff anyway: The Doors, Elton John, Pink Floyd, and his favorite, Led Zeppelin. But when he was six, that marriage failed too. Mary married for a third time, and they moved to a nice house for a while—Mary, Scotty, and his baby brother, Corey. At one point his mom moved away to find work, and Scotty stayed with Mary's sister, Peggy and her husband. He never lived in a trailer, but later Jeff would sometimes refer to his upbringing as "typical rootless trailer trash." It was shorthand for how he felt. To me he just said, "Mom tried hard, but sometimes I felt ashamed at school, you know, always the new kid catching up."

Suddenly, when he was eight years old, he was told he was going to meet his dad. Mary took him to see Tim play a show in Huntington Beach. He ran backstage afterward and sat on his dad's lap and tried to tell him everything about himself. He did his George Carlin impression and everything. He remembered how hot and sweaty Tim was. Tim and his new wife, Judy, were nice to him and invited him to stay with them for a week over Easter. Judy had a son, Taylor. Jeff remembered having a great time. He came home with his dad's phone number on a matchbook. But a few months later, he was told Tim had died suddenly. It was an accidental overdose. But nobody told Scotty that then.

He took the news in stride, but it must have really affected him. Soon after that, he didn't want to be Scotty Moorhead any more. He was going to take the name that was on his birth certificate, Jeffrey Scott Buckley.

Now, nearly twenty years later, that little kid had a complex set of feelings about his complex family tree. He loved and hated all of them. Loved them for doing their best and making him who he was, hated them for being flaky and making him who he was. Sometimes he was proud of his mom; sometimes he wished she'd tried harder with the men he'd wanted to look up to, men he wished had been less weak and selfish and more aware of his feelings when they slipped out of his life. But it all stemmed back to Tim, the first to let him down. Whatever his memories of the few times they met, whatever his thoughts about his music—and he'd certainly absorbed it over the years, gone to it alone occasionally in search of some answers—his overriding feeling about Tim Buckley, as he spoke to me, was that the guy hadn't loved him enough to stick around. And Jeff had forged his own sound without

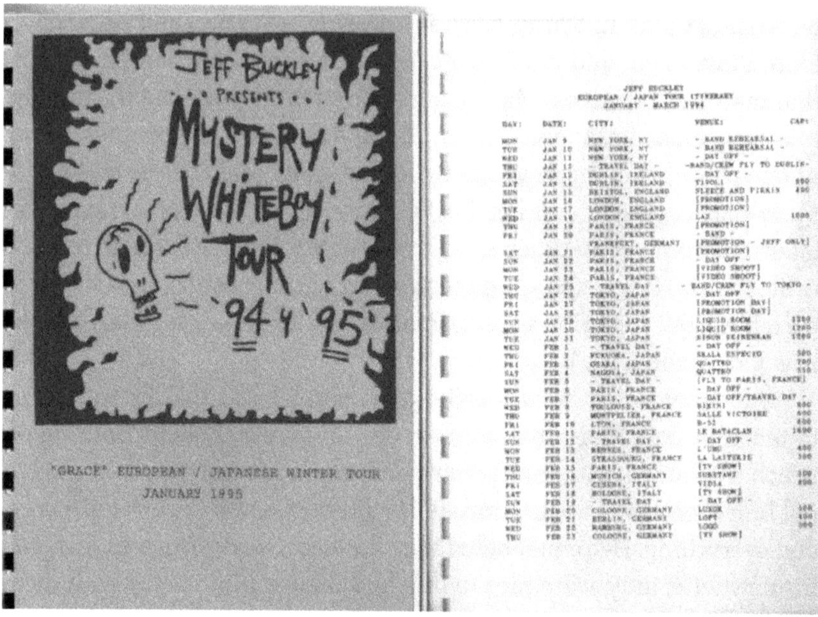

JEFF BUCKLEY
EUROPEAN / JAPAN TOUR ITINERARY
JANUARY - MARCH 1994

DAY:	DATE:	CITY:	VENUE:	CAP:
MON	JAN 9	NEW YORK, NY	- BAND REHEARSAL -	
TUE	JAN 10	NEW YORK, NY	- BAND REHEARSAL -	
WED	JAN 11	NEW YORK, NY	- DAY OFF -	
THU	JAN 12	- TRAVEL DAY -	-BAND/CREW FLY TO DUBLIN-	
FRI	JAN 13	DUBLIN, IRELAND	- DAY OFF -	
SAT	JAN 14	DUBLIN, IRELAND	TIVOLI	850
SUN	JAN 15	BRISTOL, ENGLAND	FLEECE AND FIRKIN	400
MON	JAN 16	LONDON, ENGLAND	[PROMOTION]	
TUE	JAN 17	LONDON, ENGLAND	[PROMOTION]	
WED	JAN 18	LONDON, ENGLAND	LA2	1000
THU	JAN 19	PARIS, FRANCE	[PROMOTION]	
FRI	JAN 20	PARIS, FRANCE	- BAND -	
		FRANKFURT, GERMANY	[PROMOTION - JEFF ONLY]	
SAT	JAN 21	PARIS, FRANCE	[PROMOTION]	
SUN	JAN 22	PARIS, FRANCE	- DAY OFF -	
MON	JAN 23	PARIS, FRANCE	[VIDEO SHOOT]	
TUE	JAN 24	PARIS, FRANCE	[VIDEO SHOOT]	
WED	JAN 25	- TRAVEL DAY -	- BAND/CREW FLY TO TOKYO -	
THU	JAN 26	TOKYO, JAPAN	- DAY OFF -	
FRI	JAN 27	TOKYO, JAPAN	[PROMOTION DAY]	
SAT	JAN 28	TOKYO, JAPAN	[PROMOTION DAY]	
SUN	JAN 29	TOKYO, JAPAN	LIQUID ROOM	1200
MON	JAN 30	TOKYO, JAPAN	LIQUID ROOM	1200
TUE	JAN 31	TOKYO, JAPAN	NIHON SEINENKAN	1200
WED	FEB 1	- TRAVEL DAY -	- DAY OFF -	
THU	FEB 2	FUKUOKA, JAPAN	SKALA ESPACIO	500
FRI	FEB 3	OSAKA, JAPAN	QUATTRO	700
SAT	FEB 4	NAGOYA, JAPAN	QUATTRO	550
SUN	FEB 5	- TRAVEL DAY -	[FLY TO PARIS, FRANCE]	
MON	FEB 6	PARIS, FRANCE	- DAY OFF -	
TUE	FEB 7	PARIS, FRANCE	- DAY OFF/TRAVEL DAY -	
WED	FEB 8	TOULOUSE, FRANCE	BIKINI	800
THU	FEB 9	MONTPELIER, FRANCE	SALLE VICTOIRE	600
FRI	FEB 10	LYON, FRANCE	B-52	400
SAT	FEB 11	PARIS, FRANCE	LE BATACLAN	1400
SUN	FEB 12	- TRAVEL DAY -	- DAY OFF -	
MON	FEB 13	RENNES, FRANCE	L'UBU	400
TUE	FEB 14	STRASBOURG, FRANCE	LA LAITERIE	300
WED	FEB 15	PARIS, FRANCE	[TV SHOW]	
THU	FEB 16	MUNICH, GERMANY	SUBSTANZ	300
FRI	FEB 17	CESENA, ITALY	VIDIA	800
SAT	FEB 18	BOLOGNE, ITALY	[TV SHOW]	
SUN	FEB 19	- TRAVEL DAY -	- DAY OFF -	
MON	FEB 20	COLOGNE, GERMANY	LUXOR	500
TUE	FEB 21	BERLIN, GERMANY	LOFT	400
WED	FEB 22	HAMBURG, GERMANY	LOGO	300
THU	FEB 23	COLOGNE, GERMANY	[TV SHOW]	

One of Jeff Buckley's tour books (above) and itineraries (right).

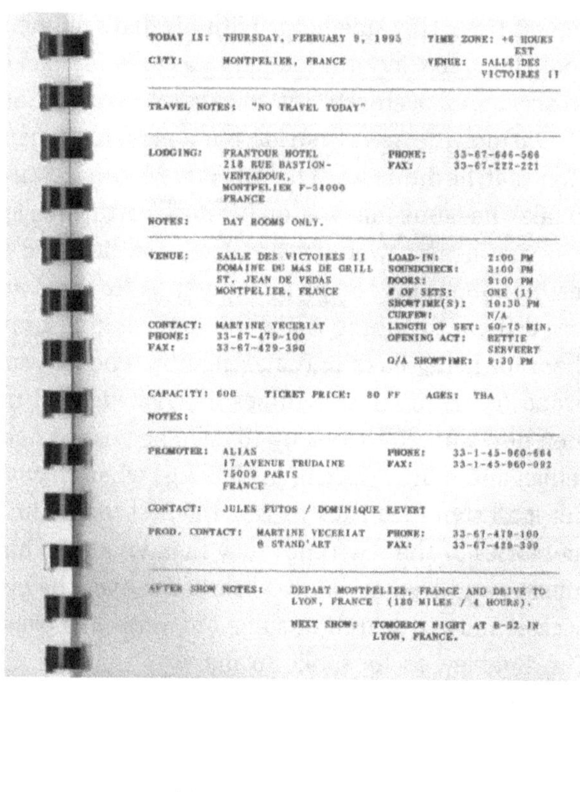

TODAY IS: THURSDAY, FEBRUARY 9, 1995 — TIME ZONE: +6 HOURS EST

CITY: MONTPELIER, FRANCE — VENUE: SALLE DES VICTOIRES II

TRAVEL NOTES: "NO TRAVEL TODAY"

LODGING: FRANTOUR HOTEL
218 RUE BASTION-
VENTADOUR,
MONTPELIER F-34000
FRANCE
PHONE: 33-67-646-566
FAX: 33-67-222-221

NOTES: DAY ROOMS ONLY.

VENUE: SALLE DES VICTOIRES II
DOMAINE DU MAS DE GRILL
ST. JEAN DE VEDAS
MONTPELIER, FRANCE

LOAD-IN: 2:00 PM
SOUNDCHECK: 3:00 PM
DOORS: 9:00 PM
OF SETS: ONE (1)
SHOWTIME(S): 10:30 PM
CURFEW: N/A
LENGTH OF SET: 60-75 MIN.
OPENING ACT: BETTIE SERVEERT
O/A SHOWTIME: 9:30 PM

CONTACT: MARTINE VECERIAT
PHONE: 33-67-479-100
FAX: 33-67-429-390

CAPACITY: 600 — TICKET PRICE: 80 FF — AGES: TBA

NOTES:

PROMOTER: ALIAS
17 AVENUE TRUDAINE
75009 PARIS
FRANCE
PHONE: 33-1-45-960-664
FAX: 33-1-45-960-092

CONTACT: JULES FUTOS / DOMINIQUE REVERT

PROD. CONTACT: MARTINE VECERIAT
@ STAND'ART
PHONE: 33-67-479-100
FAX: 33-67-429-390

AFTER SHOW NOTES: DEPART MONTPELIER, FRANCE AND DRIVE TO LYON, FRANCE (180 MILES / 4 HOURS).

NEXT SHOW: TOMORROW NIGHT AT B-52 IN LYON, FRANCE.

using Tim as an influence, so it made him angry when people assumed that he was just carrying on the family business, conversant with his dad's old classics and happy to sing a few for old times' sake. His reality was the opposite of that.

"Where are your family now?" I asked.

"Mom and Corey are in LA," he said.

"You gonna invite them to the show?"

"Nope."

"Why not?"

"I don't wanna talk about it now."

"Is there anyone you want me to send a tour book, so they can keep track of you?"

"No. Don't send one to my mom."

That was my cue to drop the subject.

Through the windscreen, the highway was turning to a paler gray. There was a rumor of dawn.

My childhood danced into my head. My dad worked for a chain of shoe stores and was away all week. On the weekends, he would come home and beat the crap out of me and my brothers and sister, or ground us for whatever we'd done in the week. That was my experience of fatherhood. So maybe Jeff was better off without one of those. I also turned to music as a kind of medicine. I just beat the crap out of my drums. My dad had a sweet side too. He loved growing roses, and would leave one for my mom on top of the TV every day when he was home.

Funny that both of our mothers played the piano and we both remembered coming home from school and hearing classical music in the house. My mom used to teach music too. Sometimes I'd come back and hear some kid murdering a trumpet or violin in our house, from the street. Other times I'd come home and mom had baked twenty cakes, all of them cooling around the house, smelling delicious. She sold them to help make ends meet.

Nobody said "I love you" in our house. We showed it when we could. But I was confused by it. It took me a long time to show love to anyone. In fact, right at that moment, staring at the wakening horizon through the windscreen of a rental car, I still hadn't found a love I could devote my life to. Apart from music. Jeff and I agreed on that. Music never lets you down.

Love was somewhere on that horizon, I hoped.

Jeff leaned over and turned on the stereo.

CHAPTER 3

Company Ink

"Jeff Buckley can get away with anything."
—Daina Darzin, *Rolling Stone*, February 24, 1994

I'M IN CEDARS-SINAI HOSPITAL, Hollywood, in a private room I can't afford, wondering what the hell just happened. It's been a weird few days. We've been staying at the Mondrian hotel on Sunset Boulevard, a trendy place where thumping music plays constantly. Jeff has done a bunch of shows, and my lung has collapsed three times.

For a guy used to controlling a busload of hairy head cases and their fucked-up dramas, you'd think this little jaunt with one comparatively sober guy and his borrowed Telecaster would be a walk in the park, but somehow it's taken its toll on me. Perhaps I'm paying for past excesses and my forty-a-day cigarette habit, but I really wasn't expecting this.

The room is stuffed with flowers from well-wishers at Sony Music. That's a good sign.

I have just had my lung attached to my chest wall. Lord knows how. Staples? Duct tape? There's a tube hanging out of me, just below my rib cage. It is my third this week. Occasionally, bizarrely, I have to lower it into a glass of water and see if there are bubbles. I cannot go anywhere else, can't get on a plane, until this tube has done its work and my lung has re-inflated. I'm stuck in LA. I really don't need this right now.

And I'm watching Jeff Buckley throw shit around the room...now he's kicking a chair. He's shouting. Seems like he's pissed about something.

Wednesday, January 19, 1994

San Francisco, a day off. Jeff slept through most of it. The long drive—me driving—had worn him out, poor boy, so I left him alone until the early evening.

This was my first time back in San Francisco since Bill Graham had died, and I missed calling him like I usually did when I hit town. The legendary promoter died in a helicopter crash in 1991. He'd let me use that same helicopter a few weeks earlier to leave the Shoreline Amphitheatre after an Allman Brothers show. Stevie Ray Vaughn died in a helicopter, and I'd been on that one just a couple of weeks beforehand too. I figure I wouldn't be lucky three times in a row, so I've never flown in another.

In the evening, Jeff and I did a reconnaissance of the Paradise Lounge. The place had multiple levels, neon lights everywhere, flamboyant drinks and matching dancers. The clientele included hippie married couples and outrageous drag queens. It wasn't Jeff's usual coffee shop vibe, but somehow it felt like a place where he could have a great show. After a drink, he announced he was heading back to our motel, the Phoenix, a colorful art deco jewel in the Tenderloin district, which he loved. I could see he was thinking about what we'd discussed on the drive.

Thursday, January 20, 1994
Paradise Lounge, San Francisco

Seven a.m. I had my morning stack of faxes to go through. Every night, Jack Bookbinder or Becky Yeagel from my office would fax over all the messages I needed to address. I'd strike up a Marlboro and work my way through the pile—interview and guest list requests, licensing agreements, Sound Scan information showing sales in places we'd just played, press cuttings, technical specs from upcoming venues for the other bands we managed, that kind of thing—writing notes on them and faxing them back from the hotel's business center. I might do this three times a day.

I got coffee, and then Steve Berkowitz was on the phone.

"Hey, Dave, just checking in that everything is fine for Reggie Griffith flying in on Sunday."

Reggie was a sound engineer from Gramercy Park who'd run into Jeff at Sin-é, seen him play there a couple of times, and was working the sound desk at a Sony conference when Berkowitz announced Jeff's signing; Reggie had asked Berkowitz if Jeff needed someone to do sound. Reggie and Jeff met up shortly before this tour. He was a black guy who loved rock but was also deep into R&B. They shared a lot of their musical taste. Though I hadn't met Reggie yet, I trusted Berkowitz's recommendation, so I had hired him and had been keeping him up to date by phone.

Jeff came to my room before the sound check to show me the set he'd been working on. He'd written down a tight list, beginning with "Mojo Pin" and "Grace" and ending with "Hallelujah." He showed me how the set built and said he was ready to perform this each night as an entity.

"Looks great," I said. "You did pack a parachute, right? I'm taking you down the crooked street."

Jeff laughed. "Criminal activity?"

"No, Lombard," I said. "We're going to the venue by the scenic route."

I was taking Jeff down Lombard Street, the steep, twisting street in the Russian Hill neighborhood with eight hairpin turns, down a hill full of flower beds and fancy mansions. It's one of the strangest neighborhoods in America, like someone built a bunch of dream homes on a roller coaster, and all the tourists have to see it when they come to the city. It's a steep walk, and you only crawl down it in a car. It gets really crowded too. Must be a bitch to live there.

Jeff stared at the vista below us as we approached the top of Lombard. The road banked sharply left and there, out in the distance, was the bay and the Golden Gate Bridge under a misty blue sky that was startlingly cloudless for the time of year.

"I have a good feeling about tonight," he said.

"Me too."

Jeff found some Deep Purple on the radio and started singing along to it.

"Let's have some group therapy!" he shouted, and started air guitar shredding. He'd often do this when rock music came on. It was some time before I realized this was a reference to the band he'd played in while at the Guitar Institute. Group Therapy was a metal band.

I looked out at the bay with Jeff sitting next to me, singing along to rock music, and something told me to treasure this snapshot. I got a weird sensation that this was as good as an American life can get. A feeling that was thrilling and chilling in equal measure. Jeff must have been feeling a buzz too.

"You know, Dave, I want to make a lot of records," he said, putting his boots up on the dashboard. "Like, eighteen albums in three years or something. Really mess people's heads with all the music. I want to make an album that people can mosh their asses off to, big music, not overwrought but ecstatic. And for album three, I wanna do *MTV Unplugged* with strings and horns and backing singers." He turned to see my reaction.

"Sounds great," I said. "Expensive, maybe. And we're all gonna be busy. We'll need a whole bunch of parachutes!"

That night's show was the first where any industry and media were due to show up. Jeff was booked to do an in-store at Rough Trade the following day, and a lot of the store's staff would be there too. These were the kind of people we were doing this tour to attract: the ground force, the tastemakers we wanted on side. San Francisco's diverse community with eclectic tastes was a perfect market for Jeff. We'd noticed a lot of our posters on the street—a blurred image of Jeff, handwritten script, no Columbia logo—designed to make him look like an indie artist who was just starting up. Which he was; he just happened to be signed to a major label. People cared about the distinction back then. They don't anymore.

When we arrived at the venue, we knew that our promo had worked. Sean Sullivan, Columbia's college rep, was a personable, burly guy, instantly likable and obviously a fan of what Jeff was doing. He'd been working hard to fill the place with cool music fans and had done a great job. The place was packed, people pressed against the stage.

Jeff wandered on with no introduction and went straight into the a capella opening of "Mojo Pin." The place fell silent. I'd asked the bar staff to cool it with the bottles and cash registers while Jeff was playing, and they did. The sound was incredible, and after each song the applause was overwhelming. Jeff didn't ramble between songs, just went through the prepared set with the occasional thank-you. It was a near-faultless performance. And no one shouted out for any Tim Buckley songs.

During the encore of "Hallelujah," you could have heard a feather falling. When he finished, a piercing whistle of approval broke the silence, then the crowd roared and stomped. The difference in reaction from the previous shows was unbelievable.

I was already in the dressing room when Jeff came offstage. He looked at me and said, "Like that?"

I held up both hands. "Yeah, like that. Nailed it."

We toasted San Francisco with a couple of JDs and then stepped out of the dressing room to see Sean surrounded by people lining up to pay their respects—local kids who were musicians, workers from record stores, students, writers, and radio DJs. Exactly who we needed. After Jeff had met a bunch of people, I packed the gear into our shitty car and told him I was going back to the motel and would call him at 8 a.m. He said he'd hang out with the Rough Trade crowd.

"Good idea," I thought.

Friday, January 21, 1994
Hotel Utah, San Francisco

I got up at 6 a.m., so I could catch Columbia early and convey the excitement of last night's show, then finalize the rest of the dates—which would carry on until March 3 in Athens, Georgia—with Jeff's American agent, Don Muller, and Missy Worth, our rock at Columbia. Missy was smart, creative and very strong, which turned off some of the people at the label, but not me. I always knew where we stood with Missy, whether or not I liked her decision, and I respected her for that. We needed to arrange some more recording time for when Jeff returned to New York, B-sides and extra tracks for Japan.

To go and get coffee, I put on my suit. I figured I should be in manager mode in this town, rather than tour manager. I called Jeff at 8 a.m. No reply. So I went to knock on his door. Just then, a car pulled into the Phoenix parking lot. It was Jeff with a woman from Rough Trade. He'd spent the night with her. He kissed her goodbye, and I saw a look on her face I would come to recognize on the faces of people who had an intimate encounter with Jeff—a look both besotted and bereft as he walked out of their lives. I bundled him into his room. I was furious.

"Are you fucking crazy?" I bawled. "We're here to schmooze these people, not fuck them!"

Jeff looked like a confused child.

"You don't dip your pen in company ink! Do you get that?"

"I guess."

"We're polite, we're accommodating, you can even flirt a little, but don't stir up any emotional stuff. You break one of these girls' hearts and you're not just screwing her, you're screwing your career." I told him about the time a guy in one of my bands bedded the daughter of the promoter in a major market. Word got back to Daddy and they could never play in that lucrative state again.

"Fuck someone outside of the music business!" I advised at some volume.

"You're different in a suit," he said softly.

Of course, I couldn't blame him. He couldn't resist, and I understood that. But this would become a recurring theme for Jeff around the globe. His sex drive created a lot more work for me, dealing with distraught product managers or lovesick PR people in every territory. They would swoon around Jeff, who would happily catch them, say what they wanted to hear by way of pillow talk, and then wander off the following morning, never to return. Or Jeff would swoon and they'd catch him. Either way, it's a wonder he got anything released in some places.

So, with Jeff still wearing the rumpled ensemble from the night before, we went to Rough Trade for a three-song performance and a meet-and-greet, trying not to catch the eye of his date too often, and it went very well.

Afterward, I took Jeff down to Alioto's on Fisherman's Wharf for seafood. He was really apologetic. I was also sorry for losing my shit, and admitted I had made the same mistake in my time.

"You must have had your fair share of liaisons on the road," he said.

"Yes, I have," I said. "But I never mix business and pleasure." I had no idea at that moment that I would soon break this golden rule in a spectacular way.

I ordered a seafood platter: a mountain of lobster, crab, mussels, and shrimp. We pigged out and started to talk about the band and rehearsing for the full tour for *Grace*, which still needed some work. He told me the majority of his songs on the record were about his girlfriend Rebecca, whom he'd adored, but they had just broken up. He said he always let people go first, as he'd been hurt so much by love in his life.

"Hey, Dave, you know that song 'Forget Her?'"

"Great song."

"I don't want it on the album like it is."

"Jesus, that's the label's favorite track," I said.

"It's not right. It's not finished."

"Columbia thinks it's the only hit," I said.

"Even worse," he said, cringing, then laughed.

I hammered a crab claw with extra vigor. That was a conversation with the label I wasn't relishing.

That night, Jeff nailed it again. His set was even better than the previous night's. He kept the talking to a minimum, little more than "This is for Leonard" before playing "Hallelujah." The audience hung on every move and cheered every song. This was exactly why we'd booked multiple shows in key places, to let word of mouth take hold and let people see him a few times to really get it.

When he came offstage, nothing needed to be said. I threw him a towel and laughed. We were in a rhythm now. One more show before LA, and he was ready.

The next gig was in Berkeley, just half an hour away from San Francisco. Jeff was looking sheepish on the drive.

"Dave," he said, "do I have to go on with Reggie? I don't really want to be with another guy on the road except you."

"That's sweet of you, man," I said. "But I've got to get back to New York. There's a ton to do. Besides, you liked Reggie, and you two can start working properly on your sound."

The show at the Starry Plow, a hip Irish pub where everyone played, was like San Francisco's shows, with an engaged, responsive audience. It had become obvious that "Hallelujah" was the clincher, the showstopper that won the crowd. Every night he did it slightly differently, gauging the mood of the room and disappearing into another world as he sang, his eyes tightly shut—not what you'd usually recommend to hold an audience, but by this point in the show they were all his anyway.

Word was getting back to Sony in New York from the local street teams about how good these shows were, how personable Jeff was being with the tastemakers and retailers and Columbia reps. In the weeks and months to come, when we returned to some of these venues, I started getting weird calls that I'd never experienced before, reps and pluggers who had become obsessed with Jeff calling to complain that he hadn't given them enough attention, not spoken to them for long enough. People had to meet him only once, it seemed, to believe they were best friends forever.

We hung around until about 2 a.m. before undertaking the six-hour drive to LA so we could check into the Mondrian hotel first thing in the morning. The Mondrian was a moody, mirrored, trendy place on Sunset Boulevard where loud music shook the bar and lobby twenty-four hours a day. Not great if you actually wanted to sleep, but a good place to hang out and be seen. It was a cool alternative to the Hyatt opposite, the rock 'n' roll flophouse of choice for many years, nicknamed the Hyatt Riot—the place where Led Zeppelin's drummer John Bohnam had supposedly, at the urging of Keith Moon, sent a revved-up Harley Davidson through a fifth-floor-landing window just because he could.[17] The Hyatt was known for discretion about who was staying there, allowing artists to check in under assumed names and making sure that no one who worked there ratted on guests to the tabloids. I'd had several artists who needed emergency treatment for a drug problem while staying at the Hyatt, but the *National Enquirer* never got to hear of it. You got the impression that the idea of the Mondrian was the opposite: to let everyone know you were there.

Reggie Griffith showed up right on time. My room was a suite; Reggie took the spare bed. I was showing him the tour-management ropes because it was down to him to take over all the things that I'd been doing, like escorting Jeff to promotional events and interviews. We had a meet-and-greet booked at McCabe's Guitar Shop, one of the coolest stores in LA, a great place to play a few songs and impress the right kind of people.

---

[17] This story might be apocryphal, but I like it.

I sent Reggie to tell Jeff they were leaving in half an hour. Reggie came back a few minutes later.

"He doesn't want to do that," he said, matter-of-factly.

I didn't intend to shoot the messenger, but my response was pretty fierce. Reggie hadn't quite grasped how important these things were and that they weren't optional once agreed upon. And then I went to Jeff's room to repeat the information until he pulled on his Doc Martens and picked up his borrowed guitar.

I got that he was nervous before the big LA show, but this was a useful way to warm up and start spreading the word that someone interesting was in town. I also got that these in-store things could be embarrassing or tedious, but you learn how to make them bearable and then they're like any of the other tedious things you have to do to be allowed to pursue the thing you love so much. It's about the music, stupid, and this is how people get to hear about it.

The next day, Jeff decided he was sick, might not make it to the second show. He probably just had the grandmother of all hangovers, but he insisted it was serious. The Mondrian had, as I knew it would, a list of "rock docs," that legendary breed of physician with a bottomless bag of Class A meds and a blind eye, practiced at dealing with recalcitrant rockers feeling "under the weather," whether that weather was chemically induced or not.

One time in Nashville I took Gregg Allman to see Dr. Nick, the physician who had looked after Elvis Presley. I was trying to get some Librium to ease Gregg off alcohol. Jerry Lee Lewis was in the waiting room and had just fired his manager. Gregg, in his delirium, suggested to Lewis that he hire me as his manager. Jerry is as crazy as they come, and he got right up in my face and snarled, "I hate managers and I wanna kill all of them." As job interviews go, it left something to be desired.

Reggie and Jeff drove to some part of town that was way past its heyday, where this doctor lived in a small, dark abode. He turned out to be in his nineties, clearly too old to be practicing. Jeff described his symptoms: "I got a fever; I'm not energized," and this guy opens up his magic bag and gives Jeff some unspecified pill and a B12 shot in the ass.

"Holy shit, what was that?!" said Jeff when he came back, laughing about this ancient guy and his eerie house and looking, it had to be said, a lot fresher than when he left. But then, a needle in the ass is going to wake you up from whatever.

Nerves affect artists in different ways. Jeff was pretty controlled; there'd be the occasional bullshit cry for attention, but he wasn't a diva. If he was feeling pressure before a show, he was more likely to withdraw for a while, shut himself in his room or go for a walk, than create problems for everyone. He never, at this point, went onstage drunk or high. He would smoke a little weed sometimes to relax, or have a few a drinks after a show, but I didn't have any concerns about his ability to handle the attention or whether he was overindulging in anything illegal or mind-altering.

We were all on a high after the LA shows. The sound was good, the reviews were ecstatic, and everyone was buzzing. George Stein was in town to see how the tour was progressing and to finalize our management agreement. I was always rather blunt with George and kept it strictly business, but this was one night we relaxed and congratulated ourselves on working with the hottest talent in town. We arranged to meet at 9:30 a.m. to talk through our management agreement.

Something had bugged me about the shows, however. The audiences had been full of music biz freeloaders who didn't need to be there, effectively keeping out the people we wanted to reach. I made a mental note to tell Sony that the guest lists were going to be super tight from now on. No rival agents and their co-workers, no employees of other record companies who were just curious to see the hot ticket. Those people could pay like everybody else from now on. I wanted the audience to be fans and enthusiastic newcomers, with only a few essential business and media guests.

This was counterintuitive for me. In the past I'd have been happy to pepper the joint with any people in the business and their families, but I sensed that Jeff needed a different approach. We wanted kids who were in awe of him, not old hands who were feeling smug that they got in the room. Get rid of the latter type and there's a completely different feeling in the audience and a more natural, fervent after-effect. I faxed Sony my stipulations, drank a nightcap, and went to bed.

I woke up feeling a little weird. Not a particularly unusual state of affairs, if I'm being honest, but I felt strangely lightheaded and short of breath this morning. I waded through my usual, comprehensive room service breakfast. But on this morning, all that orange juice, toast, eggs over easy, hash browns, and sausage didn't make me feel any better.

My hair was really long in those days, and in the mornings I'd wear it down, sitting at the desk in just sweatpants and a bathrobe, going through the morning's stack of faxes. That's how George found me at 9:30 a.m. He walked in looking like some preppy throwback—khaki chinos, loafers, button-down chambray shirt, and a pastel-colored sweater draped over his shoulders. I think he thought this made him look drop-dead cool, but it couldn't have screamed "lawyer on his day off" any louder if he'd tried.

He was carrying an old brown leather portfolio his dad had given him. Dad was the senior partner in George's firm. From it he took the draft management agreement between us and Jeff. We had submitted this to Jeff's temporary lawyer—George obviously couldn't oversee a contract he was party to—who'd sent it back with amendments. George had agreed to these in principle, and this was my opportunity to check through them, supposedly a formality. But the first thing I noticed was that our 20 percent commission had been cut to 15 percent.

"You agreed to that?" I said, with my customary bluntness toward George. "What the fuck? So I'm busting my ass for 7½ percent now?!"

"Ah, but Dave, it's in perpetuity," said George, clearly pleased with this.

"I just want it in my account, man," I said.

"Yes, but this guarantees that whatever happens down the line, we will still receive this percentage."

"I know what 'perpetuity' means, George," I snapped. "But I'm not interested in pie in the sky."

"Think of it like a pension on full pay," said George. "Whenever it stops, you're set up."

"And what do I live on until I draw this pension, George? I'm gonna need every cent I can. I've got overhead, an office, staff, a growing company. I can't live off New Potato Caboose forever." They were a jam band I managed that had signed to RCA. They were pulling in good money on the weekends doing the jam band circuit. It was my commission from those gigs that was enabling me to take on Jeff Buckley for precisely no income.

George went on congratulating himself about what a great piece of negotiation this was, but I'd stopped listening. I was feeling really weird now. George was sitting in front of me. I was shirtless. You'd think he might have noticed that half my chest had caved in. I mean, I was skinny, sure, but not concave. I was now, though.

I didn't notice it until I stood up and caught sight of myself in the mirror.

"Jesus, George, my fucking chest has collapsed," I said, suddenly feeling a lot worse. It was actually just one side of my body. The rib cage had dropped and was sagging under my skin. It looked, and now felt, really peculiar. "I think I'd better call an ambulance."

"I'll drive you to the hospital," said George.

He drove me agonizingly slowly to Cedars-Sinai in his car that had pretensions of being a sports car but wasn't. I'd have laughed, but it hurt.

I know it sounds as if I am being hard on George. I liked him, but we were wildly different people, and I had very quickly come to resent his enjoyment of "managing" a hot property while I brought all my practical experience to the job and did all the heavy lifting.

At the ER they put me on a gurney, and one of the nurses saw the pack of Marlboros in my shirt pocket. She plucked it out and dumped it in the trash can. "You won't be needing *those* again," she announced.

The doctor took one look and said: "Spontaneous pneumothorax." Sounded like a band I'd once toured with. It just means "lung collapse without warning." Apparently, it's surprisingly common in tall, skinny white males, and that described me to a T. Guys of my build can develop a bubble at the top of the lung, and anything, even a car door slam, can cause it to pop and deflate the lung.[18]

They told me they were going to stick a tube in me to re-inflate the lung and send me on my way. It hurt like hell getting it in—they basically stab you under the rib cage and put this thing in the wound—and then they told me that every twenty-four hours I had to lower the other end of the tube into a glass of water. When it stopped creating bubbles, it meant the lung was healed. That could take about two weeks. Then I

[18] Later that year, when I was hanging out at the Royal Garden hotel in London with the crew of Soundgarden, three of the crew members, tall and skinny to a man, told me they'd had the same thing happen to them.

would go back to them so they could remove the tube. In the meantime, I couldn't fly. I was going to be stuck in LA as an outpatient.

After several hours, I left the ER with the tube hanging out of my chest, covered by a T-shirt and a jacket. I managed to attend the next show, and no one was the wiser. I'm not sure I even told anyone there was a problem. As far as everyone was concerned, I'd been to the ER for a Band-Aid.

But the next morning, I felt it go again. I looked down and my chest had collapsed on the same side. It was like some awful scene from *Groundhog Day* when I went back to Cedars and they re-did the tube.

At this time, I was dating an anesthesiologist in New York. Dana worked at a hospital in Brooklyn, a gruesome place where all the cops and criminals who get gunshot wounds are treated. She was a sexy blonde, super smart, who always spoke her mind. She would come over to see me and be bouncing off the walls of my tiny apartment because she witnessed life-threatening shit all the time. I took her to a music business lunch once and she was really annoyed by it.

"All these people think they're such big shots, but I'm dealing with life and death every day," she said. And she was right.

I knew I needed to call her and check if I was getting the best treatment.

"Dave, you've got no insurance," she reminded me. "Cedars wants to get you out of there as quickly as possible. That's the hospital of the stars. They expect money."

Dana loved me, but I didn't feel quite the same way about her. I didn't want a relationship to hold back my career, which was unfair to her. I'd been a little preoccupied since taking Jeff on, and I was trying to find the right time to break up with her. She knew instinctively what I was doing, but she was a compassionate person, so she said she'd take time off work and fly to LA to look after me. Jeff was due to continue on tour with Reggie in the next forty-eight hours, so I was glad for the company.

I was genuinely pleased to see her, but when she arrived she really wanted to have sex. Maybe she found a guy with a tube hanging out of him really hot. I said, "You've gotta be kidding." But she reminded me she'd come a long way, she hadn't seen me for a couple of weeks...

I really wasn't in the mood, which I thought was only fair under the circumstances. But she reacted like I was casting doubt upon her attractiveness. "Are you serious, baby?" I said. "I'm pretty sick." But she insisted, and so I started having dutiful sex with her—which is never the best kind. And right in the middle of it, my lung popped again.

"Erm, my lung just popped," I said, coming to an abrupt halt.

Dana's bedside manner suddenly fell away.

"You're fucking lying," she said. "You've been like this for the last month. You'll do anything not to have sex with me." She was totally losing it.

"No, really, my lung popped again. I can fucking feel it. Look."

It was true. Dana looked at my chest, calmed down, and got practical. "You gotta go back and make them put it right," she said.

We went to Cedars-Sinai and the receptionist more or less tried to turn us away. Dana gave her the medical terminology for "fix his fucking lung" and reminded her of the hospital's liability. The receptionist disappeared and finally came back to announce that they could give me the operation, but there would be a two-thousand-dollar excess charge. I said, "Okay, that's fine." And then she said they wanted the money upfront. I leaned in and scanned her nametag. "Okay, Rosanna." I gave her the eye. "This is above your pay grade. I suggest you get someone to make the decision to admit me immediately, or there's going to be a press release going out this afternoon accusing Cedars-Sinai of negligence. Now, let me in, fix my lung, and send me a fucking invoice."

Amazingly, it worked. I would be operated on that evening and kept in overnight. This was the operation I should have had at the start. The business with the tube was the cheap, clumsy option for grouchy douchebags with no insurance. After a day or so, I'd be discharged and have to rest at the Mondrian as an outpatient until I was well enough to fly home.

I came to in a private room that looked like a florist's shop. Now that I had actually been admitted to the hospital, word had spread. Jeff, the band, Reggie, and Sony all knew what was going on.

George, bless him, still needed me to finalize the management agreement. So he came to pay me an early visit. I was too tired to really give it my full attention. Stupidly, I let the question of our cut in commission go unchallenged. While we were still discussing it, Jeff turned up with Reggie. He and I had to go over what was happening on the next leg of the tour.

Jeff made light of everything when he arrived. No one looks great in a paper gown and a bunch of tubing, but he pretended not to be too shocked when he saw me propped up in bed like a corpse with attitude.

"Look at this," I said, gesturing at all the flowers around the room. "Boy, are you a priority!"

"They're addressed to you, Dave," he said.

"No, they're addressed to *you*, bro," I said, tapping my nose. We laughed. "They only want me to get better 'cuz you're the next big thing."

"Fuck you," said Jeff brightly, but then his smile kind of dropped. He went and sat down in a chair and stared out of the window while I finished talking with George and went over the tour book with Reggie, pointing out things to check in each venue, making sure we had contacts for the promoters, the name of the guy who'd be paying us, and so on.

Nurses came in to check my drips. More flowers and fruit arrived. It was pretty busy in there. Jeff wasn't saying very much. George left and Reggie needed to go and get something. Jeff said he'd stay with me and wait for him.

When we were finally alone, Jeff got up and came over to the bed.

"This is bullshit," he said.

"I'm sorry?" I said.

"Is there something you've not been telling me?" he said.

"What do you mean?"

"Were you sick when you took this gig on?" he said. He was getting agitated now.

"No way. This was a lovely surprise," I said.

"Don't lie to me," he said. "I trusted you." His voice went up a notch in volume. He was angry.

"What are you suggesting, man? That I took this gig on despite knowing my chest was gonna collapse? That's ridiculous."

"Don't lie," he said again, seething. And he brushed something off the bedside cabinet, a medical chart on a clipboard, which clattered across the floor.

I looked at him working himself up, getting aggressive with the furniture, and I suddenly knew what he was getting at.

"Jeff, I'm no junkie," I said. "I've had to clean up after too many addicts to ever go near the stuff. I smoke a bunch of cigarettes and I like a JD in the evening, but that's it."

He leaned forward, looking pained. "Are you going to die on me?" he asked, choking up. And then he asked me what he really wanted to know: "Are you going to leave me like everybody does?"

By "everybody," I assumed he meant his father. Tim Buckley had died, making the classic recovering junkie's error of taking something for old times' sake, falling off the wagon by snorting the same dosage he'd been used to, which his body could no longer withstand.

"I'll be fine in two weeks," I said. "You're going off with Reggie. I can run things from the hotel. I'll be doing push-ups by the time you get back to New York. You won't even notice the difference."

"You'd better not fucking die on me," he said, smiling now.

"Not planning to," I said. "Dying would be kinda inconvenient. I solemnly promise that I will never leave you. Help yourself to some grapes."

CHAPTER 4

White Roses and Black Rocks

JEFF LOVED BRITISH MUSIC. He had an affinity for it. He loved the nervous energy in British punk, the wired consciousness of The Clash, the way Siouxsie and the Banshees went from gun-metal moodiness to skies full of fireworks. He adored the Cocteau Twins, of course. He loved how The Smiths called to outsiders and nerds. He loved the textures of Johnny Marr's supple guitar and the mordant presence of Steve Jones's guitar in the Sex Pistols. Jeff, whose own nervous energy was considerable, became even more wired whenever we went to the UK; he was stimulated by its variety. He appreciated its compactness—the lack of eight-hour drives between cities was refreshing.

I wasn't quite up to Jeff's speed as we approached his first professional visit there. Once I finally had the tube plucked from my lung, I had only a couple of weeks to recuperate before we were due to fly over for shows later in March. Sony had passed on *Live at Sin-é* in Europe, so this trip had a slightly different focus from the one in the US. When Julie Borchard announced that the UK wasn't going to release the EP, we were understandably disappointed, but there was a solution close at hand: Steve Abbott, known to everyone as Abbo, who ran the eccentric indie record label Big Cat with his business partner, Linda Obediah. They had also managed pop band EMF, which had blown up internationally, so

Steven "Abbo" Abbott, president, Big Cat Records.

they had opened an office on Broadway and persuaded EMI to rent an apartment for them on First Avenue. From this base, Abbo had picked up on many of the promising un-signed bands playing in New York, like Pavement, Mercury Rev, and Luscious Jackson. He had approached Jeff after Gods & Monsters and Sin-é shows and asked him if he'd like to record with Big Cat, but then Sony stepped in. Jeff felt that he owed Abbo a record, so when Columbia UK passed on *Live at Sin-é* and Michele Anthony instigated a funding deal with Big Cat, it seemed the perfect opportunity for them to become involved. Abbo jumped at the chance.

"For Columbia it was like a positioning thing, with minimal ambition," he said. "But I thought we could sell a lot of records through the independent network. Part of that conversation was that we were going to do *Grace* as well. We had a good team across all the distributors for Big Cat. They were like family rather than businesspeople, putting our records out all over Europe."

EMPLOYMENT DEPARTMENT
OVERSEAS LABOUR SERVICE

Group Application

Our reference JCM/9402936/01

KATHERINE MAYNERD
WASTED TALENT ARTISTES
AGENCY LTD
321 FULHAM ROAD
LONDON
SW10 9QL

Attached below is a work permit for issue to

JEFFREY SCOTT BUCKLEY

WORK PERMIT

Permit number E 265835

Worker reference No. 9402936
Date of issue 24FEB94
Period covered by permit: Permit valid to 25MAR94

PARTICULARS OF PERMIT HOLDER

Surname: BUCKLEY
Other names: JEFFREY SCOTT
Date of birth: 17NOV66 Sex: Male
Passport number: 062668830
Issuing government: UNITED STATES OF AMERICA

PARTICULARS OF EMPLOYMENT

Employer's name: WASTED TALENT ARTISTES AGENCY LTD
Occupation: MUSICIAN
Salary/remuneration: GROUP FEE
Employer's address: 321 FULHAM ROAD LONDON
Phone number: 071 351 7421
Official stamp

With JEFF BUCKLEY

E265835

EMPLOYMENT DEPARTMENT
OVERSEAS LABOUR SERVICE

Group Application

Our reference JCM/9402938/01

KATHERINE MAYNERD
WASTED TALENT ARTISTES
AGENCY LTD
321 FULHAM ROAD
LONDON
SW10 9QL

Attached below is a work permit for issue to

DAVID JOSEPH LORY

WORK PERMIT

Permit number E 265836

Worker reference No. 9402938
Date of issue 24FEB94
Period covered by permit: Permit valid to 25MAR94

PARTICULARS OF PERMIT HOLDER

Surname: LORY
Other names: DAVID JOSEPH
Date of birth: 02APR59 Sex: Male
Passport number: 110004142
Issuing government: UNITED STATES OF AMERICA

PARTICULARS OF EMPLOYMENT

Employer's name: WASTED TALENT ARTISTES AGENCY LTD
Occupation: TOURING MANAGER
Salary/remuneration: GROUP FEE
Employer's address: 321 FULHAM ROAD LONDON
Phone number: 071 351 7421
Official stamp

With JEFF BUCKLEY

E265836

UK work visas for Jeff Buckley and Dave Lory for the Live at Sin-é tour, March 1994.

Abbo's small team—Linda, Frank Neidlich in marketing, and Jacqui Rice in press—did such a good job that the week it was released in Europe, *Live at Sin-é* sold over four thousand copies, which was amazing for a complete unknown.

That also meant Jeff arrived in the UK with a decent buzz around him. We felt a heat wave of interest that was extraordinary considering he'd not played there before. The first thing Jeff was booked to do was appear at the Sony international convention being held that year at Gleneagles in Scotland. Sony staff came in from all over the globe, a temporary village of suits gathering to celebrate the previous year's successes and to see what was coming up. There would be a ton of presentations, huge lunches and dinners, bands playing in the evenings and, of course, if you so desired, eighteen holes of golf on a world-class course.

Naturally, many acts wanted to play in front of these people that could make a difference to their careers, so it was a pretty big deal to be invited to play. Jeff, of course, was DWI.[19]

[19] Standing for "Donnie wants it." i.e. Donnie Ienner, president of Columbia Records.

He was just going to do a few select tunes, Sin-é style. But I thought he had completely blown it when, during the sound check, he had tested the mic by singing The Beatles' "Eleanor Rigby" with an adapted lyric: "Tommy Mottola / Died in the church / And was buried along with his name / Nobody came..." etc., which would have been mildly amusing if Mottola, unbeknownst to Jeff, hadn't come into the ballroom and stood in the front row at that very moment.[20] Nothing happened, so I suppose Tommy missed it, thought he'd been hearing things, or didn't give a shit.

"Jesus, you gave me a heart attack there, man," I said to Jeff.

"What'd I do?" he said, genuinely unaware. I pointed to where the king of Sony and his court were gathering. "Gah, he loves it!" Jeff laughed.

The actual performance sounded great to me. I was looking around the room to see the reaction, and there were some appreciative faces—Virginie Auclair, the French rep, seemed pretty into it—but I didn't feel he'd set the place on fire. I could tell the difference because the next act on was Oasis, playing to their parent company for the very first time, and they got a standing ovation.

Julie Borchard was the one to gather the feedback: "Virginie was mesmerized by him, but others came up to me and said, 'Time and a place,' meaning, 'This is not the right time or the right place.' He was polarizing."

"Boys don't like the music," Jeff once told KASR (Arizona college radio). "Girls like the music. Women like the music. The boys I meet don't like the music. Those are the same guys I've known all my life, pretty much. I've always been on the fringe of any social thing I've been into. I don't really travel around in packs."

While Oasis was being carried out of the building on the shoulders of the CEO, I wondered if we needed to regroup.[21] Meanwhile, a new member of the team was just arriving. Sara Silver had just been poached from Polydor in France to be Columbia's new vice president of European marketing. She'd been at Polydor's Parisian office for five years, had met her husband there, and had just started a family when he was suddenly killed in a motorbike accident. It was in the immediate aftermath of this tragedy that she had been hired by Sony, and she was still feeling

[20] Tommy Mottola was the CEO of Sony US, Donnie Ienner's immediate boss.

[21] Poetic license. This didn't happen.

Sara Silver (right), vice president at Columbia Records Europe with Juliette Joseph, promotion.

somewhat disoriented when she touched down in Scotland on her first day at work with instructions to meet the president of the label.

"Anyone who did that job simply *had* to get on with Donnie," she says. "I was aware that he was a firebrand and a very big force. He had no idea I'd been taken on. I spent twenty-four hours trying to meet him until, eventually, he and a fleet of people met me in some corridor of this hotel and we sat down, supposedly for a quick chat—because he was the *president* of Columbia Records—but it lasted over forty minutes and we got on really well. All these people were standing back, saying nothing, and then when he signaled I was okay, they all spoke to me! At the very end of this conversation, he said, 'Now, the first thing I want you to do is go to London and see this artist we've just signed, Jeff Buckley,' and that was where it began. I was dispatched back to London to see him."

Sara would see Jeff at The Borderline, his first London show. But we had a couple of other dates first. Jeff's first public appearance on British soil was at Ratner's Bar, a tiny venue in Sheffield, now long gone, and was attended by about forty people, each of whom received a cassette with the Sin-é versions of "Mojo Pin" and "Je N'en Connais Pas La Fin" and an interview recorded in February.

The next day we took a train down to London. Michele Anthony had put Jeff and me into the five-star Dorchester Hotel and arranged for us to see Soundgarden at Shepherd's Bush Empire. It was the former music hall's grand reopening night as a music venue after having been the BBC Television Theatre for forty years, and the show was only for fans and competition winners, not open to the public. When we arrived at the deluxe Dorchester, the bellboy was slightly bemused by Jeff's luggage—a large, grubby pillowcase stuffed with rumpled clothes and his ever-present ghetto blaster.

"It's okay, I got this," Jeff said, taking his worldly goods up to our luxury suite, saving himself a tip.

Jeff loved the old music hall, which felt intimate but held two thousand people. I told him that in a year he would sell out this venue.

"Get outta here," he said.

I called agent Emma Banks and asked her to book the place for one year's time. Missy Worth bet me a dollar that Jeff would not sell the place out.

Our next show was in Dublin. We flew in and had the night off there. I woke up with some weird fever. I was shaking and feeling strange and thought my lung was about to collapse again. Jeff's bedside manner kicked in; he started getting annoyed that I wasn't in peak condition and might have to leave the party feet first. He came with me to Blackrock Clinic in Dublin for an x-ray, and the doctor told me my lung was fine but I'd been having an anxiety attack—which was good news but also a little disturbing. I didn't know it was possible to wake up having an anxiety attack. I must have been having night terrors without any pictures.

When we got back to the hotel, there was a thick pile of messages for me. Half the population of Dublin, it seemed, was proud of the Buckley boy's Irish heritage and "would love to be on the guest list, plus one, for tonight's show."[22] When we arrived for the sound check, there was a long

[22] Jeff always said his voice wasn't his, or his father's; it belonged to the whole Irish side of his family. Jeff's grandfather apparently had a beautiful singing voice too, and certainly wasn't the first in the family line to have one.

line of people outside the tiny venue, which had already sold out. I wondered if any of them had seen Jeff play the Trinity Ball in a Sex Pistols T-shirt a couple of years earlier.

By the time Jeff came on, the crowd, several drinks into its evening, had become a little boisterous. He said hello softly, as usual, but no one was really paying attention. Jeff just stood there, waiting. People started to watch to see what he would do. There was a pint of his favorite beer, Guinness, sitting on the stool next to him. Jeff lifted the glass to his lips and downed it in one hit. Everyone cheered, and Jeff began the show with the crowd completely on his side.

The audience was more blasé the next night at his London debut at The Borderline, a Western-themed venue under a dubious Mexican diner in Soho, right in the heart of London. It had an unusual booking policy, hosting country, blues, and Americana as well as local indie bands. People expected the music there to be eclectic, so it seemed a perfect spot for Jeff. There was a good selection of local media present, including Martin Aston, who'd done the first press interview with Jeff in the summer of 1992—who interviewed him again for *Q* magazine during the sound check—and Jim Irvin, who was with *Melody Maker*, the UK's longest-running weekly music newspaper at the time, where he was the reviews editor.[23] (Jim is the co-author of this book.)

"Jeff came on with no fanfare and started singing 'Mojo Pin,'" Jim recalls. "I remember a group of local reps for hip American indie labels like Sub Pop and Merge yacking away rather disrespectfully at the bar. I went and told them to shut up and they did, probably because they all needed reviews in my pages! Jeff became softer and softer until the room fell silent. It was such a refreshing show. So much in that time of Pearl Jam, Husker Du, Guns N' Roses, and Spin Doctors was so male and dry. I was tired of music that operated only on the surface. Here was

[23] Martin Aston: "I did the first piece on Jeff in Q magazine. But unfortunately, my editor said to me, 'I want you to do a feature on sons and daughters of...' and you didn't argue. You're a freelancer; you do the piece. So I contacted Michael Nesmith's son and Stephen Stills' son [and] Dweezil Zappa—there were a few around—and then I said to [my editor], 'Please, if I do this, can you keep Jeff separate from this feature?' And he promised he would, and then when the feature ran, he hadn't. Jeff was in it—they ran it as all one thing. And when that appeared, Jeff hit the roof and blamed me, and I never spoke to him again. It was really upsetting. It just haunted me."

someone on a completely different trajectory, unafraid of being emotional, without all the bluster of grunge. I wasn't entirely convinced by the EP, but when I watched him perform that night and then heard early samples of *Grace*, I realized he was a huge talent."

"It was an epiphany for me," says Sara Silver, who had gone to the show on her own. "There are some shows where it just feels like you're a voyeur, looking into someone's soul. This was one of those. He was very charismatic but also haunting, and I think because of my particular situation at the time, still suffering from my bereavement, he resonated hugely. This haunting sound was a powerful force, and it was my job to work out how we took it to the world."

A gig the next night in Glasgow meant an early-morning flight back to Heathrow the following morning to catch a session with GLR, London's local BBC station, a slot designed to alert people to the next couple of gigs at The Garage in Islington and at Bunjies, a cute little basement folk club in Central London that dated back to the early 1960s and made Sin-é seem generously proportioned.

As I was still obviously a bit shaky from my collapsed lung, Abbo was accompanying Jeff on this run. By this time they'd become close.

"We'd meet regularly at a bar called Tom & Jerry's in New York, hang out and drink Guinness together," Abbo says, "I suppose I became a friend of his, and he didn't seem to have many real friends. I'd only discovered I liked the blues since living in New York, so it was great hanging with him, because he was a huge blues and jazz fan and if there was a guitar around he had to pick it up and show off. He knew every Robert Johnson song, every Muddy Waters tune, Bessie Smith; he introduced me to the physicality of the blues, watching it at close quarters. Everybody talks about his voice, but he was a brilliant guitarist. The guitar was an extension of his body.

"Tim Buckley hadn't really entered my line of vision growing up listening to black music. Singer-songwriters with fluffy hairstyles were not currency on my council estate in Luton! We were in Tom & Jerry's and someone said to Jeff, 'I've been listening to your dad,' and I said, 'Who's your dad?' and he said, 'Tim Buckley.' I knew the name from record shopping; I'd seen the sleeves in the racks, but that's it. But when he came over to Britain there were loads of Tim Buckley fans. And it was a real problem early on, because he really didn't like talking about him."

The traffic from the airport to the GLR studios just off Baker Street was awful. A road accident had slowed everything to a standstill. Jeff's slot on the mid-morning show was fast approaching. "Of course, this was before mobile phones, so I had no way of communicating with the radio station that we were stuck in traffic," says Abbo. "For the last few days on this tour, everyone who'd interviewed Jeff had been asking about his dad. How did Tim write 'Song To The Siren'? Was there stuff in his lyrics that he might have related to? Things Jeff couldn't answer.

"We were listening to GLR while we waited in traffic and the presenter kept saying, 'We're supposed to have this artist, Tim Buckley's son, turning up, but he's late....Will he or won't he turn up?' This went on and on. She must have said 'Tim Buckley's son' about four times and didn't mention Jeff once. Suddenly, he just kicked my radio in with his big DMs [Doc Martens], just smashed the fascia and then sat back sulking all the way there. I could get another radio, of course, but I was mostly worried he wasn't going to do the performance.

"We finally arrived about forty minutes late and they were all so rude to us, and yet they knew what the problem was, as they were broadcasting traffic updates and warnings of delays themselves. If I were him, I'd have walked out. The female presenter was a typical local radio DJ, a bit gushy and knew nothing about him and his music. I had a word with the station manager to ask her to stop mentioning Tim Buckley, and he handed her a note to that effect. Jeff just sat there silently and she said, 'What are you going to play?' and Jeff said, 'A song.' I'm thinking, 'Oh god, here we go.' And he started to play "Grace." He did this long guitar introduction, went on for about a minute, like he needed to calm himself down before he got to the actual start of the song, and then he launched into the most electrifying performance. The best I ever heard him do it.

"There were about six phones in the control room, and they all started lighting up. 'Who is this? Who is this? It's amazing!' And all the time, Jeff's getting more and more into it. The presenter went from being this standoffish woman to...I swear she would have thrown herself on him given half a chance, the second he finished singing. You could see she was totally enthralled."

Presenter: "You looked quite exhausted at the end of the song."

Jeff: "I was getting a lot of anger out. Something happened on the way here..."

"The phones didn't stop throughout the next song. The station manager said that in all his twelve years at the station, he'd never seen a reaction like it."

Abbo thinks this performance sparked Jeff's breakthrough. There were certainly plenty of people in line outside The Garage in North London that night. Inside, the first stars were taking note. Chrissie Hynde and Jon McEnroe were in the audience. Chrissie had been a big fan and a friend of Tim's, had actually interviewed him while she was briefly a music journalist with the NME, and she was obviously curious to see how his offspring compared. They struck up a conversation after the show and she clearly said the right thing, because he went off with her to jam with The Pretenders in a nearby rehearsal room. I wasn't carrying anything heavy because of my lung, and I didn't want Jeff to pull any important muscles, so I asked McEnroe if he wouldn't mind. He happily hauled Jeff's amp downstairs to the car. The Pretenders' jam with special guests Buckley and Mac went on all night.

Bunjies, as I've said, was tiny, a basement folk club and coffee bar on West Street in Soho, with gingham tablecloths and melted candles in wine bottles on the tables and a performance area tucked into a couple of arches in what must have been a wine cellar at one point. It looked unchanged since it had begun in the early 1960s, and had seen a couple of folk booms come and go. It was more of a cafe with an open-mic policy by this point, which felt like a good place for Jeff.[24] There wasn't really any need for amplification, so when we arrived for a sound check, there was very little to do but see where Jeff was going to stand in the cramped space and gauge how his voice reflected off the nicotine-stained ceilings. While Jeff did that, I went outside for some fresh air and was stunned to see a line of people already waiting to get into the show.

I took a look at the guest list and realized we'd be lucky to fit twenty of this assembling crowd in the tiny space. Every time I looked up, the

---

[24] I couldn't find any record of Tim Buckley's playing Bunjies, but Tim actually lived in London for a while in 1967–68 and certainly played on the local circuit, including at nearby sister folk club Les Cousins, on Greek Street, so he may have appeared at Bunjies too.

line was getting further down West Street. I went back into the venue and found Jeff talking to Emma Banks, the agent. He was saying how great the venue was and that he'd like to do something like hand out flowers to everyone before he went on.

"Jesus, you won't believe what's happening out there," I said to them. "The line goes about four blocks. There's no way these people are going to get in. Is there any way we can do two sets?" Jeff was happy to. Emma spoke to the club owner and was told they had some regular club night happening later on. She came back and said, "They can't do it but I've had an idea!" She disappeared up the steps onto the street, and I spoke to Jeff.

"What flowers would you like?"

"White roses," he said.

"I'll get them," I said, and went back up to the street, where the line had grown even longer.

I walked around looking for a florist and bumped into Emma. "I've booked Andy's Forge," she said. "It's a little place just around the corner in Denmark Street. He can go on at 10:30."

I bought as many white roses as I could find. They reminded me of my dad's cutting a rose from the garden for my mom every day. Jeff handed them to people waiting outside and those lucky enough to get into the club, as he squeezed himself into the corner that passed for a stage. He sang upward, listening to his voice reflect off the curved ceiling into this hot, crowded, and attentive space.

There must have been a hundred people stuffed in there. It was a terrible fire risk.

When the show was over, Jeff walked up the steps to the huddle of patient people that Emma had gathered, plus anyone from the first show who wanted to tag along, and led this crowd like the Pied Piper toward Andy's Forge. Abbo was alongside me. "Have you ever seen anything like this before?" I said.

"Never!" he said. And we laughed liked idiots at the wonderful absurdity of hanging out with Jeff.

It was during those London shows that I truly began to realize how great Jeff could be, a mega-star, the biggest thing in my lifetime. I saw him as Bruce Springsteen and me as Jon Landau, a couple of lifers

Bunjies Folk Cellar, London, March 18, 1994. *Top photo:* Jeff Buckley passing out white roses to fans. Journalist Martin Aston is far left. *Bottom photo:* Jeff singing toward the curved ceiling to project his voice to the back of the room.

dedicated to the same career. That's the dream if you're a manager. The potential shone out of those shows. But I knew I'd have to work hard to keep up. Maybe that's what my anxiety attack had been about!

There was one show I didn't get to. It was a lunchtime gig in a pub in somewhere called Hitchin. Abbo and his family were in attendance.

"Emma Banks and I were both Luton Town football fans, so she had booked this thing ten miles up the road on a match day," he says. "Jeff had seen my four-year-old daughter, Hope, wandering about just before he went on, and he picked her up and sat her on a stool next to his mic stand, facing the audience. As soon as Jeff started to sing, there was a woman in the bar who was goggle-eyed at him, and she walked to the front of the stage and just took her top off, then her bra, and let loose her huge boobs right in front of Jeff—just stood there topless. It was lunchtime! My daughter's gazing up at him while he's singing, and this big pair of old boobs is wobbling around in front of the two of them. It was surreal. Hope's twenty-five now and can legitimately claim she's been onstage with Jeff Buckley."

I missed this delightful scene, as I was on my way up from London to drive to the next show. With me I had a cassette of the latest—and, I hoped, the last—*Grace* mixes. The sound filled the car as Jeff and I soaked it up, him checking that all the tweaks he'd ordered were present and correct. Meanwhile, in the back, Abbo wasn't having such a great time.

"I thought they sounded absolutely awful," he recalls. "I couldn't understand how all that raw energy Jeff had live had been turned into this mild-mannered, polite record. There was no roaring guitar; the voice had been contained. I'd been listening to performances like the GLR session every day and seeing what it did to people and I thought, 'Jesus, this is Andy Wallace who's done Rage Against The Machine and Nirvana?' It just seemed very, very tame. I didn't know what to say, and I had to ride in the car with them for two hours afterwards....But now I take it all back. I think it's a beautiful record, and the experience of Andy Wallace means it still sounds good twenty-five years later, but compared to that instant live experience, this version was initially such a shock."

The European leg of the *Live at Sin-é* tour ended in Amsterdam at the Paradiso. We had some time off there, and Jeff was like a kid in a candy store. He loved the coffeehouses that sold multiple varieties of hash; he loved the people and the atmosphere of liberation. Plus, the city is beautiful, with its canals and tramways, cobbled streets and waterside dwellings. We had a great tourist's night out wandering through the bars and clubs and the neon-bright red-light district.

The next morning, back at the hotel, Jeff came pounding on my door and asked me to come to his room. He said, "I've been throwing up all night, Dave. And have a look at this." He pointed to the toilet bowl. Something as black as tar was bobbing in the water.

I'll be honest. My initial thought was, "Cancer!" I called Mojo Concerts, our promoter, and asked for the phone number of a rock doctor and made an appointment. When we arrived, there was a waiting area but no receptionist, so I had to wander out back to locate a nurse. When we came out, Jeff was bent over puking in the clinic's sink. The nurse hurried him in to see the doctor. I must have waited an hour before the nurse took me in to where Jeff was being examined. The doctor immediately started chewing me out, criticizing me for working Jeff too hard on this tour (this was like, day 11), saying that it was managers like me that gave the business a bad name, and that Jeff needed total rest. He totally tore me a new one.

I was stunned. As we left, Jeff kept apologizing to me.

"Sorry, Dave. Sorry, man. So sorry you had to hear that, dude. Sorry."

I called Emma to cancel the Paris show booked that night. Then I went back to Jeff's room. "Okay, we're going to have to get you some proper rest. I'll cancel the rest of the shows, and I'll book us in here for another few nights until you feel well enough to fly home."

"Er, Dave, I've got something to tell you." He gave me his "don't hate me" look.

So it turns out that because I'd told him under no circumstances to bring any hash over the borders from Amsterdam, he'd swallowed the lump he'd bought as soon as he got back to the hotel last night. It could have killed him.

I could have killed him. All the shit that doctor gave me, plus I thought Jeff was dying, plus I'd canceled a show, and all for this. Of course he hadn't said anything to the esteemed doctor about this.

The rest of the tour was fine and we flew back to New York. We landed at JFK, and a Sony car was waiting for us. When we climbed into the back, exhausted, Jeff kicked off his shoe and there was a huge chunk of black hash on the floor.

"Are you fucking serious?!" I said. I'll admit I raised my voice slightly.

Jeff started laughing, but I was not in the mood. I was having visions of being perp-walked somewhere in an orange suit. The one thing you did not do back then was import hash from Amsterdam, especially as a musician, because customs officials were always suspicious of visitors from Holland bringing it into the country. But back then, there wasn't the same level of post-9/11 paranoia and security—full-body scans and sniffer dogs in the line for immigration. We were very lucky.

CHAPTER 5

Grace

"It's funny to hear his work described as blues, modified rock 'n' roll, and raga rock when, in fact, there is no name yet for the places he and his voice can go."

—Lillian Roxon on Tim Buckley, Lillian Roxon's Rock Encyclopedia (1969)

WHEN REGGIE GRIFFITH TOOK OVER for me on tour, one stop on the itinerary was a forgotten address in LA. Jeff was still receiving royalty checks from the estate of Tim Buckley at this time, small sums he was entitled to as a dependent. (He voluntarily gave up his right to this income a couple of years later.) Reggie drove him to a place in downtown LA to pick up the latest check. Neither of us can recall whose house this was, maybe a relative's or perhaps the home of Herb Cohen, Tim's former manager, who had once given Jeff money to cut that demo in LA. And we can't remember why Jeff handed the check over to Reggie. We didn't need it as cash for the tour, because Sony was providing that, so the reason for this errand has been forgotten. But Reggie does recall how this trip prompted Jeff to talk about his father: "When we drove there he was talking to me about how, when his dad was still alive, he'd been going to a Montessori school, really progressive. He loved it. He was having a

Photo by Merri Cyr

Dave Lory and Jeff Buckley outside Sony Studios, New York City, discussing the final sequence for the songs on *Grace*.

great time learning in this relaxed way, with all these great kids, and then, once his dad died, boom, he got hit with public school, and he said, 'I was, "What the fuck is going on?!" I was having fun with my friends and suddenly I'm in this really different environment, so disorientating I shut down into myself.'

"We listened to a Tim Buckley cassette a few times in the car during that tour, then Jeff threw it out of the window while we were on the highway. But he dug his dad. The way he talked about him, I'd never have imagined it was only one visit where he met him. It felt like he was talking about a relationship that lasted a long time, and maybe in his mind it did. It meant a lot to him.

"He told me that he didn't really get on with his mom. I didn't like my mom, so it was easy for us to share that stuff. He'd say: 'She's doing her own thing; I'm doing mine. She's not gonna get in the way of me doing my thing...' It wasn't like a visceral hatred or anything, but Jeff didn't want Mary involved in his life."

Also on that leg of the tour was a three-day layover in San Diego so Jeff could complete work on one of the unfinished songs on *Grace.* They'd talked about keeping it as an instrumental, but then it was decided the track definitely needed a lyric. That was Jeff's job on this stop. They were put in adjacent rooms in what Reggie describes evocatively as "the shittiest fucking motel." There were compensations. Jeff knew how to rig the TVs so they could watch movies for free. "I would stop by and see if he wanted anything to eat," Reggie says. "I supposed he was working on songs, but I'd get him out of there sometimes. I like to walk around and sightsee. I'd go back and say, 'Hey, dude, come and check this out.'

"On the last day, I found this spot on the coast—you could see seals hanging out there. And I took him up there and we were standing on this rock formation; waves are crashing and we didn't talk much, just hanging out, and we suddenly got hit by a huge wave that knocked us both over, and we're rolling around trying to stay on these rocks. It was kinda sobering: 'Oh shit, now we've got to drive back to LA.'

"We drive there all soaking wet, and I say to him on the drive, 'Did you write a song?' And he's like, 'Nah, but I think I got the start of one.' So I say, 'Do you think Berkowitz will be pissed that after being here three days, you didn't come up with anything?' And he's like, 'Oh we'll see.'

"We drive to Sound City studios, and Clif Norrell, his recording engineer, is there. Jeff went straight in and started singing 'Dream Brother,' and I thought, 'Holy fuck, you got nothing and you came out with *that*?!' Chris Dowd of Fishbone was there, and that's who 'Dream Brother' was about."

Though Reggie thought this was spontaneous, Jeff had been playing with lyric ideas for a while, and the "Dream Brother" poem dedicated to Chris had been written before the band came together. Jeff was delighted that those first rehearsals had resulted in some new music that he liked. Mick Grondahl told Gayle Keleman, curator of an early Jeff fan website, how it came about, in 1995. "We had been taking out of the air whatever came our way. Then Jeff turned to me: 'Do you have any grooves?' So I started playing this simple F/A/G thing I had come across on my own in another jam, that had never really taken off. I knew there was something in it, and Mattie laid in this really nice cymbal, snare, and bass drum figure, and then Jeff started to do this very trailing, snakelike pattern to it....

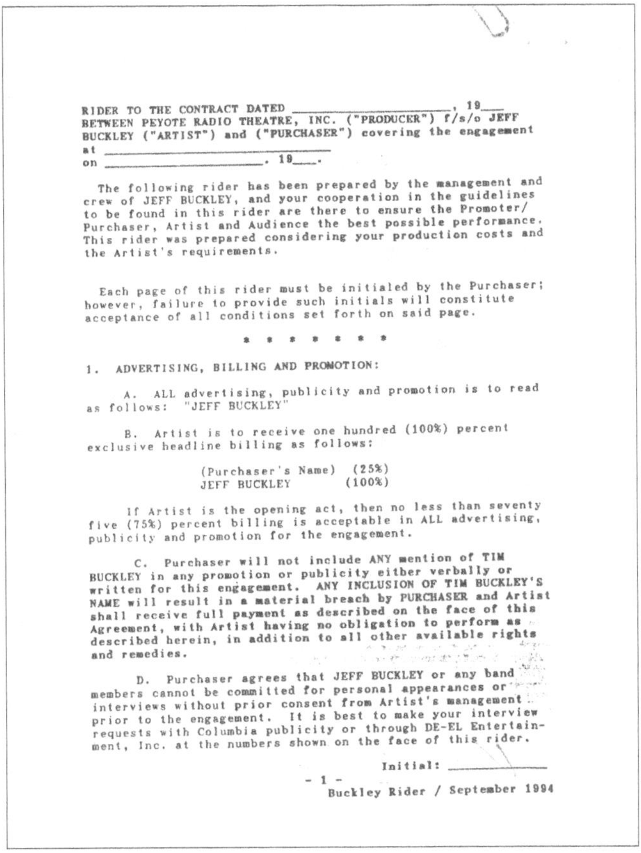

RIDER TO THE CONTRACT DATED ____________________, 19___
BETWEEN PEYOTE RADIO THEATRE, INC. ("PRODUCER") f/s/o JEFF BUCKLEY ("ARTIST") and ("PURCHASER") covering the engagement
at ______________________________
on ____________________, 19___.

The following rider has been prepared by the management and crew of JEFF BUCKLEY, and your cooperation in the guidelines to be found in this rider are there to ensure the Promoter/Purchaser, Artist and Audience the best possible performance. This rider was prepared considering your production costs and the Artist's requirements.

Each page of this rider must be initialed by the Purchaser; however, failure to provide such initials will constitute acceptance of all conditions set forth on said page.

* * * * * * *

1. ADVERTISING, BILLING AND PROMOTION:

A. ALL advertising, publicity and promotion is to read as follows: "JEFF BUCKLEY"

B. Artist is to receive one hundred (100%) percent exclusive headline billing as follows:

(Purchaser's Name) (25%)
JEFF BUCKLEY (100%)

If Artist is the opening act, then no less than seventy five (75%) percent billing is acceptable in ALL advertising, publicity and promotion for the engagement.

C. Purchaser will not include ANY mention of TIM BUCKLEY in any promotion or publicity either verbally or written for this engagement. ANY INCLUSION OF TIM BUCKLEY'S NAME will result in a material breach by PURCHASER and Artist shall receive full payment as described on the face of this Agreement, with Artist having no obligation to perform as described herein, in addition to all other available rights and remedies.

D. Purchaser agrees that JEFF BUCKLEY or any band members cannot be committed for personal appearances or interviews without prior consent from Artist's management prior to the engagement. It is best to make your interview requests with Columbia publicity or through DE-EL Entertainment, Inc. at the numbers shown on the face of this rider.

Initial: ____________

- 1 -

Buckley Rider / September 1994

The front page of the tour rider sent to promoters, stating that they could not use Tim Buckley in any promotion for Jeff's live shows. I told Jeff that when journalists asked about his father, he should say, "I only met him once, a couple of months before his death, but I have some phone numbers of people you can call to find out about him." That killed all further inquiries.

It wasn't until we came to Bearsville that it started to take shape. We got a good version without any lyrics."

Jeff often turned to his dreams for lyrics. But "Dream Brother" is a tribute to a relationship—Jeff and Chris as each other's fantasy siblings. They bonded on so many things and had a huge respect for each other as writers and musicians.

"I have been fortunate to grow up with some incredible musicians who were my peers, but Jeff was a freak of nature," Chris says. "He could pick up something he'd never played before, like a violin, and get a great sound out of it. He went through this whole phase of Indian instruments. When he signed and got money, most people would buy a Porsche or something. Not Jeff. He bought every Indian instrument you can imagine. I'd be at his apartment and he'd have some crazy harmonium thing. When he discovered Nusrat, it was all about that; he wanted to learn how to play tablas and everything. Not like that 'fresh out of Guitar Institute' shit he had when we first met: 'I can play all this but it has zero soul behind it.' With GIT he felt that he had been duped. I don't think so at all. It informed him, and you have to be able to play. But I taught him 'The One' and once Jeff understood this is how you write parts for a song, this is what a hook is, this is the right feel for this kind of song—and we went through all that the entire time we lived together—once he finally got a grasp of that...*Grace*."

I take for granted now that *Grace* works, but it's an unlikely collection of material that shouldn't hang together, as it swings from "Last Goodbye" to "Lilac Wine" to "Corpus Christi Carol" to "Eternal Life." Then consider what's happening within those songs. Some of them are hushed and empty; some are crowded with ideas, the guitar textures, Mick's melodic bass lines, the jazz inflections of Mattie's drumming, and then, a really unexpected touch, the strings, which on "Last Goodbye" sound like the orchestra from a Bollywood movie.

Jeff's head was so full of ideas—those eighteen albums he was anxious to make[25]—that finding out where to begin had been the biggest challenge he faced approaching this record. He set his bar high. He'd say he wanted a record that would hit harder than *Led Zeppelin II*. If you knew him, you didn't doubt he was capable of it. He was constantly surprising us with what he could do.

"Somewhere I might have a video. My sons, Nick and Ben, are four and two," says Steve Berkowitz. "They would watch *Silly Symphonies* and *Merry Melodies* while Mom and Dad made dinner. Jeff was over, lying on the couch watching these cartoons with the kids, and then, all of a sudden, he is standing next to the television and mouthing all the words and music of the cartoons and acting them out and being silly. Nick looks at me and says, 'Daddy, why does he *know* that?'

"'I don't know why, Nick, just watch him...'

"He would do that, whether it was TV themes, German *lieder*, Count Basie, or James Brown. He had ingested all the nuances and dynamics

[25] One of them, he told me, would be *Live in Pakistan*.

and levels of those things; like in the cartoons, the juxtaposition of large and small sounds, a dynamite explosion followed by the small sound of someone picking a cloth off their head—he would replicate the nuance of all of that. Which we hear in *Grace.* He was able to assess those dynamics and turn them into equal, impactful parts of a performance.

"On tour, hurtling through the night in the back of the bus, Jeff would put on Count Basie or James Brown and entertain everybody by being the entire band, especially Basie, where, as the different solos came on, he would move to different places and be that guy on his spot in the orchestra, just in the back of the bus. It was like Jerry Lewis or Jim Carey or someone, that kind of physical comedy. It was hysterically funny. That's why at his funeral I played some of the James Brown CD *Love, Power, Peace: Live at the Olympia, Paris, 1971.* He knew all the raps, all the solos, all the crowd screams on that record."

Grace could have been a crazy outpouring of influences and technique, like Frank Zappa on speed. Instead, it's a carefully balanced object. Some people who knew Jeff well—like Abbo, as we've heard—were initially disappointed that it didn't display the nerve-shredding intensity that Jeff could deliver during his stage performances. But maybe a whole record of that would have been too much. Too exhausting. By underplaying its emotional peaks and troughs, he created a space where people could find their own story. By avoiding contemporary trends, he made a record that has lasted longer in the public's affection than many other once feted albums of the '90s—something timeless.

Steve Berkowitz fired the starting pistol when they still had only four original songs and a bunch of cover versions. It was a classic "you did pack a parachute, right?" move. As Andy Wallace said, "I wasn't worried. I trusted in the team."

"The whole process of this album [was] ass-backwards," Jeff said in his interview for the EPK (electronic press kit) that was distributed to the media with *Grace.* "The date was chosen, the studio was chosen, the producer was chosen, but I didn't have a band. Thought I'd get it together by that time. 'Last-minute'—that's my middle name, hyphenated. But it all worked out. I knew I was going to work with Andy after I talked with him at Sony. We talked about Sun Ra and Little Willie John and how to record things and the way I wanted to do it. I wanted to get a big room with the band and the material, twelve mics, live, and virtually we did that."

Andy Wallace says that he approached the making of *Grace* with an "anything goes" mentality, and rigged the space accordingly.

"The production method was very different from a normal album. We didn't stick with one sound for the whole record. We changed drums around a lot, changed position, tried different mics—each song was a unique production. It wasn't a conscious decision; it's just that each song had such a different nature, so we couldn't do it like a production line."

"Andy and the band had set up three different stations in the big room at Bearsville," says Berkowitz. "One was a rock band setting, with a set of drums and some amps. Then, over to one side, there was a little platform like a folk club, with a stool, an acoustic setup. And then there was this lean-to cave made out of canvas, which Jeff could just go into to write lyrics and play solo. So whatever he felt like doing, he could go from place to place, rock out, be in the dark, make music. It was all mic-ed all the time."[26]

Any of a dozen of Jeff's Sin-é staples could have made the record, and he tried them all.

"The idea was to capture a body of work to choose from," Andy says. "Usually in the evenings, after dinner, after some wine, Jeff would just go in and sing things—the covers that ended up on the record and others, like 'Satisfied Mind,' 'Lost Highway,' 'Alligator Wine'; things that have come out since. Whoever was around would be the audience, and it was all very casual. I didn't direct them at all. 'Alligator Wine' sung in the style of Screaming Jay Hawkins was as much of a surprise to me as anyone. But so engaging. I liked the fact that they brought an element of the humor that was so good in the solo shows. He did 'Night Flight,' the Led Zeppelin tune, and a beautiful version of 'Calling You' from the movie *Bagdad Cafe.* That's one I wish we'd put on the album; there was something magical about it.

[26] Steve Berkowitz asked Columbia for fifty thousand dollars to film the sessions. When asked why, he said: 'Imagine if someone had filmed the making of The Beatles' first two albums. What if this was that and we hadn't filmed it?' Filmmaker Ernie Fritz shot many sessions, including the recording of "Hallelujah."

"Jeff wouldn't necessarily sing a song the same way twice. On some tracks it was difficult to match vocals. If I had a track that was 90 percent there and I needed some repairs, he would sing it in a style that was different enough from the original take for me to say, 'You're not helping me out here!' and he'd say, 'Well, the new way's better,' and I'd say, 'Well, maybe not!' I remember playing that game a number of times! We never really butted heads, but sometimes I'd be frustrated.

"All four of us seemed to get on well up there. There weren't any issues, anyone being an outsider; this one's giddy and this one's moody. Everyone co-existed well. Mickey and Matt are really good musicians, very good at taking direction, and I had no problem giving directions. I knew how I wanted things to sound. Jeff was the major filter of the arrangement ideas. He would sit down and illustrate an idea on the drums or bass, but he never said, 'You've got to play exactly this or that.' He wanted a band feeling where there was that participation."

"Jeff would keep improvising the whole way," says Berkowitz. "We were in final mix mode, and he'd want to record more: 'Give me the microphone. I wanna put this part in.' He never wanted to stop."

As a former drummer, I was delighted that Matt Johnson was the guy behind the traps. I loved the way he played, simultaneously tough and tasteful, right in the pocket and clearly a great listener. He knew precisely when to accent and when to stay out of the way. What's amazing when you hear him on *Grace* is how little recording Mattie had done by that point and how nervous he was.

"I had done several recordings, but local-yokel things," he says. "The stakes weren't the same as when there's a budget and a record company and the establishment of a career. A lot of my own need for playing music was wrapped up in the deep insecurities of a young man. At every moment I was terrified of absolute failure. White-knuckling it. I was also feeling around for how the money works. How do we get paid? What does the record company do? It was a learning experience about how the industry works. I was incredibly green."

Although I didn't attend any of the *Grace* sessions, because I wasn't on board yet, I went to Bearsville with other artists and it was a terrific space—rambling, relaxed, and creative. Woodstock had retained something, thirty years after its hippie heyday, that made it somehow intoxicating. That country air was a hit of good grass. Something about the place made you want to kick back, stick around, and lose some inhibitions.

"I think Bearsville was chosen because of the lack of distractions there," says Matt. "You were out of the city. And there were little huts where the artists could live, a feeling of splendid isolation in a bucolic little town. It was just beautiful—the light, the trees. It was just coming into fall, so it was an extraordinarily serene place. There were little local bars that you could pop out to for a minute, Tinker Street, the grocery store, and we went there and got fish sticks or something and cooked stuff at home, and relaxed and listened to music in our huts. So, relative to doing it in the city with Jeff and his friends and the bars and all the distractions, it was a no-brainer.

"We'd do our session each day, and at night it would be food and hanging out, watching *Beavis & Butthead*, playing pool. We did one set of basic tracks per day. Andy would get us in around 11 a.m. and we'd be done by 7 or 8 p.m. to make sure everybody was well rested for the next day. Andy had made so many records. He didn't want to get into enabling an artist's night owl habits or being chronically late all the time."

"I had no idea what a great compositional editor Andy Wallace was going to be," says Berkowitz. "It was similar to what Teo Macero did with Miles Davis—the guys would just come in and play, and Teo would edit it up into a song. Compositional mixing. If you were to listen to the original takes on the *Grace* multi-tracks...to hear where those songs started and where they ended up is an unbelievable journey. Andy's involvement was really important in the way *Grace* came together. *Grace* was not the record we went in to make. No one had a fucking clue, especially Jeff Buckley, that that was the record they were going to make. But it was in him, and out it came."

"Songs just come," Jeff said in the EPK interview. "I have these notebooks that I fetishize over daily. Run to in times of need. I always have something with me. And usually they're just rambling verse. My songs come out of poems, and sometimes poems come out of dreams, or reality, or something I want to say. Sometimes some tune will come down on me first or I'll sit absorbed in something on the guitar, something that my hands need to do, and music will come out of that. But mostly it's what my heart wants to say."

But while he had a lot of material in his notebooks, he was taking his time turning that into new songs. It felt as if Jeff needed to live with a song for some time before he was happy with it. Most of the originals were at least a couple of years old and had been through numerous stages.

Jeff was bunking with friends in Harlem in 1990, and struggling to make ends meet, when Tim Buckley's former manager Herb Cohen called out of the blue and offered him some money to cut a demo. He accepted the offer and returned to LA to stay with Kathryn Grimm and Mark Frere, fellow former members of his GIT band Group Therapy. Recorded over two days with Jeff playing every instrument himself, the four-song demo he made, *The Babylon Dungeon Sessions*, contained early versions of "Last Goodbye," then named "Unforgiven," and "Eternal Life."[27]

Jeff gave an intriguing insight into the birth of the latter in his EPK interview.

"I wrote [it] on my friend's couch in Los Angeles. There was a week where I couldn't sleep. I was possessed by the feeling of anger, because there's a grave imbalance in the psyche in America, where a person can do their best all of his or her life, get their family together, get their shit together, never hurt a soul, and then somebody will break into their house, break into their car, mow them down in the convenience store or fast-food place or any other incredibly crappy environment to die in. People are still messing with each other racially, sexually. Nothing's really changed. It's just a song that's saying life is too short to be endeavoring to fuck up anybody's life. There's too much to be aware of just about being a human being, just about living. There's too much at stake to be trying to fuck up anybody else's life, because life is bigger than anything. And afterwards is bigger than anything. It makes burning a cross completely useless—burning a cross in any form, whether it be against your wife

[27] The other songs from this session were "Radio" and "Strawberry Street." In the program notes for *Greetings From Tim Buckley*, the St. Ann's tribute show, Jeff wrote that Carole King heard this demo and contacted him, and that they'd written together. If that really happened, I'd like to hear that song!

or against two gay lovers walking down the street. He don't fuck with anyone, the cardinal. You don't do that. Or pay the consequences."

That's what kept Jeff awake. "Eternal Life" meant a lot to him and was the one song that he came to think should have been handled differently on *Grace*, and we'll come to that later.

The album's stunning opening pair of songs, "Mojo Pin" and "Grace," were written with Gary Lucas during Jeff's time with Gods & Monsters. After meeting Jeff at the St. Ann's show, Lucas had indeed, as he'd mentioned to Berkowitz, invited Jeff to join his already functioning band as its new vocalist. Jeff, however, felt duty-bound to return to LA, possibly to follow up on his earlier demo. While he was there, Gary sent him some instrumental tracks on cassette for Jeff to add words and melody to. The topline for "Grace" was written over a piece Gary had called "Rise Up To Be." "Mojo Pin" started life as "And You Will."

Gary was invited up to Bearsville for three days (and for fifteen hundred dollars) to play on those songs. His short but fruitful working relationship with Jeff (whom Gary's wife, Caroline, referred to sarcastically as "the Precious One") was a source of some consternation to him. He got a whole, very candid book out of it.[28] Like everyone else, he'd been seduced by Jeff's presence and talent, but ultimately felt jerked around by Jeff's non-communication over what he was prepared to commit to while they worked together. Gary saw them as a potentially great two-man creative force, a new Page and Plant. Jeff dangled that possibility in front of him for a couple of gigs (and "signed" a joint development deal with Imago Records) and then, having demanded that Gary completely restructure the band by sacking his friend Jared who was playing bass, Jeff suddenly announced he didn't want to do it anymore.[29] Gary felt there was something Oedipal in the betrayal, seeing himself as the father figure being stabbed in the back.[30] Jeff, who was too set on finding his own unique path to consider any kind of serious creative partnership, did feel guilty about it, so while he respected Gary, he subsequently felt uncomfortable around him, like Gary knew him too well, and there

[28] *Touched By Grace: My Time With Jeff Buckley* (Jawbone 2013).

[29] Jeff agreed to the deal only in principle and, having shown it to George Stein, did not actually sign it.

[30] Gary was 14 years older than Jeff.

was an edge to their encounters. Two fulsome egos jostling for center stage—with the nagging sense that Gary reckoned Jeff's whole persona was a schtick that he no longer bought.

All that aside, he did a great job in his three days there, playing extraordinary guitar on his two songs, which set the tone for the double-guitar interplay that Jeff and his band would employ from then on. It's Gary who supplied many of the detailed textures that give these songs their unique character: the little backward loop that runs in back of "Mojo Pin," the dreamy drone in the intro, the string-like tones played with an EBow. For "Grace," he created the ghostly chiming violin sound that's on the intro and between and behind the verses. The long, shivery glissando in verse two is, according to Gary, "glass bottleneck on the Strat through a pitch-shifter and a delay pedal."

In a dense little book about *Grace*, academic and fan Daphne A. Brooks calls out "Mojo Pin" as a ballsy way to open a debut album: "a slow-burning howl of a track...that has you wading through the hummingbird serenade of Buckley's lullaby falsetto into the wonderland world of ugly addiction."[31]

Though sometimes "Mojo Pin" is announced as a song about a dream, the term "mojo pin" does indeed refer to a syringe full of heroin. Jeff used this as a visual once or twice, miming jacking up when introducing the song live. Gary Lucas recalls his doing something similar when he first explained the lyrics to him.

Jeff's songs aren't all autobiographical, but he certainly dabbled in all the most popular narcotics at one time or another. This instance, however, could be a reference to his father's weakness for the opiate that ended his life.

In his book, Gary asserts that Jeff was "obsessed with his father's death." Jeff certainly had a morbid preoccupation unusual in someone so young. Tim's death had thrown an immovable shadow over Jeff and bequeathed to him a lingering sense of impermanence, of the brevity of life. He was afraid of falling down the same rabbit hole as his dad, assumed he was programmed to do something similar, and both flirted with it and fought it. Jeff referred to death all the time, not least in his

[31] "Grace", *331/3* series (Continuum, 2005).

songs. He'd also say things like: "Oh, when's it my turn to die?" jokingly, as an expression of frustration if things weren't going right. He spoke about death like it was an acquaintance that could show up anytime. "Grace" itself is full of it.[32]

Gary came away from his time in Bearsville—contributing the "magical guitarness" that Jeff credited him for in the *Grace* liner notes—with the impression that *Grace* was being made under pressure.[33] He felt that Jeff, hunkered down in the "writers cottage" at Bearsville, was aware of the expensive clock ticking away while they tried to create music from scratch in this luxurious environment, and Gary wondered how anyone could cope with that.

Until I came to write this book, I hadn't fully appreciated how much pressure Jeff put upon himself to deliver. I saw how annoyed he'd get when a show went badly or something didn't go according to plan, but I now see those reactions went deeper than I'd realized. Jeff was good at concealing his true feelings. He'd navigate social awkwardness by doing something silly, easing the tension with humor. But there were outbursts I might have read better.

He would veer from being really grateful to Sony to being really resentful that it was making him "do all this bullshit to sell records." But of course, he wanted to sell records too. He would love his inexperienced bandmates one minute and then express dismay at them the next. He would moan to me about George and vice versa. He would swing in his relationships between giddy love and conflicted resentment. And there was a simple reason for this: that was how he treated himself. Jeff was riddled with doubt. He knew what he was capable of and was scared of not delivering it. "I want to write song after song after song," he said to me during one of our first meetings. Yet there were only three totally solo compositions on *Grace.*

---

[32] In one interview, Jeff remembered that he was "anticipating leaving LA for New York" when he wrote the "Grace" lyrics, and proposed that "my time has come" is a positive line about what lay ahead in New York—so the song, instead of being morbid, could be about not being afraid to leave his old home for a new one. Performing live with Gods & Monsters, however, he announced it was about "my obsession with death and dying."

[33] In an earlier version of the credits, Jeff thanked "Gary Lucas and his special guitar voodoo."

Were his standards too high? Was he afraid of letting it all out? Was he kidding himself? All of the above. Jeff's art was born in the moments when his turmoil and his genius were in sync, and he came to recognize that was a rare occurrence. "Wait in the fire," the refrain of "Grace," may be a reference to waiting for inspiration to strike during an episode of pain.

"Lover, You Should Have Come Over" is a real highlight of the album and considered by many to be the most perfectly Jeff-like thing he ever recorded, opening with an introduction Jeff played on his Indian harmonium. It was one of the tunes that really blossomed at Bearsville. He described the song as being partly about the "delicious feeling" of lying on the floor waiting for someone to call, while also being too busy to wait. He also noted that the song "has a lot of connotations other than just being lonely and wanting to make love."

Jeff didn't discuss his lyrics. They weren't even a topic of conversation between him and Andy Wallace during the *Grace* sessions. It strikes me, however, that the lyrics don't carry all the information in a Jeff Buckley song. They are signposts pointing somewhere in the direction of what he wants to convey. For me, the real information is in his voice—its timbre, its dynamic, the melodies he chooses, and the way he leans into those melodies and flies.

I'd never experienced before, from rock music, the feelings I got when Jeff was in form. It seemed like he was finding a new way to communicate, pulling together all the things he had fed on as a kid and a student of music: rock and jazz and gospel and blues are all in there—that's a given—but the colors that are unexpected are the ones that made him special. He adored Siouxsie Sioux; her metallic tone and punky energy are somewhere in Jeff.[34] Then there was Elizabeth Fraser. Her "unique, impossible" voice, as he described it, and her unpredictable melodies were a huge influence upon him. The fact that he came to have a relationship with her was mind-blowing for him.[35] The things that Fraser did with her voice echoed in Jeff's deepest, most recent influence, Nusrat Fateh Ali Khan, whom he referred to as "my Elvis." Nusrat's voice

[34] His Siouxsie and the Banshees influence is most obvious on songs like "Nightmares by the Sea" and "Witches Rave," from the *Sketches for My Sweetheart the Drunk* album.

[35] You can hear him work a little bit of her song "Ivo" into the "Live at the Bataclan" version of "The Way Young Lovers Do," to the delight of the Parisian crowd.

transfixed him when he was in Harlem in 1990 and his roommate Kevin brought home one of the singer's albums. Jeff wrote about that moment in some liner notes for a 1997 compilation of the singer's recordings, and his choice of metaphor is interesting:

"Part Buddha, part demon, part mad angel...his voice is velvet fire, incomparable...I felt a rush of adrenaline in my chest, like I was on the edge of a cliff, wondering when I would jump and how well the ocean would catch me: two questions that would never be answered until I experienced the first leap."

Jeff eloquently describes how the repetition of the lyrics keeps going until the corporeal meaning of the words falls away and the sense is simply felt. Somehow Jeff understood this immediately without being able to speak Urdu, the language in which Khan sang. He was so moved by Khan that he resolved to discover all he could about that incredible voice and that style of singing, qawwali. Which was not a simple thing to research then—it's easier now that the internet is so vast—and Jeff must have gone to some lengths to investigate his newfound passion. One obstacle was that the techniques of qawwali are never written down, but only passed through the family line from fathers to sons. The spiritual aspect of the technique makes it all the more mysterious. Jeff's enthusiasm branched out into wanting to learn about playing the tabla—another discipline people spend a lifetime perfecting—and replicating the drones and strange tunings of Indian and Pakistani music with his guitar.[36] I have no idea where he found the time to go so deep into this music that "healed the fuck" out of him, as he said, but he was very committed to it, saw Khan play four times—even interviewed him in 1996—and often talked animatedly about him.

Eastern music provided Jeff with a palette that wasn't being used in Western rock then. One reason *Grace* was a slow burner, from a sales point of view, is that it didn't play by the same sonic rules as the big rock records of the time—albums by Nirvana, Pearl Jam, or Soundgarden, all of which, despite their supposed freshness, were basically traditional, employing gruff male voices and loud guitars with different strengths of

[36] Jeff put some of his Khan influences, especially vocally, into "New Year's Prayer" from the *Sketches for My Sweetheart the Drunk* album.

abrasion. Jeff approached his vocals from a different viewpoint. He could do the visceral howls too, if he wished, but just as Louis Armstrong or Billie Holiday sang like a trumpet, Jeff's sound resembled a guitar tuned in the direction of India. As Chris Dowd has said, finding your hat—your own voice—on any kind of instrument is every player's mission. Unusually, Jeff had found something of his own by the time of his very first public recordings.

It was also very important to him, at this stage, that his music wasn't macho. The guy in his "Judy Garland jacket," as seen on the cover of *Grace*, liked to tap into his female energy. Jeff wanted to explore emotion from multiple perspectives, and he wasn't remotely interested in following trends.

"I don't write my music for Sony. I write it for the people who are screaming down the road, crying to a full-blast stereo," he wrote in one of his notebooks.[37]

"I don't have any recollection of there ever being an issue of how the record should sound, fitting in with the grunge thing, or whatever," says Andy. "We all felt confident that this album would find its way and be a great record. It was a lot of work, a lot of experimenting in the studio. If there was any static from the label, I think Steve Berkowitz ran interference pretty well. I don't recall any conversation with anybody from Columbia saying that we were going in the wrong direction. I like variety, so it was a lot of fun for me."

The three cover versions were the songs that emphasized the tender, almost sentimental side of Jeff's character. Though way more traditional in form than his own material, their selection seemed daring in the era of grunge.

"Lilac Wine" is a standard, written in 1950 for a show called *Dance Me A Song*, that has been revived several times. Like "Mojo Pin," it equates love with addiction and intoxication. The song isn't clear whether the drink is hallucinogenic or a poison, but it has a powerful effect on the protagonist. "I learned it from Nina Simone, who secretly, I think, I want to be. Although she would advise against it strongly, I'm sure," Jeff said. Perhaps he identified with Nina because she was another unique,

[37] Quoted in *Grace*, by Daphne A. Brooks.

At one point Columbia preferred this shot as the cover of *Grace*. Jeff disagreed. We turned it into a backstage pass so that the executive who liked it could feel vindicated when he wore it.

unmistakable stylist who took risks with her voice, who was untrained as a singer but an expert in another instrument, and who disregarded genre barriers. A lifelong champion of Nina's work, Jeff was drawn to her expressive delivery and refusal to be categorized.[38] He covered several of her songs at Sin-é, among them "Be My Husband" and "Four Women." She had also sung great versions of "Strange Fruit" and Bob Dylan's "Just Like a Woman," both of which Jeff sang too. In fact, you could say Jeff's whole act and approach to his Sin-é sets took Nina's style as a template—the vertiginous shifts in mood, the humorous asides, the bursts of French chanson and exotic songs from far afield, the arrangements that blurred musical boundaries.

[38] Soul singer Jhelisa Anderson, whom Jeff had played with briefly while in LA but who later made a name for herself in England, admitted that despite having once met the great woman and indeed driven her to the hospital, she had been largely ignorant of Nina Simone's work until Jeff turned her on to it.

"Corpus Christi Carol" is a Benjamin Britten song. Britten was a British composer who rose to prominence in the 1940s and '50s. A friend named Roy, who used to make Jeff classical mix tapes, introduced him to the piece in his teens.

And then there's "Hallelujah." "It's a Leonard Cohen song," Jeff said in the EPK. "But I do the version that has other verses that Leonard didn't record on *Various Positions.* I first heard it when John Cale did a version on *I'm Your Fan* (a Leonard Cohen tribute album). That was my favorite. I just learned it one night before a gig at Sin-é. Somebody suggested that it should be on the album. And I said okay. I was ready not to do it, again because it's from Sin-é and I wanted to move on. But it's a great song. I wish I wrote it."

Jeff's reading of this beautiful, many-layered song has become the definitive one for many people, and his take on it has been covered many times. His version's blend of sexual tension and choirboy purity was a perfect fit. He understood that duality and milked it. He always enjoyed singing that ascending melody, and got a kick out of its effect upon an audience who'd not heard it before. I don't know if Jeff was aware that Cohen had written, as he'd once reckoned, "possibly 80 verses for the song over the space of at least four years," filling several notebooks. But he noted that John Cale's version differed in tone from the original.[39]

The performance captured on *Grace* is actually a composite of five different takes. Andy Wallace selected which lines to splice together, with Jeff's approval. The final effect is a beautifully measured delivery. Jeff is never tempted to become overwrought, and he infers the weight of

[39] When agreeing to cover the song for the *I'm Your Fan* tribute album, Cale, rather than transcribing the lyric, called up his friend Cohen and asked for a copy. Cohen faxed over everything he had. Cale came home to find his floor littered with fax paper. Cohen had recorded two distinct versions. The one on 1984's *Various Positions* had four verses and began with the one about King David and is religious in tone, though it includes the famous second verse. The one he sang on *Cohen Live*, a version recorded in 1988, has only the fourth, final verse in common with the original. The only hint of religious imagery is the third verse. When Cale made his selection, he took five verses, the original recording's opening two followed by the first three verses of the live version, losing the final verse Cohen had used on both his recordings. This makes the song a more equivocal work than (either of) Cohen's, mixing the religious and sexual imagery, with the ripest lines from each version.

the song without the use of an orchestra, a choir, or the other trappings subsequent cover versions have leaned upon.[40]

One thing that always intrigued me was Jeff's decision to place this song, with which he had closed so many of his shows, smack in the middle of the album—a counterintuitive move that worked great.

"After a few weeks, Jeff said, 'That's it; that's all I've got. We're done,'" says Berkowitz. "I said, 'Are you sure? Why don't you guys think about it?' Andy and I went out of the studio and took a long walk into downtown Bearsville, had lunch at a Chinese restaurant, threw stones into a stream, and then walked back, and Jeff says, 'We got another one!' and that's when they played 'Forget Her.' I'm in the control room with Andy when they start playing it, and I say, 'You've got the tape rolling, right?' And he had. Where did *this* come from?"

When I came on board, "Forget Her" was the song everyone at Columbia was buzzing about as the record's potential smash. It was a simple, blues-shaped thing with a moody guitar intro and a powerful simplicity. It got under your skin because it was a sincere piece of work that actually had a chorus that repeated. It also had a good old-fashioned guitar solo on it and a prominent Hammond organ part. It reminded me of The Beatles' "While My Guitar Gently Weeps," the one with Eric Clapton on it.

"When he played that, I called Don Ienner and said, 'His head's exploding with ideas. We're not coming back; we're going to spend some more time,'" says Berkowitz. "After 'Forget Her,' in Jeff's head, some switch flips and all that resource and ability, all those ideas, all that woodshedding, which I assumed was going to happen on his third record, comes pouring out. He seemed to unlock all of that music. The trepidation of that first step, thinking, 'Which Jeff Buckley am I going to be?'—he'd finally got past it."

Jeff's increased confidence shows in the way he approached the out-of-left-field idea to add strings to the album.

"The strings were a complete accident," says Berkowitz. "I'd always liked the first Colin Blunstone album, *One Year*, the way the strings bridge the songs on that record, and I thought Jeff might like the idea. I had just met this guy Karl Berger, a fine musician, who in the '50s and

[40] In 2014, the Library of Congress announced that "Hallelujah" would be preserved in the National Recording Registry.

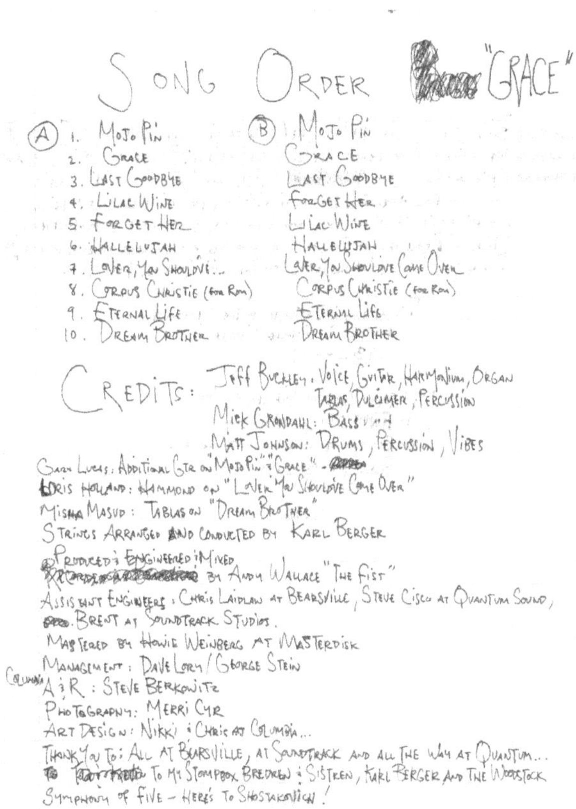
SONG ORDER "GRACE"

(A) 1. MOJO PIN
2. GRACE
3. LAST GOODBYE
4. LILAC WINE
5. FORGET HER
6. HALLELUJAH
7. LOVER, YOU SHOULD'VE...
8. CORPUS CHRISTIE (FOR RON)
9. ETERNAL LIFE
10. DREAM BROTHER

(B) MOJO PIN
GRACE
LAST GOODBYE
FORGET HER
LILAC WINE
HALLELUJAH
LOVER, YOU SHOULD'VE COME OVER
CORPUS CHRISTIE (FOR RON)
ETERNAL LIFE
DREAM BROTHER

CREDITS: JEFF BUCKLEY: VOICE, GUITAR, HARMONIUM, ORGAN, TABLAS, DULCIMER, PERCUSSION
MICK GRONDAHL: BASS
MATT JOHNSON: DRUMS, PERCUSSION, VIBES
GARY LUCAS: ADDITIONAL GTR ON "MOJO PIN" & "GRACE"
LORIS HOLLAND: HAMMOND ON "LOVER YOU SHOULD'VE COME OVER"
MISHA MASUD: TABLAS ON "DREAM BROTHER"
STRINGS ARRANGED AND CONDUCTED BY KARL BERGER
PRODUCED, ENGINEERED & MIXED BY ANDY WALLACE "THE FIST"
ASSISTANT ENGINEERS: CHRIS LAIDLAW AT BEARSVILLE, STEVE CISCO AT QUANTUM SOUND, BRENT AT SOUNDTRACK STUDIOS.
MASTERED BY HOWIE WEINBERG AT MASTERDISK
MANAGEMENT: DAVE LORY / GEORGE STEIN
COLUMBIA A & R: STEVE BERKOWITZ
PHOTOGRAPHY: MERRI CYR
ART DESIGN: NIKKI & CHRIS AT COLUMBIA...
THANK YOU TO: ALL AT BEARSVILLE, AT SOUNDTRACK AND ALL THE WAY AT QUANTUM... TO MY STOMPBOX BRETHREN & SISTREN, KARL BERGER AND THE WOODSTOCK SYMPHONY OF FIVE – HERE'S TO SHOSTAKOVICH!

Jeff's initial handwritten credits and two song sequences for *Grace*, both of which included "Forget Her" before "So Real" was recorded.

'60s was competing with Gary Burton to be the coolest young jazz vibraphone player. He was an arranger, and also a conductor of the Frankfurt Philharmonic Radio Orchestra, a hip German guy, and he happened to live in Woodstock. I call Jeff up and suggest we get him in, and he's into it. They meet once in my office, and Jeff plays the stuff on acoustic guitar. Karl and the players could only come in on certain days, so we had to record improvised basic tracks for some of the songs. Karl [took these recordings] home and wrote all the charts. Then we had the string quartet come in."

"Karl was thrilled to have that gig. I don't think he had worked on many rock records," says Andy. "Jeff had some ideas, like bouncing the bow on the string, something he had heard that he wanted to incorporate into one song."

"That was a spectacular day," says Berkowitz. "I have a vivid picture of Jeff. He's in the bunker at Bearsville in a dirty, tattered wife-beater shirt and suspenders with his pants hanging down off his ass, and he's working with Karl and the players and all of sudden he goes: [*hums to himself*] 'Got a pencil?' And Jeff starts erasing the arrangement and writing other notes in, and Karl takes it over to the piano and says, 'Yah, that will work. That's good.' And I'm saying, 'I didn't know he knew how to write for strings!' There were way more strings recorded for *Grace* than we used—longer, almost symphonic versions of some songs. Jeff and I discussed doing something with those parts. He said, 'Someday we can take those strings off and do something else with them.' But we never got to that."

When the six weeks at Bearsville were up, they more or less had complete multi-tracks for nine songs: "Grace," "Mojo Pin," "Last Goodbye," "Forget Her," "Lilac Wine," "Lover, You Should Have Come Over," "Corpus Christi Carol," "Hallelujah," and "Eternal Life."

The mixes took months. Tweaks were still happening several months after I started work, when the album was still slated for a spring release—a quick turnaround after the EP. Two other things held up that planned release. First, it was decided we needed a second guitar player to replicate the intricate arrangements on the album. Second was Jeff's decision to drop "Forget Her."

When promo cassettes of *Grace* were sent out in anticipation of the spring release date, "Forget Her" was on the record. The song had started to bug Jeff. He'd mentioned this to me on the road. I found a fax that George and I had sent to Berkowitz on April 22, 1994, saying that Jeff was unhappy with the latest mix of "Forget Her" because "the material recorded in Los Angeles was not used and the current version is not what he wants on the record." I don't recall extra stuff being recorded, but there it is. Shortly after that, Jeff became adamant that he didn't want it on the record at all.

Everybody thought this was a bad idea. "That was a song that resonated with me and I thought would resonate with other women," says Julie Borchard. "It was a beautiful song that was heartbreaking and deserved to be out there."

Over the years, there's been dispute and speculation about Jeff's motives for dropping it from *Grace*—mainly because, typically, he told everybody a slightly different story.

"Too much of a balladeering melodrama, the 6/8 waltz thing," says Matt Johnson. "The white-man blues. He might have been embarrassed about it, thought it wasn't his best writing." Jeff had developed a thing about "white blues." He loved blues music but thought it was something that should be felt, not copied. On one of our drives, he said, "I want to sing the blues in private, not in public. It's in everything I do, but it's my blues."

"I don't usually get too adamant about things the artist doesn't want," says Andy, "but on this occasion I really went to bat to try and get him to put it on the record, as it was such a strong song. The track was finished, and though he always felt he could sing it better, he wouldn't go in and re-sing it. I'm not sure why his objections were so strong. I was mostly concerned with making a great album, and that was Jeff's main concern too. But I thought that 'Forget Her' was a prime candidate for a single."

Steve Berkowitz says, "It's a beautiful song—accessible, emotional, with verses and choruses, and for Don Ienner, who was a radio man, it was the perfect choice as a single. He wants it back on the record. Jeff says no. This goes on for a month or two, and finally Don Ienner says, 'We've got to talk to him.' So there's a dinner arranged at an Italian restaurant on the West Side, on Eighth Avenue, and attending is Jeff, me, Ienner, Michele Anthony. It's a nice dinner and finally Donnie says, '"Forget Her" is gonna be the big hit of the record,' and Jeff looks around and says quietly, 'If I ever hear that song again, I'm gonna throw up,' and Donnie says, 'Well...okay,' and Jeff says, 'I gotta go,' and gets up and leaves."

Jeff gave me a bunch of reasons too. One was that he didn't want Rebecca to hear it. Some have assumed that was because the song is a brush-off, but it isn't; it's about being unable to forget someone you still love, and that was pretty much the state of things when I first knew Jeff. Maybe he just didn't want her to know that.

Weighing it all up, what he told Leah Reid sounds most convincing: "What you're hearing is only twelve-karat, and in my head that song is twenty-four-karat and I don't want it to come out until it's twenty-four-karat."

He just didn't think it was ready. Looking at various notes and memos of mine, I noticed that in 1995, Jeff had listed "Forget Her" as a contender for a between-album EP that was being discussed for a while, so he can't have been completely down on the song.

We quickly realized that reproducing *Grace* live would require a second guitar player in the band. Both Mattie and Mickey had come via random meetings. Jeff didn't have time to sit around and wait for one of those to bear fruit again—the clock was ticking on *Grace*'s release date; tours were being booked.

According to Gary Lucas, Mickey turned up at his apartment one day to ask him if he'd consider being their second guitar player. Gary was pleased that Mick rated him enough to ask, but quite rightly pointed out that the offer had to come directly from Jeff or he couldn't consider it. I was surprised when I read that in Gary's book; it seems unlikely on a few counts. But no more unlikely than what actually happened. Jeff invited a friend from his Harlem days, a budding actor named Michael Tighe, whom Jeff called "Chico," to come and sit in with them, and almost on a whim asked him to be the second guitar player. Jeff announced to me as a fait accompli that Michael, who was twenty-one and had never played professionally with anyone, was his new guitarist: "I've found my guitar player, Dave!" I was going to meet him at Montana Studios on 57th Street and 11th Avenue.

He looked about twelve, a skinny, cherubic insect in black clothes. The entirety of our first conversation was, "Hi." He wasn't the most talkative musician I'd ever met. Or the most musical. His battered, anonymous guitar seemed to be attached to his amp with a really short cable. He stood glued to it with his back to us. They started to play. It was a jam, a formless free-for-all. It went on for some time. I couldn't hear a thing this kid was doing. I was starting to get the picture: he was perfect for the gig—he could barely play guitar and had no equipment. On the plus side, he was a good-looking kid and Jeff really liked him, so he was someone to hang out with on the road. But, fuck.

The studio manager came into the room. There was a phone call for me. Who could this be?

"Dave!"

Donnie Ienner. Shit.

"So Jeff's got a new guitarist. What's his name?"

"Michael. Michael Tighe."

"Uh-huh. Who's he played with?"

I gulped. "Oh, everyone, everyone, whole bunch of people. Hey, Donnie, about the EPK..."

I got away with it, I think, but I knew it was going to be obvious to everyone that this guy had no experience. Mattie was pretty outgoing behind the drums, but Mick and Michael were literally shoe-gazing. Michael was playing hardly anything. I went back into the room hoping for a sudden transformation. The jam was still lumbering on.

"Donnie," I said to Berkowitz. "I told him the kid has played with everyone."

Berkowitz laughed and shook his head in despair. Remember, he was a guitar player, so this was doubly painful for him. Michael had only fooled around with two bands in high school or something.

"Don't you play the actual songs?" I asked Jeff, slightly pissed off, my whole career flashing before me.

"Don't worry about it. It'll be fine," he said, smiling. He was training his players to expect the unexpected, to *listen*, to take note of where he was going.

I was going to have heart failure. I turned to Berkowitz.

"Jesus, this needs work."

Actually, Michael soon turned out to be an asset.[41] He provided the inspiration Jeff needed to finish the album, the germ of an idea, a little chord sequence that became "So Real." Jeff quickly got an idea for the chorus but couldn't find the rest. We needed some B-side material, so decided to use the day Jeff had asked for in Sony Studios to cut this track and see where it went. That night, Chris Dowd dropped by for a visit. Jeff, Michael, and Chris were going to the corner store for something, and Jeff suddenly announced he was going for a walk. He came back a half an hour later with the rest of the lyrics and melody in his head, and laid down the vocal in one take.

---

[41] Michael turned into a dedicated musician. After Jeff's death, he formed a band called The 3AM, and has recently cropped up as a co-writer on Liam Gallagher's *As You Were* album.

Jeff loved "So Real," another song with a golden, Eastern aspect. To him, it was too good to be a B-side. It was the missing puzzle piece for *Grace*.

"When he saw *Grace* with 'So Real' on it, he saw that the album had not only a family of songs that captured a moment, but also that 'So Real' expressed where he was going," says Matt Johnson. "He thought that song saved the record."

The "So Real" session was in April 1994, just after we came back from the solo European tour and just when *Grace* was originally supposed to have come out.

I had to take Jeff aside and tell him that he couldn't tinker with the album anymore; it was done. It had now been pushed back to August.[42]

When asked about the album's title on the EPK, Jeff answered: "Grace is what matters in anything. Especially in life, tragedy, pain, love, death.... Grace is a quality I admire in people. It keeps you from reaching for the gun too quickly; it keeps you from destroying things too foolishly; it keeps you alive and keeps you open for more understanding."

Discussions about the artwork were well advanced by the time I came aboard in December 1993. The *Grace* cover shoot had been a month earlier.

"From a marketing perspective, the solo sleeve portrait is obviously what you want to do with a solo artist," says Leah Reid. "If you want to make some connection with the people in a record store, it's easier to do it with a large picture of somebody. Genesis or Pink Floyd can have conceptual covers, but Dylan and Springsteen and Billie Holiday, they're all on their record sleeves. It's page-one marketing, but it's that way for a reason. It helps to make the artist visible and to tie everything together. We decided [the cover of *Grace*] needed to be a portrait of Jeff."

"We shot it in this loft belonging to my friend Billy," says Merri Cyr. "His boyfriend Jamie is an artist, so there were really beautiful objects and settings that already existed within the space, and I created some different setups and combined my props with Jamie's art pieces. The loft had weird architecture, vaulted ceilings, and a lot of natural light in the stairwells, which was beautiful.

---

[42] August is not quite as strong a release slot as spring. It can be hard to get the media and record buyers to focus during the vacation season.

"Billy had made a small stage area inside the loft; he actually did little events there with cabaret acts. Jeff had brought this duffel bag full of his clothes, all smashed in there, none of them pressed or even clean. There was a giant bed and Jeff just emptied the bag onto it, spread his clothes all over the bed. I selected items from what he'd brought to go with each setup. The gold sequined jacket was his. He called it his 'Judy Garland jacket.' Jeff was hamming it up with an antique microphone on that little stage. I took a couple of rolls of that, and the cover image came from those shots.

"I was taking natural-light pictures of him in the stairwell, and he just jumped up at me at one point and I caught him in midair. They used that on the back cover. Later in the day, Mattie and Mickey came in and I took a few shots of them with Jeff. That was the first time I had met them.

"A couple of weeks after the shoot, we had a meeting in [Sony art director] Chris Austopchuk's office. I can't remember why, but for some reason Jeff and I had gotten into a tiff again. I wouldn't talk to him, so he called and got Chris to call me in for a meeting. At one point when looking through the contact sheets, Jeff said, 'That's the one.' He just points at the shot that became the cover of *Grace.* I'd made prints of all the ones that I liked, and that wasn't one of them. Jeff saw something there that I hadn't been compelled by initially. I understand it now, but at that time I thought that one was a little generic. Now it's hard to imagine it would be anything else."

Even though Jeff had picked that image, some of Merri's preferred shots and those selected by Chris Austopchuk and sleeve designer Nicky Lindeman went forward to the dummy sleeve process.

"There were a lot of versions of the *Grace* sleeve," confirms Leah. "Nicky Lindeman did up a bunch of rough versions of the artwork in CD boxes to see how it would look in the store. There was one I thought was really cool, a shot of him reflected in a broken mirror, and one senior executive said, 'If you think that's who Jeff Buckley is, then you have *no* idea who he is.' Really! It was a great picture and I absolutely loved that shot.

"I was sent down to Philadelphia, where they were playing in the Grape Street Pub, with six or seven comps of the sleeve, and I laid them all down on the table. There was the one of him sitting in the park under the Temperance sign; there was a shot of him under a table covered in clocks, writing in a book, and the broken mirror shot. And he looked straight at the one that became the cover and said, 'This is the one. I love this one because I'm listening to music.' He loved the look on his face, listening to music and at peace. That started the controversy."

Jeff's choice was not popular at 550 Madison. Donnie Ienner's ire could be heard echoing down the corridors. "He looks like a fucking lounge singer!" (Albeit a half-dressed one.) Someone said it looked like an Adam Ant album. Someone else suggested there should at least be some eye contact. Jeff held firm. Leah and I backed him 100 percent. Like with the "Forget Her" furor, Donnie was seriously annoyed. But he'd agreed to the contract that allowed Jeff full artistic control, and this was one of those occasions when Jeff intended to exercise that clause. The shot stayed.

We officially delivered *Grace* to Sony on May 31, 1994.

Three days later, the band snuck out on a low-key tour of New York state, just to warm up before the full weight of the *Grace* promotion kicked in. Berkowitz and I drove to a show at the Stephen Talkhouse in Amagansett in the Hamptons, about a week into the run. After what I'd witnessed in rehearsal, I was very nervous, and those nerves turned out to be warranted. Jeff positioned himself stage right (left to the audience), with Mattie center stage and Mickey and Michael over at stage left.[43] Mick and Michael faced their amps the entire show and didn't turn around for another few weeks. It looked like Johnny Solo & His Shambling Novices. The lack of experience was obvious. They sounded okay, they played songs off *Grace*, but man they still needed work.

That was one reason we turned down some big TV slots that Columbia offered to chase up shortly after *Grace* came out, like *Late Night with David Letterman* and *Saturday Night Live*. Jeff loved those shows, but even he had to admit that his band wasn't quite ready for national exposure. We decided to wait.

Grace was finally released on August 23, 1994.

From where I was standing, it was a classic. But it was by no means a triumph from the get-go. There were great reviews, and there were a

---

[43] I recently saw footage of Nusrat Fateh Ali Khan playing live and realized he positioned himself stage right too, so that may be where Jeff got the idea. This stage arrangement continued until the very end of the *Grace* tour in 1996.

couple of absolute stinkers. Robert Christgau of *The Village Voice* called Jeff "a syncretic asshole." (Yeah, I had to look it up, too.)[44] Considering this was effectively Jeff's local paper, that had to hurt. Luckily, we were in the UK when the album came out and the reception there was way more positive, though first-week sales peaked just outside the Top 30 album chart.

It wasn't a smash, then. Was Columbia worried?

"Columbia was a company that was about hit records. It always was," says Berkowitz. "But everybody there got how great he was when they saw him play.

"[For Jeff,] coming through the side door of the music business was a good idea. Coming through the front door was not a good idea, because it could eat you up and spit you back out."

We knew the contract was solid, and Columbia had already made a sizable investment; they weren't about to throw us under the bus. Dylan and Springsteen had both delivered flop debut albums. This was about development. Christgau and his kind could go fuck themselves. Jeff knew that doing anything to please critics was a waste of time. He also knew that one day he'd make a record that would blow everyone's minds. Thing is, for a lot of people we were meeting, he already had.

"I loved *Grace*, aside from being involved in making it. I thought it was really strong. But I wasn't shocked that it wasn't an out-of-the-box success," says Andy Wallace. "It was a first album and it didn't have any instant radio hits. It took repeated listening to be hypnotized by it. Once you're familiar with it though, it has so much depth and passion that you become addicted to it."

Hallelujah.

[44] Syncretic: Attempting to amalgamate different religions, cultures, or schools of thought.

CHAPTER 6

Peyote Radio Theatre and the Mystery White Boy

BECOME A PROFESSIONAL MUSICIAN and you will soon, for tax and legal purposes, have to form various entities—touring, merchandise, publishing companies, and so on—through which to conduct your business. Jeff's touring company was named Peyote Radio Theatre, and touring was what we were going to be doing for the immediate future. After talking to Jeff on the solo tour, I had a clear idea of how he wanted to present himself. We talked about how he imagined the band. "I want it to be mesmerizing—the sexiest, scariest, dreamiest, hardest, most sensual band in the land," he declared, and in his usual understated delivery, it sounded plausible. "I want to smell the sex for miles," he added, laughing. He talked about how eventually he'd like to make music that no one could pinpoint, something stripped of all his influences, something beyond genre, something "all original and all *soul*, Dave!" That phrase stuck in my mind.

Early on, I had worried about Jeff's apparent lack of an image and kept mentioning it to Berkowitz and Abbo, one of whom turned to me eventually and said, "Dave, his image is fine. Stop being so Brian

JEFF BUCKLEY
C/O DE-EL ENTERTAINMENT, INC.
P.O. BOX 20131
COLUMBUS CIRCLE STATION
NEW YORK, NY 10023-1483

Postcard for the *Mystery White Boy* tour with artwork by Jeff Buckley.

JEFF BUCKLEY ON TOUR NOW

DATE:	CITY:	VENUE:	DATE:	CITY:	VENUE:
OCT 19	NEW YORK	CBGB	NOV 18	PORTLAND	LA LUNA
OCT 20	ASBURY PARK	T-BIRDS	NOV 20	SAN FRANCISCO	NOE VALLEY MIN.
OCT 21	ALBANY	VALENTINES	NOV 22	LOS ANGELES	LUNA PARK
OCT 22	BROOKLYN	ST. ANNS	NOV 23	LOS ANGELES	THE ROXY
OCT 24	BOSTON	CHARLES PLAYHSE	NOV 25	SAN DIEGO	LA PALOMA THTRE
OCT 25	MONTREAL	CLUB SODA	NOV 26	PHOENIX	VALLEY ART THTRE
OCT 28	TORONTO	TRINITY CTR	NOV 29	AUSTIN	ELECTRIC LNGE-TENT
OCT 29	DETROIT	MAGIC BAG	NOV 30	DALLAS	21 AMENDMENT
OCT 31	ANN ARBOR	THE ARK	DEC 1	HOUSTON	URBAN ART BAR
NOV 1	CLEVELAND	WILBERT'S	DEC 2	NEW ORLEANS	HOWLING WOLF
NOV 2	CINCINNATI	SUDSY MALONE'S	DEC 4	MIAMI	TALK HOUSE
NOV 4	ST. LOUIS	SHELDON BLRM	DEC 5	ORLANDO	JAZZ&BLUES CLUB
NOV 5	LAWRENCE	MULLIGAN'S	DEC 7	ATLANTA	VARIETY THEATER
NOV 6	MINNEAPOLIS	UPTOWN LOUNGE	DEC 8	NASHVILLE	ACE OF CLUBS
NOV 8	CHICAGO	GREEN MILL	DEC 10	RALEIGH	THE BREWERY
NOV 9	CHICAGO	GREEN MILL	DEC 12	WASHINGTON,DC	9:30 CLUB
NOV 12	DENVER	BUG THEATER	DEC 13	PHILADELPHIA	DOBB'S-TENT.
NOV 13	SALT LAKE	ZEPHYR CLUB	DEC 14	NEW YORK	IRVING PLAZA
NOV 16	VANCOUVER	STARFISH ROOM	DEC 15	HOBOKEN	MAXWELL'S
NOV 17	SEATTLE	BACKSTAGE	DEC 16	PROVIDENCE	CLUB BABY HEAD

(ALL DATES ARE SUBJECT TO CHANGE)

Epstein-y."[45] Once I realized that the white T-shirt, keychain, saggy pants, and Doc Martens actually comprised a distinctive look, I also began to see that there was a real advantage to keeping him anchored to the ground, at least for the first year or so, to let things build naturally. Jeff and I called it "The No-Promotion Promotion Plan," designed to keep a lid on any hype or hysteria about him and allow people to discover him at a natural pace and for the right reasons. Just arrive in a city, talk to fanzines and local radio, play a great show, and let the word grow the old-fashioned way. It meant months of dogged slog on his part and a good investment of cash on Sony's, but we all felt that "one fan at a time, sweet Jesus" was the way to go if he wanted a long and fruitful career.

[45] Epstein, The Beatles' manager, took them out of their biker leathers and put them in neat suits and ties.

Jeff was wary of being either a flash in the pan or allied to a scene that would consign him to the dumpster as soon as tastes changed. He was playing the long game.

One of the keys to being a good manager is realizing that your main role is to find good people and let them do their jobs, so the artist can get on with his or hers. With a marketing plan based around constant touring, we needed a good tour manager.

Gene Bowen and I had met when I attended NYU, and we'd kept in touch. After studying music business, Gene had gone into tour management. He'd had a rough time with addiction as a younger man, had worked hard to get clean, and had landed a job at Columbia Artist Management International (CAMI), a company that set up and managed tours for ballet companies and orchestras coming into America from other countries. It was very corporate, a suit-and-tie gig, and incredibly complex, handling sixty to eighty musicians and dancers going across the US and through airports, dealing with customs, carnets, visas, and hell knows what else. Gene was getting really tired of it and wanted to get back into rock 'n' roll. I told him I might have something for him down the road with Jeff. I knew that once the solo shows were done, we'd need someone to handle the upcoming band tour, so I gave him a call. I figured if he could handle sixty foreign classical musicians, four kids and a van would be like a paid vacation. I also thought it was useful to have someone on the road who was sober, just to keep an eye on the guys and make sure no one was overindulging in anything detrimental to themselves or the enterprise. Gene knew what he was doing regarding accounts and planning and he had a relaxed presence, schlubbing around in a baseball cap, saggy jeans, and a pale sweatshirt. With a shock of dark, curly hair and a goofy smile, he made us think of the cheery figure in checkered pants who stands outside Big Boy burger restaurants. He'd occasionally be reminded of this.

We quickly developed a smooth system for promotion: Howard Wuelfing, Leah Read and I would put together the plan and hand it on to Gene, and Gene would make sure it fit in with the road schedule. Having set an itinerary, we turned it into a tour book with a page for each day listing the flight times, hotel, venue, load-in time, and showtime, and the names and numbers of every local contact, venue manger, promoter, and so on. At the front of the book, every show would be listed and then a calendar would map out each week, showing which were travel days, days off, promotion days, video shoots, or rehearsals. The names and numbers (phone and fax) of all the key personnel for all the Sony branches in every country would be there, plus those for the promoters in each territory, the relevant travel agencies and hire companies. Every person on the tour, band and crew, carried one of these. So everyone knew precisely where they would be on any given day, what they were expected to turn up for, and whom to call if anything unexpected happened. A tour manager's job is to make sure nothing unexpected happens. He's with the band the whole time and keeps them on track. This tour was just Jeff, Matt, Mickey, Michael, Gene, and sound man Reggie Griffiths in the van. The band would still have to do some of their own loading and unloading, and would do a lot of night driving and sleeping in the van. Sometimes after an overnight drive, we'd book a day room in a hotel or motel so everyone could shower and rest.

Later, they'd graduate to a tour bus and there'd be a production manager, some road techs for guitars and drums, front-of-house and monitor engineers, and a lighting guy. At that level the band would not be touching any equipment, but would simply be shepherded to the hotel, radio station, record signing, or whatever else the day contained, and when they arrived at the venue the gear would all be onstage, set up, and ready for sound check.[46]

The *Mystery White Boy* shows were due to begin on June 2. One of the first things we needed to deal with was that Reggie wasn't working out. His work was solid, but there seemed to be some other issues.

"Jeff had talked me up to the guys, and I thought this was going to be great. I'm looking forward to it; I looked up to them because they were the guys who played on *Grace*!" he recalls. "For whatever reason, Mick wasn't having any of it. It felt very, very strange. I don't know what

[46] Tour managers should also be prepared in other ways. Once when I was on the road with Savatage, we drove from Minneapolis to Indianapolis. I walked out to introduce the band and shouted to a packed stadium: "Are you ready to rock, Mindiapolis?!" The band went on to the sound of fifteen thousand people going, "Huh? What he say?" I wanted to die. "Thanks for warming them up, Dave," said the singer. From that show onward, I always asked one of the crew to write the name of the city on a strip of white tape placed directly under the center microphone, where any idiot could see it.

we fought over. Small stuff. Whenever there was a decision to make—Where do we eat? Where do we hang out?—Gene would say, 'Reg, why don't you pick a spot and drive them there?' And I'm like, 'Okay, fine.' I'd pick an Olive Garden or something, and Mick was like, 'Dude, let's go to a real Italian place.' And he'd get into it.

"I did a bunch of gigs on the East Coast. I shopped for some instruments for them, helped Mick buy a bass rig. I watched Jeff teach Michael how to play guitar, saw him putting his fingers on the frets. Matt was great. But I just couldn't get along with Mick; I don't know why. I've worked with so many way more difficult people since then, but that got me fired, after we played Long Island."

That was the gig at Stephen Talkhouse in Amagansett when I first saw the band play and was appalled. The sound wasn't a problem, but Gene told me about the tension in the camp. Jeff finally had to break the news to Reggie.

"Jeff cried when he fired me. He sat down with me and said, 'You're not hitting it off with the guys. We have to let you go.' And we both cried and I said, 'That's cool, I'll get something else.' He knew that I wasn't gonna get mad or anything."[47]

We had a prime two-night slot at the Fez in New York coming up and needed a replacement quickly. Mick knew a guy called Paul Wilke who was young and inexperienced—come in, join the gang—but seemed capable and enthusiastic and got a good sound at those shows.

The Fez had been a regular spot for Jeff on the same circuit as Sin-é when he was just starting out, and he'd played there many times. These shows were billed as "Kiss Me Goodbye," marking where the yearlong campaign began in earnest.

I liked the band on a small stage. They needed to hear each other and get out of the habit of looking at their amps and their hands, and a cramped stage drew less attention to their lack of experience.

Fez was located in the East Village at 380 Lafayette Street under a restaurant. A small, rectangular room with a stage, and a silver strip curtain as a backdrop. Everyone seated at tables. Very Jeff and very cabaret. A

---

[47] Reggie went on to work with Prince at Paisley Park, and he's a highly in-demand front of house engineer still.

JEFF BUCKLEY
"Kiss Me Goodbye Gig"
FEZ
(Under "Time Cafe")
380 Lafayette Street
(212) 533-2680

FRIDAY, JUNE 17th:	SHOWTIME:	10:00 PM
	DOORS:	9:00 PM
SATURDAY, JUNE 18th:	SHOWTIME:	10:00 PM
	DOORS:	9:00 PM
SUNDAY, JUNE 19th:	SHOWTIME:	8:30 PM
	DOORS:	8:00 PM

Tickets are $8.00 per person each night. Special early and guaranteed admittance for you and a guest "only if" you present this card and arrive no later than one half hour prior to scheduled door times.

Postcard for the Fez shows in New York City.

woman called Ellen booked the room and loved Jeff. She once asked him to meet Joni Mitchell, and he was so nervous that he got roaring drunk and then, when he came down the stairs and saw Joni sitting there, just slid under one of the tables, only slightly drawing attention to himself by throwing up. I'm assuming he never actually met her, or if he did, she wasn't impressed.

The Fez shows went really well. Among those who showed were The Edge from U2, Chris Cornell from Soundgarden, and actress Winona Ryder.

People outside the company had early copies of *Grace* by this time, and the buzz was very positive—as it should have been, but reassuring to know.

One show on this run was especially significant. In Iowa on July 9 at Gabe's Oasis—a three hundred-seat venue with only about forty people in it—Jeff met two bands: The Grifters and The Dambuilders, who would play key roles in his life. The Grifters, from Memphis, made noisy records for local label Shangri-La. Jeff took an instant liking to their wonky Pavement-meets-Alex Chilton sound and especially bonded with drummer Dave Shouse. The Dambuilders were an unusual indie band who'd formed in Honolulu, made a name for themselves releasing indie records in Boston, and had just signed to Atlantic. Their unique feature was a violin player who provided rhythm and lead—like a guitar player—and also sang backing vocals. Her name was Joan Wasser. She had striking black-and white-dreadlocked hair and a carefree but intense charisma that Jeff found irresistible. Watching him play, she immediately identified him as "such a ham." Later on, Jeff tried his miming to James Brown Live at Olympia on her, and it went down well. "I felt like a queen," she told author David Browne. Named after Joan of Arc and adopted at birth, Joan had hidden depths that Jeff recognized, but she'd had a stable upbringing in Norwalk, Connecticut, which meant she was more self-assured than he was and provided a grounding influence. She loved to free-associate with him, whether that meant taking magic mushrooms or lying in tall grass all morning. She didn't judge him, make him feel either beholden or superior and, of course, she was creative and musical too. She didn't appear threatened or overwhelmed by him but simply happy in his company. There was an equality between them that Jeff desperately needed with a partner. He shone whenever they were together.

The summer of 1994, it seems, was the new summer of love. On August 6, we pulled into The Point in Atlanta. For reasons that were never entirely clear, it had been decided that Atlanta would be a good spot to entertain a group of French journalists who were excited to see Jeff play after hearing advance copies of *Grace*. The European head of promotion, Samantha Way, was coming with French product manager Sophie Zannettacci, to accompany the French media.

Jeff definitely had his Francophile side. He loved Edith Piaf and Jacques Brel and the Parisian chanson tradition, which leans heavily on the lyrical content and emotional clout of a song, and isn't about perfect voices so much as great sellers of a story.[48] Although this wasn't necessarily the kind of song Jeff wrote himself, he certainly understood it in his dramatic renditions of "Lilac Wine" and "Hallelujah" and, of course Piaf's "Je N'en Connais Pas Le Fin" from *Live at Sin-é*. The French quickly recognized the connection and celebrated him for it.

[48] Yes, all right, Brel is Belgian. I know.

Samantha Way, promotions manager at Sony Europe, in her office in London, 1994.

Missy Worth had also come in for the show from her LA base, and we arranged to meet these two women to see what ideas they could give us regarding Jeff's impact in Europe. We'd booked a table at the Ritz-Carlton, but because we were staying in the same hotel, I arranged to go up to Samantha's room to meet them first. The door was ajar, and when I walked in, I saw two gorgeous women in short skirts and high heels—one a vivacious blonde, one sultry and dark-haired—both of them sitting on the king-size bed, laughing and waving champagne flutes like parade flags. It was obvious that these marketing executives were not from up the stuffy end of the music business, had no intention of ever going there, and saw absolutely no point in having a boring time; in fact, with their classy European look and their champagne on ice, these savvy young women, charged with the welfare and development of multi-million-dollar artists, seemed to epitomize "work hard, play hard." I'll admit I fancied them both. However, as I approached, the blonde gave me a look that I recognized as interest, while the brunette coolly appraised me and carried on saying whatever she was saying in a sexy French accent. The blonde introduced herself as Samantha Way, and when she spoke she sounded to me like a real cut-glass Brit. She could have been a member of the royal family for all I knew.

I have asked Samantha to recall that evening too:

"This was my first adventure in Buckley land. There were a lot of Europeans flying over to see him play and do introductory interviews. The Germans had done a similar trip to Washington, DC, I believe. Sara Silver, a huge fan, was behind getting the European press out there to see him. Sophie and I were having a lovely relaxed drink at the hotel before we had to go and have this business dinner at the Ritz-Carlton with you and Missy Worth from the LA office. She was a pistol, very charismatic; everyone was a bit in awe of her. You wanted to hear our ideas about Europe, and then you walked into where we were having this drink, and I thought, 'Wow, he's attractive.'"

See, I told you. I knew it. We had dinner, and I can't recall much except that I was finding Samantha increasingly alluring as the evening went on. And then we went to the show. She had never seen Jeff before and was totally blown away. Sophie was utterly in awe of him. The French journalists also thought he was sensational. The interviews went well. "Jeff was absolutely charming," says Samantha. "That soft-spoken, boyish quality would bring out the maternal streak in anyone. He was absolutely open with me as someone from the record company. I didn't get any sense of 'them and us' from him regarding Columbia, but then I don't think I came across as the typical record company type. My role was to make things as comfortable as possible, to facilitate the exchange between him and the media, make sure that everything flowed, so I don't think he had anything to be negative about in that respect."

I flew home the next day, and Samantha and Sophie came on a later flight. They went to a meeting at George's office, and I casually called while they were there and wondered if anyone would like a guided tour of New York. Samantha agreed and was so delightful as we took in the sights, I was soon hoping we would conclude with a guided tour of my cozy live/work area and anything else she cared to see while she was in the vicinity...(fade to black—company ink, mostly).

On August 19, Jeff flew into London by himself in advance of the band and went to visit Liz Fraser again. It was during this visit, I think, that they went into the Cocteau Twins' studio in Richmond and recorded a song they'd written together. "All Flowers in Time" is a pretty thing, but sounds tentative and not nearly as transcendent as you might hope a song featuring those two voices would be—the start of something that was never fully realized.

The day that *Grace* was finally released, we were in Ireland for Jeff's third visit to Dublin, once again at Whelan's. Samantha joined us for the British and Irish leg of the tour, and I was very pleased to see her again. After the Dublin show, we had to drive for a couple of hours to get to Belfast, but it meant we had to cross the border into Northern Ireland, a tense maneuver in those days. Although the "troubles" had erupted in the late '60s, the violence in Northern Ireland was still going on in the mid-'90s. I couldn't believe the border crossing point. They had these metal blocks set into the road that could spring up and overturn a truck at the push of a button. There were snipers in gun turrets all around us. It reminded me of Checkpoint Charlie in Berlin. Samantha was sitting next to me in the bus and she gripped my hand as we approached this scary scenario. She later told me that she looked back and saw Jeff grinning; he had noticed our connection. He was the first.

Samantha had been filling us in on the exploits of the IRA. When we pulled up to the American Hotel, I said to her, "Oh, it's under construction," and she said, "No, the IRA bombed it last week, so it's safe to stay here." During the show that night, Gene came and tapped me on the shoulder and said I might want to come outside, as the British military were interested in our bus. When I walked outside, there were tanks flanking our vehicle. An officer came over to me and said that because we had British plates on the bus, they would protect it during the show and would be escorting us back to the hotel. That freaked me out.

The next morning, Jeff, Mattie, and I drove to the airport while the others took the bus. On the way there, our driver kept pointing to the pubs we were passing, telling us about when each one was bombed and how many people had died. I have to say we were happy to get out of Belfast.

August 30, 1994, was a red-letter day. Jeff officially received his publishing advance of two hundred thousand dollars from Sony Music Publishing. Thus I received my first—and my only that year—commission check, in the amount of fifteen thousand dollars. Managing Jeff Buckley was not a get-rich-quick scheme.

On September 1, Jeff returned to The Garage in Islington, the venue where he'd met Chrissie Hynde. The album had made it into the UK charts by this point, and this was the first crowd I'd seen where people knew (almost) all the material. This time he was playing at the downstairs venue—a large, open room with two levels and good sight lines, a long bar at the back, and a deep stage opposite. Jim Irvin, my co-author, was there, though we wouldn't actually meet in person for another twenty-three years. Jeff, positioned at stage right, was obviously the focus of attention for the three rows of adoring girls at the front. At one point it was so hot in the room that Jeff took his shirt off. The first three rows seemed to crumple in unison. "Have my babies!" shouted someone. "I got a show to do first," said Jeff.

"There were a lot of musicians there," recalls Jim. "Bernard Butler of Suede was over by the sound desk. Evan Dando of The Lemonheads, completely off his face, kept heckling the stage, though Jeff never seemed to take the bait. And shortly before the show began, the whole of Radiohead walked in. This was about 18 months after their first album, *Pablo Honey*. They were at RAK Studios having a hard time recording its follow-up, *The Bends*, and producer John Leckie decided they needed a night out. He'd heard *Grace* and thought they'd enjoy it. Seeing Jeff, it turned out, showed them a way forward."

"[Jeff] just had a Telecaster and a pint of Guinness. And it was just fucking amazing, really inspirational," Colin Greenwood, Radiohead's bassist, told *Uncut* magazine. "We went back to the studio and tried an acoustic version of 'Fake Plastic Trees.' Thom sat down and played it in three takes, then just burst into tears afterwards. And that's what we used for the record."

"I won't forget 'Kanga Roo,'" says Jim. "That really tested the crowd's resolve. After it had been going on for about ten minutes, people were looking at their watches, shrugging at each other and mouthing, 'Shall we go?' The crowd at the back began to thin. I went for a pee, bought a drink, and had a chat to someone, and it was still going on. But somewhere around the twentieth minute, the looping monotony started to get to me and I found myself being drawn toward the stage. When it ended, after about twenty-five minutes, I felt uplifted, like I'd run a marathon. Playing that was a brave move that literally divided the crowd. I suspect it was way more exhilarating to play than to watch. Jeff looked

Photo by Merri Cyr

Jeff Buckley signing at Tower Records with Dave Lory, New York City, December 1994.

radiant when he left the stage, bare-chested and perspiring, feedback ringing in our ears."

This old Big Star song, which Jeff may have first heard as the opening track on This Mortal Coil's *It'll End In Tears*, the album that included Liz Fraser's version of Tim Buckley's "Song To The Siren," had quickly become a source of bewilderment to audience members on this tour. The original is a fragile, oblique little song, rather like something by The Velvet Underground, deliberately ragged with amateurish drumming and blasts of feedback and Mellotron, not pretty but atmospheric. Jeff had turned it into a ringing, roaring tour de force that went on some nights until somebody pulled the plugs. I recognized it as a useful way for the band to get tight and transcend together, relying on intense concentration to make it through. I was cool with it, but as Jim says, audiences and critics were bemused by it, calling it a mistake, a rude breaking of the spell cast by the rest of the show.

A week or so after The Garage, Jeff was about to play at the Cruise Cafe in Oslo when he received a phone call from someone at Sony. The gist of the call was to tell Jeff to stop playing "Kanga Roo." Someone in the UK office had reported back about crowds getting restless and that press reviews had been negative. Jeff was told the song was damaging to his career. He took the call in stride while on it, but when he got off the phone, he hit the roof. This was precisely the kind of interference he was wary of and angered by. It may have been meant as a good-natured piece of advice: "Hey, kid, cool it with the 'Kanga Roo,' huh?" But it was received as the worst kind of philistine bullshit. After raving that his contract gave him total artistic control, Jeff simply carried on playing the song whenever he felt like it. It was back in the set in Frankfurt and Antwerp. He left it out in Berlin and Amsterdam.

It didn't end there. When a group of Sony executives flew in to see him play in Hamburg, "Eternal Life," already heavier onstage than its album version, had become a raging, up-tempo beast, like Nirvana with the brakes off. The band stopped in the middle of the song, and Jeff screamed out the line about "white noise of the world"—the white noise being meddling executives at Sony and the British media who had fucked him over. Some nights they would go straight from this into "Kanga Roo" to test everyone's mettle.

The band had about a month off before the main US tour started, this time in a deluxe Eagle tour bus with its own beds, galley, stereo, and TV. For decoration, Jeff hung up a portrait of Kurt Cobain, a totem of integrity but one who'd let the bastards grind him down. The picture functioned as a warning sign.[49] This run took in some unusual venues, none weirder than Sudsy Malone's Rock 'n' Roll Laundry & Bar in Cincinnati, a bar with a Laundromat in it. Lord knows how this place stayed open—it was such a weird proposition—but if nothing else it provided an opportunity to get some washing done during the sound check.

"Kangaroogate" seemed to trigger something in Jeff. His dream was being skewered; his attempt at the "most sensual band in the world" had been tainted. Plus he was starting to receive a kind of attention he hadn't bargained for. Sales of *Grace* may not have been spectacular but, judging by the kind of adulation he was suddenly receiving—from not

[49] In an interview in *The Observer*, Jeff said of Kurt: "[He] didn't feel loved, or maybe he didn't know how to recognize it...Independence has to come or you will die. You'll end up like someone's puppet and you'll be gone like a chump before you're 30."

just people who attended the shows, but the people from the local offices of Sony, the promoters, and the record store owners—everybody, it seemed, was in awe of *Grace* and therefore of Jeff and told him so whenever the band pulled into town. Having stepped onto a public stage, Jeff was unprepared for what ninety minutes of unconditional love from a crowd can do to a soul. The boy who felt abandoned now felt he was being abandoned by normality. And this effect was unbalanced around the world; one minute he was being feted in Frankfurt, the next he was playing to some beer-chugging indie kids in Iowa who didn't quite get it, or being told by some executive that he wasn't playing by the rules. Switching someone from intense affection to indifference is a classic alienation technique; it's mental torture to a vulnerable mind. Jeff was starting to react badly to it. I was sensing a note of disquiet in Gene's daily reports.

There were two nights booked at The Green Mill in Chicago, and on the first night Jeff just lost his shit. For the first time in memory, he went onstage roaring drunk, wasted on tequila. He was also frantically chewing gum. Songs stopped halfway when he forgot a lyric or heard a bum note and told the band to stop and then start the song all over again. He "blah blah blah-ed" his way though verses, broke strings, and fucked up in every possible way, all the while explaining to the impatient crowd, "I am *drunk*, okay?!...I'm so sorry...I suck so bad." It was a train wreck. It may have been triggered by another tactless pre-show phone call from someone at Sony telling Jeff off for being disparaging about MTV in the *Rolling Stone* interview that had just appeared. I made a mental note to clear somebody's desk.

We'd been talking for a while with Merri Cyr about going out on tour to take some pictures, work her magic in a live situation, and it occurred to me that she might provide a steadying influence on Jeff. So I submitted a budget to Sony, and we asked her to join the tour as its official photographer from November until the band returned to New York just before Christmas. She arrived at the Electric Lounge in Austin, Texas, and found Jeff in a foul mood. "Nobody would go near him—band or crew," she recalls. "They were terrified of him. It seemed as if he was losing his cookies, going crazy and getting angry. He was drinking a lot. He was depressed. He was being really ornery onstage. If he

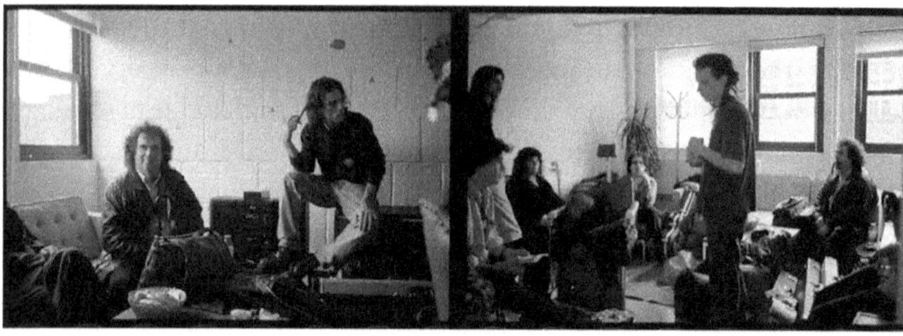

Photos by Merri Cyr

Jeff Buckley backstage at Sony Studios, New York City, prior to a radio performance. Top left: Steve Berkowitz, A&R at Columbia Records, and Matt Johnson, drummer. Top right: Dave Lory (standing); Gene Bowen, tour manager (seated); Missy Worth, senior vice president at Columbia Records; and Steve Berkowitz (seated).

Bottom left and right photos: (left to right) Dave Lory, Jeff Buckley, and George Stein, attorney and co-manager.

perceived people weren't paying attention, he would pick someone out and be adversarial with them from the stage. He could really eviscerate someone if he wanted to."

When Merri got a chance to talk with him alone, he was obviously upset.

"One of the first things he said to me was, 'I think the band's gonna break up and I'm gonna fire Dave.'"

She videotaped the set that night. Back on the bus, Jeff asked to look at the video. "I fixed it up so they could watch it, and he asked me to leave 'cuz he needed to talk to the band. I thought, 'Uh-oh, something's going to happen now.' Nobody was getting along, and they all seemed frightened of him. Sometimes he would appear meek and helpless; other times he could conjure something very ominous and intimidating. The band didn't break up that night, but he went over the video and used it to critique everyone's performance." In Merri's footage, Jeff actually appears in pretty good spirits in the sound check, fooling around on the drums, playing bits of Hendrix and Red Hot Chili Peppers on bass, and plunking out the old instrumental "Popcorn" on his guitar, but if you knew him, you can recognize the tension behind the eyes.

There was something self-destructive about the mean-spirited behavior. The idea that the band was going to split and that I'd have to be fired was just trash talk. He'd certainly shown no signs of dissatisfaction with my work. Quite the opposite. In fact, there were a couple of times when he said to me, "Dave, you work too hard. You should be getting all the money. I should fire George." And I talked him out of it. I pointed out that we had an agreement; I'd shaken on it, and I intended to stick by it as long as it was the best thing for his career, and he appreciated that.

"Jeff set up conflict situations a lot," says Merri. "One time I asked him why he had two managers. He said, 'So they can keep an eye on each other.' To me, having two managers seemed wrought with conflict. I said to Jeff, 'Maybe there are things you don't like about Dave, but he is totally devoted to you.' Jeff was kinda sensitive to everything, and Dave was like the opposite. Jeff needed that kind of protection on the outside. He took Dave on because Dave stood up to him."

The next day, Merri took the band to do a shoot in Austin. "Jeff and I went to a bar early in the afternoon, and he started lining up Cuervos. He did about three of them in a row, and I'm like, 'What are you *doing*?!! It's noon and you're getting wasted!' Jeff was surrounded by people who couldn't really stand up to him. But since my living wasn't dependent on him, I could say, 'What the fuck, Jeff? Why are you hurting yourself?'"

Jeff appreciated this and listened to Merri's pleas to ease up. Her attention meant he also wanted to resume their earlier, intimate relationship.

"It was a conflict for me, as I didn't want to be perceived as a groupie. I wanted to be seen as a photographer," says Merri. "When he tried to be openly affectionate with me in front of the other guys, it made me feel awkward. I was there to take pictures. I didn't want to be his girlfriend if it diminished my professionalism.

"I do think he needed someone who gave a shit about him who wasn't his employee. Jeff didn't know how to do some really basic things—how to take care of himself—because of how he was brought up. He didn't know how to take a break, he'd never taken a vacation, he wouldn't go to the gym, he didn't care what he ate. He was still living out of paper bags. His waif persona, the little boy with a bag, 'Help me.' Families around the globe would pick him up and take him home and let him live with them: 'He's so skinny and cute and looks so hungry.' That happened to him all the time. From my perspective, it seemed he felt desperately unloved. He would push love away and at the same time say, 'Give it to me. *Go away*, then *come back*.' What Jeff wanted and what he needed were two different things. On one level he had to control everybody; on another he didn't respect you if you didn't stand up to him and fight back when he bullied you.

"I don't know about him with other people, but my relationship with him felt familial, though there was also a sexual aspect to it. We had similar backgrounds, lower middle class; neither of us knew our fathers. We had similar father abandonment, crazy mother issues, weird family stuff. Sex can be just two kids hanging out, fooling around; it wasn't the main thing. It was like it had no context.

"I wanted to do my photography. Jeff was being respectful to me and very helpful and supportive, and that was the best gift he gave me. He was so generous on one level and so broken on another. On the road, I definitely got pulled into his orbit. That was really tough for me.

"When we went to New Orleans, I'm having a good time shooting and doing my thing, and he was being all sweet to me and said, 'We should go do this and that and have dinner.' And we arranged to do this. He was supposed to meet me at the bar, and he didn't show up. It was kids' stuff. I was so angry he'd done this big seduction thing and then not shown up: 'You don't *do* that to someone who is your friend—stand them up and leave them in a bar. Come *on*!' I was really upset and I was going to go home to New York."

A couple days later, Merri and I were having breakfast together at a place on Ocean Avenue in Miami when Jeff appeared. He'd obviously been through her stuff; he was wearing one of her shirts and he started fooling around and being super attentive and sweet to her. It was his way of saying sorry.

"I'm saying, 'Aaaarrrgggh! You're such a freakin' dick,'" says Merri. "But I couldn't help but forgive him. He looked so sweet."

Perhaps to reflect how he was feeling on the road, Jeff wanted to complete the angry new version of "Eternal Life." I thought it might make a good single for rock radio. We'd cut a new backing track at Sony Studios during our October layoff, with plans to add some overdubs later.

There was a two-day break before the show at the Florida branch of Stephen Talkhouse in Miami, which gave us a perfect opportunity to record at Criteria studios, where a bunch of classic albums had been cut. I asked my old friend Bud Snyder, the Allmans' mix engineer and one of the sweetest guys in the world, to record whatever overdubs Jeff had in mind and maybe do a mix. Something told me he and Jeff would get along.

"We worked our butts off but we didn't do much," recalls Bud. "The whole band was there, but mostly it was just me and Jeff. He exhausted everybody that weekend; he went non-stop. I don't know if he got any sleep at all. It was just experimenting; we didn't discuss anything in

Photo by Merri Cyr

At Criteria studios in Miami. Left to right: Bud Snyder, studio engineer; Jeff Buckley; Dave Lory; and Paul Wilke, Buckley's live engineer.

particular. The whole thing seemed to be about some guitar tones and feedback that he was trying to introduce into the song. At one point I said, 'What are you *doing*?' And he said, 'I'm working on tube feedback through the pre-amp stage.' And I'm like, 'I never heard of that.' He showed me what he was doing, and it was amazing. Most guitarists get feedback by putting their pickups in front of their speakers. He was putting the pickup in front of the tube on the pre-amp stage of his Marshall amp. Of all the guitar players I'd ever worked with, it was Jeff who showed me this first. He got some amazing sounds. We spent hours recording those little feedback bits."

Merri took a bunch of pictures of Jeff and Bud working. "At the Talkhouse gig, the band had a really great set and were really happy," she remembers. "They reunited in the bus after the show, all smiles. The good energy was back, and they all laughed and ate hamburgers. All that tension that had been going on for weeks just disappeared, and they were a band again. Then there was a sweet vibe for the rest of the tour. The guys in the band were really nice to me, very brotherly. I think my function on that trip was to overtly say to Jeff, 'Hey, what are you doing? Stop hurting yourself; I care about you.'"

When the Eagle landed in Philadelphia, there was one weird scene that temporarily took the shine off Jeff's new good vibe. A bunch of Tim Buckley fans made themselves known in the crowd by constantly shouting out for Tim's songs. Jeff was rattled and then suddenly, unexpectedly, gave in and started to play "Once I Was."

"I'm going to sacrifice myself right now..." he said. "Show all the hippies how good I can do this song....Let me show you how cool this song is. It's the only time you'll see me do it, I swear to fucking god."

And he sang a lullaby-soft version of his father's song. When he was done, he turned to the fans. "Are you satisfied now?" Apparently not, as some of them wanted to talk to him after the show. He took it with good grace and patiently answered their questions, but when they left, he ran agitatedly around the parking lot for some time before getting on the bus.

Jeff's Christmas letter to his fans:

Hello...um...how overwhelming can something be? Just tell everybody for me that Mickey, Michael, Matt and I love you all supremely! This has been the most surreal year of joy and utterly satanic bullshit mixed together.... Your support and your love has completely inspired us to go on with the tour with more patience and energy.... Believe me we fucking FEEL you out there.... It helps so much and I just wanted to tell you that I love you too....NO MORE CUERVO NIGHTS!

CHAPTER 7

"How's a Guy Supposed to Brood Effectively When People Go Around Calling Him Dishy?"

"Remember me, remember me, but ah / Forget my fate."
—Nahum Tate, "Dido's Lament," 1689

JEFF WAS FLYING ON THE CONCORDE on January 13, 1995, when he wrote me a memo: "This is the year of *My Sweetheart the Drunk*, baby-o!" On these sheets, torn from his notebook, he listed the contents of two records he intended to release that year, an EP called *Two Ninas* in June with the album to follow, both to be recorded, mixed, and mastered "in Seven Days in March....Bring the whole thing in for under 45,000 dollars." The tracks he listed for the EP were: "Pop Song in E," "Forget Her," "Snow Song," "Moodswing Whiskey," "Punk Boy Shine My Shoes 'Fore I Rip Out Your Styx Tattoos," and "Hymn."

Two of those I know: "Forget Her," obviously, the outtake from *Grace*, and "Moodswing Whiskey," which he was starting to play live, but I have no memory of those other titles. I can't say for sure if he'd even written them yet, or if this was a fantasy listing, his way of getting it out into the universe to give him the spur to make it actually happen. *Two Ninas* was a name that started to crop up increasingly in conversation; by the end of the year, it would become a potential new name for Jeff's band. Here, it was just a title for a Jeff Buckley record. His suggested artwork was the shot Merri took of Jeff's face reflected in a broken mirror, the image that Leah Reid had preferred for the cover of *Grace*.

Jeff's listing for the projected album is also intriguing. Housed in "devil art by Carla Avitabile" and produced by Jeff himself, *My Sweetheart the Drunk* would be composed of "Prayer," "Sequins," "I Woke Up in a Strange Place," "Moodswing Whiskey," "Medusa," "Ballad of Frank & Charlotte," "Old Man & Two Ninas," "Blood Coffee Flashback," "Chocolate No. 2," "Love Is Rebellion," "Come to Me," "The Lower East Side," "Rebecca," and "Gunshot Glitter." Again, I recognize only a few of these titles. "Chocolate" was being sung live, usually as part of a medley with "Mojo Pin," "Gunshot Glitter" would be demoed in Memphis, and "I Woke Up in a Strange Place" would also be tried live. The rest are puzzling, especially as new material would prove hard to come by once work on the album actually began. So, were these titles merely a reference to lyrics in his notebooks, or working titles for songs that became something else later? It's interesting how often he would come up with these quite detailed work plans—often while on airplanes—and yet never see them through. The reality when he hit the ground would always be slower, with more strings attached, more people to consult first. I know this bothered him. I know he was always looking for a new way to do things, yet the huge network of Columbia employees working on his behalf naturally had other ideas. Eighteen months after the release of his debut album, the world was only just catching up with *Grace*, and the more the world heard it, the more the world liked it.

Flying on the Concorde was not an indication of a sudden improvement in his fortunes. Donnie Ienner wanted Jeff to attend the Rock and Roll Hall of Fame dinner with him on the night of January 12. The invitation was partly superstitious; previous companions had broken through in the year following the event, and Donnie hoped some of that classic rock juju would levitate Jeff if he was seen at the two thousand dollars-a-plate occasion. As it turned out, Jeff, who was wearing a fluorescent pink jacket visible from space, was spotted by everyone engaging infamous publicist and scenester Danny Fields in a lingering lip-lock in the middle of the VIP area. Later, he was also seen backstage in a tearful embrace with old friend Moon Unit Zappa, whose late father, Frank Zappa, had been inducted into the Hall of Fame that evening. Jeff was also approached by one of his heroes, Robert Plant, who told him how much he liked *Grace*. Jeff was rather overcome. But like Cinderella fleeing the ball, he had to leave all these luminaries behind to make another booking, at Whelan's in Dublin, twenty-four hours later.

So Donnie had signed off on a Concorde trip. The beauty, of course, was that flying from New York to London in under five hours meant it was possible to land just before you had left! Samantha was in charge of making sure Jeff landed safely at Heathrow and then got to Dublin the following morning. Tom Petty de-planed first, drunk and weaving all over the place. Then Samantha saw Jeff, in his winter coat, with a flower in his lapel and carrying his ghetto blaster, looking like Paddington Bear, a lost creature from the other side of the world.

"We got to our hotel and I said, 'Do you want to eat, have a drink, or whatever?'" recalls Sam. "He said, 'I'd really like to go and see a friend.' I said, 'Don't do this to me. I'm supposed to keep you here.' He said, 'I'm not going to do anything outrageous. I just want to hang with a friend for the evening.' He wanted to see Liz Fraser in Twickenham. I had recently got one of those huge cell phones that were like bricks with an antenna. So I gave it to him and said, 'Okay, take this. You have to check in with me when you arrive and promise me you'll be back at such and such a time.' And I just hoped nobody checked up on us until the next day. To his credit, he came back at the appointed time. But, yes, he had lost his plane ticket to Dublin, so there was always something. And he was obsessed with getting a haircut. He insisted on getting it done at this hotel we were staying at, and I was worried about that."

Also on the itinerary was a less fraught return to GLR and a rare TV slot, on the nightly British arts program *The Late Show*. This may be the best TV performance of "Grace." You can see it on YouTube. There's Jeff with his hotel haircut, throwing his arms in the air, exasperated, when presenter Tracey McLeod mentions Tim Buckley.

Jeff Buckley on the video set in Paris for "Last Goodbye."

On January 21 we flew to Paris. We needed a video for "Last Goodbye," and this fucking thing took up a lot of headspace, too much discussion about who was shooting it and how much it would cost. Initially, Merri Cyr was going to direct; she and Jeff storyboarded something in the style of Jean Cocteau. But Sony wanted someone more experienced. Somehow, we end up hiring an East Village avant-garde theater director called John Jesurin, whom Jeff and Michael knew but who had never directed a video before. Merri's material would be projected onto the band in the new setup, which, because of time constraints, was going to have to be shot in France, in a rented warehouse space. What should have been a low-budget thing turned into a Hollywood-size location shoot.

"This was the '90s, when the record company would spend shitloads of money on a video and put it on the artist's tab,"[50] Merri reminds us. "I went to a meeting at Sony about the shoot, and they're saying, 'The catering's going to cost ten grand,' and I'm like, 'That's gotta be some pretty good food!' I went back to Jeff and told him how much the catering was going to cost and that it was his money. Sony heard about it and punished me and cut down my shooting time. I did not get any reward from Jeff for trying to protect him. I felt he didn't stand up for me."

[50] Half the cost of videos and promotion was recouped from an artist's royalties.

At the shoot, Jeff was stressed and spent all day being mean to Sony's video commissioner, Lee Rolontz. I spent all day apologizing to her. It wasn't like Jeff to behave that way, but the reality and absurdity of the whole enterprise were getting to him.

"I wish he had just been able to get a small budget, and we could have made a beautiful art film," says Merri. "The sequences I made were haphazardly used. Having those films projected onto Jeff was, to me, a metaphor for the way so many people projected their needs and emotions onto him. There's a shot of Jeff at the end of the video, and he's so pissed off he's not even mouthing the words."[51]

I disliked it at the time, particularly as I knew it had cost close to two hundred seventy-five thousand dollars. Watching it recently, however, I thought it looked pretty atmospheric. But you're definitely not seeing all that money on the screen. When the single was finally released, "Last Goodbye" managed, unlike the single of "Grace," to crawl into the US alternative charts and receive a few MTV plays, but it by no means paid back a return on its outlay.[52]

By this point, some of us were concerned about how the band sounded out front. Paul Wilke, who was mixing front of house, was a cool kid but, again, inexperienced, and didn't know how to get the best out of the bigger rooms we were now appearing in. He got a decent club sound that didn't work anywhere larger. I thought he couldn't mix a drink.

We needed to do something. The next shows were in Japan, and from there we'd be returning to Europe and the UK in decent-sized venues, including my on-a-hunch Shepherd's Bush Empire booking. I suggested to Jeff that we ask Bud Snyder, who'd recorded "Eternal Life" in Miami and was used to mixing in stadiums and sheds, to sit in on some shows and help Paul to take his craft to the next level. Jeff agreed that would be a good idea.

Bud had just gotten off the Gregg Allman Christmas tour when I called him.

---

[51] The whole "Last Goodbye" episode left Merri Cyr very unhappy: "I didn't see Jeff for a long time after that. I felt he really threw me to the wolves."

[52] The US alternative chart peak was 19. In the UK it made 54 on the national singles charts.

"Bro, would you come out and show our green sound guy what to do for these bigger shows we got coming up?"

"Sure I'd love to," he said. "Where you playing?"

"Japan."

"Oh. Cool. So when would this be?"

"Can you fly to New York tomorrow?"

"Shit, I just unpacked."

"Sorry, bro. Berkowitz would like to talk to you before we go, and then I'll fly you straight to Japan."

"Okay. How did you manage to get me a work visa so quick?" he said.

"Oh, you're just going on vacation, Bud!"

We laughed and Bud said he'd do it.

I always like to make sure there are at least a couple of free days after a long-haul flight to acclimatize and get over jet lag, but we needed a rehearsal immediately so Bud could get some idea of what Paul was doing and what the band would be playing. The band set themselves up, and Bud and I turned up about an hour in. When we walked through the door, they started playing "Jessica" by the Allman Brothers. Funny guys.

Next was something almost in the same zip code as "Kick Out the Jams," then one of their formless, interminable jams. Bud sat there listening intently. Then he put up his hand. The band stopped.

"Guys, you don't play any of these in your show, do you?" Bud has a slow, easygoing Southern delivery.

"No," said Jeff, shaking his head.

"You know why I'm here, don't you? I'm here to get some idea of how the band sounds onstage and what I'm gonna be mixing."

Jeff looked at Bud like this was a surprise. "Well, we never play the show in rehearsal."

"So what the hell are we all doing here?" said Bud. Then he smiled and continued: "Let's go get drunk!"

A friend of his happened to be doing sound for a band playing that night at the Liquid Room, the famous Tokyo venue where Jeff was booked to play the following two nights, so Bud suggested we all go there. Someone spoke up. "Well, we can't really do that. Jeff will get mobbed."

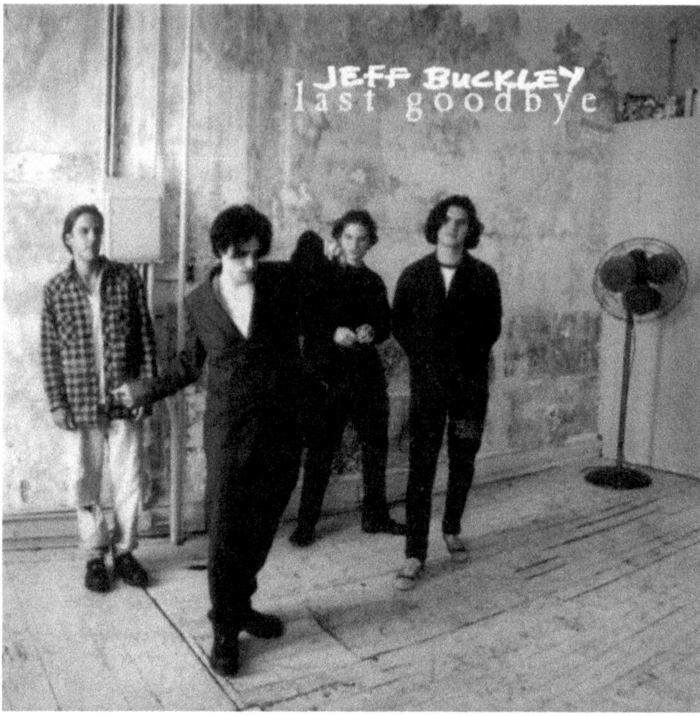

Photo by Merri Cyr

Jeff's approved artwork for the single of "Last Goodbye" that appeared outside the US.

Bud laughed and held his arms out like he was Uncle Fixit. "Guys, I know the record's doing great here and all, but trust me, we can go to the Liquid Room and everything will be cool."

We go down there and as soon as the girls found out Jeff was in the club, there was mayhem. Traditional Japanese reserve and courtesy flew out the window. We were mobbed. We managed to circle the wagons and see some of the show. Afterward, however, we were trapped—dozens of fans were waiting around to get a piece of Jeff—so we had to leave the club via the service elevator with all the band's gear and then hide in a doorway as feverish girls ran past looking for him: "Jeff! Jeff!" It was like Beatlemania.

On Saturday, January 29, we were back for our own show. The Liquid Room was a state-of-the-art space, neon-lit and chrome bright. Acoustically it was great and, as usual with Japanese venues, you could eat your sushi off the dance floor. It was all kept spotless. The Japanese had a unique system for visiting bands, which our crew grew to really appreciate. I'm not sure if it was union-related or just an extreme mark of respect, but on the first night of any tour, a team of local techs, hired by the promoter, would shadow our guys and take incredibly detailed notes and photographs of everything, checking it all with geometric tools, noting the exact angle of the boom mics and the height and tilt of all the cymbals, plus all the settings on the dials of our amps and pedals. They would compile all this information into a huge manual and then, every night, replicate the stage exactly. Our crew didn't have to lift a finger. Soon after setup, we received a visit from our promoter, Massy Hayashi. When he arrived and walked across the stage, the Japanese crew stopped what they were doing and parted like the red sea, bowing as he passed. "This guy must be powerful," I thought. He seemed very nice, but his workers obviously weren't about to displease him in a hurry.

Bud started showing Paul some tricks with the drum compression, setting it so that everything was audible individually and not just a powerful mush. Matt looked up, delighted. "Hey, I can hear my kick drum!" he said. The audience needs to feel a kick drum in the chest and wants to hear everything clearly. Even if you have a dense, distorted sound as a band, the listener wants to know where everything's sitting in the spectrum. The guitars can't get in the way of the voice; the bass can't obliterate the drums. A front-of-house mixer can't just push up faders and hope for the best. Bud was showing Paul all he knew, but Paul was not being terribly responsive and was sulking throughout the sound check. But the sound they got together at that Saturday-show was tight and clear, and I was feeling good about this experiment.

During Sunday's sound check, however, Paul was acting really pissy. I got it to some extent; he felt this guy was coming in over his head and was pissed because he didn't like being told that he didn't know what he was doing. But then I decided no, actually, I had a problem with his attitude! He was being a know-it-all and instead of taking this valuable opportunity to take some tips from a master, he was acting like a jerk.

After the show, I was sitting in the glaringly clean dressing room with Jeff and Mattie when Paul wandered in with a face like someone had shat on his lip. Jeff said, "How's it sounding, Paul?"

"He's making you sound like Toto," said Paul, moving an eyebrow like 'we all know how uncool that is.'

I felt myself bristle.

"Excuse me? Are you being fucking serious?" I began, trying to sound way more reasonable than I felt.

"He doesn't have a clue what this band should sound like!" Paul said.

"Oh, he doesn't? So he's heard the album and come to rehearsals and spoken to everybody and he has no idea? That's why he's here, to hear the band play and help you get the best out of it."

"No it's not."

"What?"

"You just want your buddy to have my job."

"Listen, this guy's trying to help you. He doesn't need a job; he's got a job!"

"He's taking all the balls out of it," he said petulantly. "This band wants to sound raw."

I looked up and saw Bud standing in the doorway. Everyone turned to look at him.

"This is insane," I said to Paul. "This guy asked you to give him three shows to get used to the band, and all you're doing is coming backstage and bitching and complaining and telling the band it sounds like shit, stabbing him in the back. You're not seeing this as an opportunity to learn, are you?"

"I just don't think it should sound like Toto."

"Nobody's gonna make it sound like fucking Toto! This band is not Toto!" I yelled. "He's gonna show you how to make *this band* sound loud and clear and you take it from there. Okay?"

Bud turned and left. I was livid. Paul snorted and went to pack his gear away.

"Can you believe that guy?" I said to Jeff that night back at the hotel. "He's behaving like a spoilt child because we're giving him a chance to learn from an expert. I can't take that kind of negative attitude. I think we should let him go." Jeff agreed with me, didn't raise any objection.

"If I can get Bud to agree to stay for this run while we look for someone else, would you be okay with that?"

"Sure," said Jeff.

"Okay. Paul's going home."

A little later, Jeff told me Mick wasn't happy with Paul being fired. Paul was his friend; he'd put him forward for the gig. Jeff made his "call a meeting" face. This was my cue to do the dirty work. If something came up that Jeff didn't want to confront—and that was most things—I'd have to call a meeting and be bad cop. I called Gene and asked that the band be gathered after sound check the following day. I spoke to Bud and asked if he'd stick around for the European dates. Thankfully, he agreed.

That day's show was an MTV Japan performance with an early curfew: a filmed public show around 7 p.m. and then the audience went and the TV crew would film an interview. The venue was the Nihon Seinekan, a lovely hall for classical music but with one of those reflective classical acoustics where if you clap, you can hear it echoing about five times. I knew Bud would have his work cut out for him, plus he'd be liaising with a TV crew.

After the sound check, I called the band together into the dressing room for our meeting. Kazy Itoh, the Japanese product manager, and his colleague Emi looked concerned.

"Something wrong?" said Emi.

"We're going in here for a meeting, and we don't want to be disturbed. Nobody comes in, okay?"

It was Mick's turn to act entitled and pissy. I got it; his friend was being pushed out. I was interested in witnessing his powers of persuasion.

"We're not happy," said Mickey, the cherubic uptown Adonis.

"We?"

"Yeah, the band."

"And the band is...?"

"All of us," Mickey said. Michael said nothing. Jeff looked sheepish. He was wearing his fluffy winter coat for some reason.

"Oh, really," I said.

"Yeah, and we don't think Paul should be fired. Paul knows what he's doing; he's had the best idea of what we should sound like. We trust him and we don't think you should tell us who our soundman is. We don't think you should be making decisions like this without talking to us first..."

He was talking like this was his band. That made me seethe. He kept going for another couple of minutes.

"Okay, you've had your time. Now I'm gonna talk," I said, sweet as a switchblade. "First of all, this is not your band—you're a hired gun, a side guy. Second of all, I got all the input I need, thanks," I said. "I ran it by *that* guy." I pointed at one of our posters on the dressing room wall. "What does that say?"

"Jeff Buckley," said Mickey.

"Yeah, and that's who everyone came to see tonight and every night. The guy that pays your wages. The guy that's signed to the record company. Not 'the band.' Okay? And do you know who makes up Jeff Buckley Enterprises, the organization that writes your very generous check every month and makes all the decisions? That's 85 percent Jeff and 15 percent me and George. That's the band I consult. And you know how much Jeff Buckley Enterprises makes from every show you get paid for? Nothing. There's no profit. 'Cuz we're paying way over the odds for know-it-alls who can't mix for shit and musicians who couldn't fucking play six months ago. We've paid for you to be any fucking good. So guess what? If you want a say in what Jeff Buckley Enterprises does, how about you get in line with the rest of the partnership, huh? Pay back every cent of what you've been paid so far, plus what we spent on your equipment, plus whatever we consider to be a fair price for a percentage of the stock, and then and only then you can have a fucking say."

I waved my finger in his face. "Here's what's happening, dude. Bud is out here until we get a replacement, and Paul is flying home tomorrow."

I walked out. Mickey probably called me all kinds of genitalia. I didn't care what he thought. He knew he was damn lucky to have this gig, and he wasn't going to push his luck too far, but I was annoyed that our problems with sound engineers somehow flowed back to this guy. I wondered if he'd been disparaging about Reggie just so he could get Paul the job in the first place.

Outside the dressing room, Emi and Kazy looked terrified as I burst through the door like my ass was ablaze. They'd heard all the shouting and thought the band was breaking up, and they were very anxious that they'd be held responsible for not having created the right atmosphere and thereby destroying Sony's great hope, and that they'd be banished to the Japanese equivalent of Siberia. I caught up with Kazy later and put his mind at ease.

Photo by Merri Cyr

Tour postcard

We had been using Soundgarden's monitor rig, custom made by the band's soundman, Mark Naficy. I discovered that Mark was about to become available, as the *Superunknown* tour was just finishing. I arranged a meeting with him for when we returned.[53] Bud would complete the European tour.

"That tour is one of the highlights of my life," says Bud today. "It was just a joy. If Jeff had asked me to stay on, I probably would have left the Allman Brothers. The music was phenomenal, but more than that, out of all the bands I've ever worked with, nobody ever controlled an audience, or a stage, like Jeff Buckley—nobody.

---

[53] Mark Naficy agreed to join us after the European dates and remained our soundman until the end of the *Grace* run, almost a year later.

"We were playing in Hamburg, I think. There were some guys at the bar who seemed to be there just to drink and didn't care who was playing, even though there was a line around the block of people who'd come to see Jeff Buckley. Jeff brought something way down to a whisper, 'Lilac Wine,' I think, and the audience went silent, except these drunks at the back, not paying attention, laughing and clinking bottles. And, I've never seen this before, but practically the entire audience turned around at the same moment, put their fingers to their lips and went, 'Shhh!' And the drunks shut up. It was an incredible sight. Every night something weird like that would happen. Women in the audience would start crying so hard, they'd have to be carried out of the club. Jeff Buckley brought me to tears on several shows, and the only time I can remember that happening before was with B.B. King. It was an experience to *be* at a Buckley show, let alone to be mixing it."

About four shows in was the Bataclan in Paris. The French label wanted us to record the show for a local EP release. Bud helped a French engineer get a jump on the band's wide dynamics, showed him how to handle the extremes of a Buckley performance, and then went and mixed the show out front. This date was where Jeff gave Sam some advice in matters of the heart related to me.

"We were in Paris and Dave was just being a real pain in the arse," she recalls. "He'd got sick and lost his voice, so he wasn't being very attentive. So while everyone was quite happy that he'd lost his voice for a while, I was upset because he wasn't being particularly friendly to me, and Jeff took me aside and said, 'You know, there are boys and there are men. And Dave's a boy.' I'm sure that a lot of the dynamic between Dave and Jeff was very paternal, and every kid has a reaction now and then. He thought Dave wasn't taking the relationship as seriously as he should—which, coming from Jeff, was an interesting observation! When Dave actually proposed, years later, onstage at a gig at Arlene's Grocery, he said to Jeff afterward, 'Am I man now, or a boy?' and Jeff said, 'Oh, you're a man now.'"

When we hit Italy, we were treated like kings by the promoter—wined and dined and shown a great time. There was also an open-air gig that appeared to be raising money for the local Communist Party. We knew Jeff had connected in Italy when the local press office sent over a pile of clippings three inches thick. Bud also recalled the Italian dates with fondness:

"There were a few nights when it was just Jeff and me—everybody else had passed out—and we would smoke some hash and drink a little wine, and one night in Italy we got talking and I told him how much I loved 'What Will You Say,' and he told me how he co-wrote it with Chris Dowd. And I said, 'I have a feeling in that song that you're talking about if you went to heaven, would your dad recognize you? Well, my take on the song is the complete opposite of that. I was separated from my son for fifteen years, and I had to wait until he was eighteen before I got to know him. The day after his eighteenth birthday, I hooked up with him. I flew him to Toronto, we got to know each other, and he ended up moving to Florida with me. Then one weekend he left to go up to Detroit, and he passed away that weekend. I had this tragic relationship with my son, and I look at that song from the father's standpoint.' We sat and talked about that a whole lot, the two of us crying into our beers. It was a good release for both of us, and it meant the world to me."

In London it was time to play the Shepherd's Bush Empire show I had asked Emma Banks to book exactly a year ago. We not only sold out, but there was a line around the block of people trying to get in. I still have the framed dollar Missy Worth sent me with the inscription: "You were right, I was wrong, Missy."

We heard that "Last Goodbye" was actually getting some traction in Australia. Sony Australia's boss, Denis Handlin, called to see when Jeff could tour there. "When the single's a hit," I said, brushing him off, because Australia felt like a smallish market a long way away. Then I got a fax from him showing that the single was high on national youth radio station Triple J's airplay chart and poised to go up the following week, with a silver bullet, golden kangaroo, or something. Scrawled in Denis's hand on the fax was: "When are you coming?" We booked some shows there for September.

Meanwhile, it was time for the *Mystery White Boy Tour* to hit the US again. Chapel Hill, Atlanta, Nashville, Memphis, New Orleans, Houston—this time on a co-headline tour with Juliana Hatfield. Mostly Jeff went on last. Playing to the current indie crowd was, in my opinion, an uncomfortable fit for Jeff. He was so much better than all of them, operating on a much higher level, but we did need to reach those kids and Jeff always nursed a strong urge to fit in somewhere. He was naturally influenced by the people around him—Rebecca, Joan, whoever—to hang with their particular crowds. He would feel in awe of them, but often they were more in awe of him.

"Last Goodbye" had opened up college and alternative radio a little. The fans were enthusiastic and the rooms were filling up, though barely half the size of the places we were playing in Europe.

We were just getting into a nice groove when, in May, something happened that seriously pissed Jeff off. He was named one of *People* magazine's 50 Most Beautiful People in the World.

The magazine did it in the May 8 issue, a full page devoted to a picture of Jeff, naming him alongside George Clooney, Elizabeth Hurley, Brad Pitt, Jared Leto, Julie Delpy, Faith Hill, Gloria Steinem, and Patrick Stewart in that year's pantheon of celebrity hotties. Exalted company, but that didn't please Jeff at all. The text was short and fluffy—the opening line was: "How's a guy supposed to brood effectively when people go around calling him dishy?"—with a quote from a British journalist who rated Jeff as "juicy." The photograph, taken by German photographer Nicola Dill, was originally shot for LA lifestyle magazine *Buzz*, and *People* had bought it from an agency.[54] In other words, they had not gone via Sony's press department or us, so we'd had no say or approval.

I first heard about it—guess where?—in Chicago, the scene of Jeff's last drunken episode, when Jeff came onstage at the Metro Cabaret looking more unkempt than usual—two-day stubble, hair like a rat's nest, dirty T-shirt—and dedicated the show to "*People* magazine and Cuervo tequila. Both induce failure." Could have been better. Offstage we didn't hear the end of it for days. Jeff veered between laughing about it and being angry. From this point on, he talked about "uglifying" himself—this was when he dyed his hair black and began wearing a battered biker's jacket.

[54] Nicola Dill: "The atmosphere was frantic. Columbia and the client, *Buzz*, seemed very nervous, probably because the shoot was completely disorganized, but I like to improvise. We set it up near Columbia Records' office in Santa Monica. I found a back alley that had good light. The moment I turned my attention to Jeff, he was great—intense and charismatic. The shoot went well."

One other thing happened that night in Chicago. I kind of broke up with Samantha. Both of us had only recently extracted ourselves from difficult, long-term relationships. Mine had been particularly fraught—too tedious and personal to go into detail here—but it had scarred me and, as I'd told Dana the nurse, I didn't really want to get back onto the commitment horse just yet. Sam was in a similar place; we were both just enjoying our fling for what it was. She had flown in with some people from European MTV, and we had a great time together, as usual, but then I started talking about how I couldn't commit to an exclusive relationship. So she said, well, in that case she was done with me, and I couldn't blame her. In my head, I was still pursuing the road-dog lifestyle with a girl in every port, which I had been accustomed to my entire adult life: no ties, no explanations. But when Sam and I were together, the connection was undeniable.

In June, Jeff finally succumbed to offers to appear on MTV. "Last Goodbye" had made enough of a dent in the alternative chart for the channel to see him as a potential guest host for their flagship alt-rock show, *120 Minutes*. The band filmed a session at MTV Studios in New York, and then Jeff and Michael co-hosted: Jeff dressed in his leather jacket and smoking a cigarette, trying his hardest not to look like one of the world's 50 Most Beautiful People; Michael with his hair cropped close to his head. Jeff began with a rundown of the delights to come: "Alanis Morissette, Garbage, Gene, Sleeper, and lots more, you lucky sods," he said in a British accent, before introducing Primus. They chose some videos they wanted to play: Melvins, Jane's Addiction; Jeff shouted "smack" and "penis" like a kid with Tourette's, just because he could, introduced the MTV audience to Alanis Morissette's "You Oughta Know," and dedicated the latest Cranberries clip to Chris Dowd.[55]

On June 6, Jeff played a show at Roseland in New York. The promoter, Ron Delsner, and I used to play tricks on each other backstage. He came out of his office during the sound check saying, "Paul McCartney is on the phone for you, Dave." And I said, "Yeah, Ron, whatever," and kept going. After a few steps I thought, "Well, you never know with Buckley." So I went back to Ron's office, and sure enough, Paul McCartney was on

[55] "One of many inside jokes," says Chris. "We both hated 'Zombie.'"

the phone asking if he, Linda, and Mary, Paul's oldest daughter, could come to the show. I said, "Of course!"

Come showtime, a dear friend of mine, Charlie Feldman of BMI, was seated at a VIP table on a raised area at the back of the club. I knew he'd worked closely on the Beatles and McCartney accounts at BMI but had never met Paul. So I went over to him.

"Hey, Charlie, I've got a friend coming down to the show that I'd really like you to meet."

"Sure, no problem, Dave. My pleasure."

A few minutes later I walked over to Charlie's table with Paul, Linda, and Mary McCartney. Charlie's face was a picture!

Charlie brought the family to the dressing room after the show, and Jeff just fell into conversation with Paul; they chatted for ages. Linda had known Tim and remarked on the family resemblance. Joan Wasser was there. Merri Cyr took a bunch of pictures. Afterward we all hung out at Le Bar Bat, and Jeff was on a high.

By the time the *Mystery White Boy* tour arrived back in Europe, the crowds were getting larger and more enthusiastic at each stop; the word on Jeff was spreading like butter on a griddle. It was exciting to see the difference, in little over a year, from the coffee shop gigs we had done to launch *Live at Sin-é*. Now that there were crowds rocking up to sold-out venues, and Beatles coming to see us, we had different concerns than bar staff noisily tossing bottles.

Jeff had an affinity for European audiences that was still eluding him in America,[56] but also he relaxed away from home, freed from record company drama, the intensity of Manhattan, and the pressures he felt around friends and family. Music fans in the UK had moved on from grunge after the death of Kurt Cobain, many toward the Britpop bands, but Jeff catered to an unspoken demand for something other than overt maleness, football-terrace sing-alongs, and wry takes on modern times; he also happened to be more musically dynamic and—let's face

[56] The US was his slowest market. A US SoundScan report dated June 18, 1995, showed that Jeff had sold 114,019 albums since the release. Out of these, 20,635 were cassettes. His biggest markets were New York (19,623, or 7.21 percent of total sales), Los Angeles (8,392, or 7.36 percent of total sales), and Boston (8,806, or 7.72 percent), then cities like Chicago, San Francisco, Philadelphia, and Minneapolis at 4,000 or more in sales.

Photo by Merri Cyr

Jeff Buckley with Paul McCartney backstage at Roseland in New York City.

it—gifted than the great mass of US indie acts of the time. People were starting to feel Jeff's impact on the culture; other bands were talking about him. Standing at the back of shows, I was beginning to get people in the industry coming over to check me out like I was the guy who knew where to drill for oil.

France was definitely our biggest European market, which was a surprise, as it has always been a really tricky country to make headway in. "Even French artists find it hard to break in France," Sara Silver says. "You have to approach it in a more personal way. Go and sing a song with a local artist, for example, and build from there." Sara reckons that in her five years working in Paris for PolyGram, she'd seen only one or two new acts per year make any headway. Success was such a rarity that every opportunity was seized upon. "The French, once they get on board, really push something, and if they've got an artist that means something to them, they'll knock on your door every day, saying they need this, need that, we have to do this, do that, and they're relentless. Some people don't understand their methods, because they don't work like we do in the UK or US." Sara had a phenomenal team who was really passionate about

Merri Cyr's pictures taken backstage at Roseland, New York City, June 6, 1995.

Top row, left to right: Missy Worth, senior vice president at Columbia Records; 2nd & 3rd photos: Michele Anthony, executive vice president at Sony Entertainment; and Donnie Ienner, president of Columbia Records; 4th photo: Donnie and Jeff embrace.

Second row, left to right: Linda McCartney; Mark Naficy, live sound engineer; Jeff Buckley; 2nd photo: Same as previous except Mick Grondahl, bassist 2nd from right; 3rd photo: Steve Berkowitz (standing), A&R at Columbia Records; Jeff Buckley; and Mark Naficy (sitting); 4th photo: Missy Worth; 5th photo: Linda and Paul McCartney with Jeff Buckley.

Third row, left to right: Paul McCartney and Jeff Buckley; 2nd & 3rd photo: Joan Wasser and Jeff Buckley; 4th photo: Paul McCartney and Jeff Buckley embrace.

Fourth row, left to right: Mary McCartney, Steve Berkowitz, and Paul McCartney; 2nd & 3rd photo: Jeff Buckley backstage; 4th photo: Front: Michael Tighe, guitarist, and Mary McCartney; Back: Charlie Feldman, vice president, writer relations, at BMI; Dave Lory; and Steve Berkowitz.

the music. French product manager Sophie Zannettacci was particularly committed and, like Sara said, constantly bugging me by phone, fax, and whatever else to get Jeff over for more appearances. Jeff was turning heads in France more than any other new artist, and it looked like it might be the first country to hand him a gold record. He had quickly sold out two nights at the prestigious Olympia theater in Paris, where James

Brown had cut the live album he loved. He was really looking forward to playing there, but first there were a bunch of festivals to play, not the least of them being Glastonbury in the UK.

Glastonbury Festival started out as the Pilton Festival in 1970 as just a few hundred hippies in a field listening to whoever was prepared to show up. Twenty-five years later, it was a temporary city, appearing like magic for three days every year in the west of England, making millions for charity. It had become what Woodstock was supposed to have been but wasn't—a vast, three-day haven of peace, love, and great music. The pervading background aroma of cow dung only added to the charm. Like mud to a boot, Glastonbury clung to its left-wing hippie origins, managing to feel organic, radical, and spontaneous while actually being a prime showcase for mainstream music—its staging, its equipment, and its artists. You needed to be a big deal to headline there, but because it always sold out whoever was playing, they liked to take risks with the booking and each year would offer a prime spot on the central Pyramid stage to an up-and-coming artist. This year, on the festival's twenty-fifth anniversary, Jeff had been chosen to play on the Saturday afternoon. It would be the biggest crowd he'd ever faced.

As a warm-up, Emma Banks had booked shows in Leeds, Glasgow, and Cambridge. I flew in for meetings and was in time for the latter show at The Junction, a cute, hexagonal venue that had hosted more than its fair share of major artists on their way up. I went with Samantha, and by the time the show was over, I was hallucinating from jet lag. She was driving, fortunately. She said she needed to talk to me, and it sounded serious, but I crashed out immediately on the drive to Bath—where we were staying, the band having driven direct to Glastonbury—and didn't wake up until we arrived. Sam wasn't happy; she really wanted to speak to me. I said, "Let's talk tomorrow," I thought it was about some promotion thing that could wait.

Bath is an ancient city but tiny, more like a swanky village. The streets were alive on Friday morning, the cafés and cute boutiques brimming with patrons. It was a beautiful day. We had a small shopping list of stuff Jeff had asked us to pick up: peppermint tea, black hair dye, and a CD of "Dido's Lament." The week after Glastonbury, Jeff had been booked to appear at Meltdown, another prestigious annual event, held

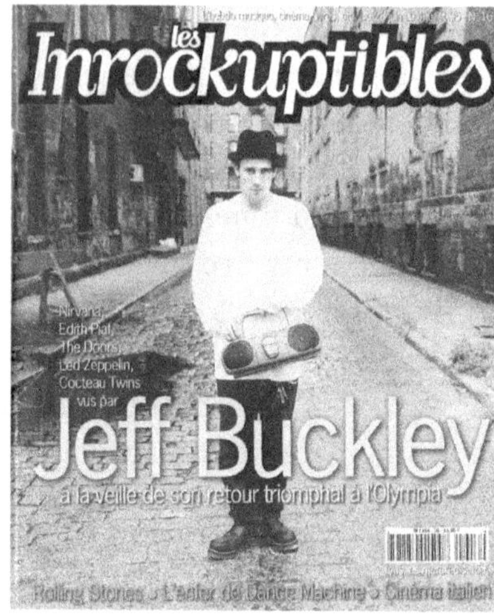

Left: The Olympia in Paris, where Jeff had two sold-out performances. *Right:* Jeff Buckley on the cover of *Les Inrockuptibles* for the Olympia shows in Paris.

in London at the Royal Festival Hall. Each year an artist known for being eclectic was made guest curator of a week of genre-crossing concerts, and that year's curator was Elvis Costello, who had invited Jeff to sing with an orchestra. After discussing singing some Mahler in the original German, Jeff decided he wanted to try "Dido's Lament." Sam had located a music shop in Bath where we could pick up the CD. It was a tiny place up a steep hill, so small that six skinny people would fill it. There were no racks; you just asked at the counter for what you wanted. An old guy was serving, and when I asked for a copy of "Dido's Lament" for one of my male artists, he laughed and told me no man could sing it. The only other person in the store was a young dude, around eighteen years old, who asked which artist it was for. "Jeff Buckley," I said. He turned to the shopkeeper and said, "Jeff Buckley can sing it." I laughed, tickled that word about Jeff had reached out here. The guy put the CD on the stereo and "Dido's Lament" filled his tiny store. The opening line , "When I am laid, am laid in earth, may my wrongs create no trouble, no trouble in thy breast," was pretty overwhelming, but I was surprised when Samantha hurried out of the shop in tears.

I paid for the CD and followed her outside. "You wanted to talk to me about something?" She nodded and blew her nose.

"I'm pregnant," she said immediately. Then, staring at this man whose face was frozen in shock, she blurted out that she was not expecting anything from me financially or even as the father, but that she was having the baby anyway and thought that I should know.

I have to admit my first thought was not one of joy and excitement. I thought, "After all these years of sleeping with every girl I could, why *now*?" My first utterance was a classic faux pas.

"Are you sure it's mine?" Jesus, my big mouth. I was confused and didn't know what else to say. I did love Sam but couldn't see myself settling down, certainly not at this point, just free of a long, toxic relationship. All I wanted to do after years climbing the ladder was to enjoy working with the best artist I'd ever known. Now I was going to be a father?! It was a scary thought. Not just for me. Who would want *me* for a dad? Sam informed me later that she almost didn't tell me. That would have sucked. I'm so glad she let me know, or I probably would have ended up with the wrong person somewhere down the road. Sam couldn't be a better mother or partner.

After my initial genius question, I started vacillating between, "Hey, this is cool!" and, "Sweet Jesus what am I going to do?" My Catholic upbringing suddenly lurched to the front of my brain. I could hear my mom lecturing me about mortal sin. I thought, "Okay, this is my child and it will have a father." Next up was my organizational side. I begin thinking about Sam and her job, and a whole lot of practical things that needed to be done before the pregnancy began showing. (The baby, apparently conceived when we were calling it quits in Chicago, wasn't due until January 1996.) I don't recall buying hair dye or peppermint tea.

At the earliest opportunity, I called Missy Worth in the US. She was the one person at the company I knew I could talk to about something private without it being all over the building three minutes later. When I told her about the pregnancy and my concerns that this news might jeopardize Sam's job, she started laughing. "Don't worry, Dave. Everyone is screwing everyone at Sony." It was true. And we all factored it in when we were looking for favors on a record. If you knew who was doing whom, you could get what you needed much faster. Different times!

Jeff adored Sam. She was his safety net, keeping the media at a distance, mothering and protecting him whenever he was in Europe. I wasn't sure when to break this news to him. I was wary of telling him, considering his own experience. I knew he'd be upset if he thought I wasn't going to do the right thing for the kid. He might even be worried that Mom and Dad might stop paying him attention with a new kid on the way. But I hadn't even really admitted to him that Sam and I had been together. I didn't really discuss my personal stuff with him, and obviously I had strongly advised him never to mix business and pleasure. But he needed to know about this. I picked a good moment and asked if I could have a word with him alone on the bus.

"So, Jeff, you know I have a soft spot for Sam?"

"Yeah, duh!" he said.

"Well, she's pregnant. With my baby. I...I just wanted you to know I'm committed to being a father. I'm gonna take care of her. And the baby."

Jeff gave me one of his intense stares, like he was scanning an audience, calculating all the implications of something. "Sam is great," he said, finally. "I really care about her, and I'm glad you're doing the right thing. Congratulations, Dad."

He gave me a hug and walked off the bus. I couldn't quite tell how that had gone down.

This string of shows was a treat, almost a reward for all the hard work so far, and the band rose to the occasion. For the Glastonbury set, there wasn't much in the way of production. Not much to see on that stage, too early in the day for many lights, and in those days, there was nothing in the way of side screens to provide close-ups for the crowd. All an act could do in this situation was woo the audience with music. Jeff, Michael, Mickey, and Mattie just sauntered onto the stage, plugged in, and played. The day was overcast, but the rain had stopped and there was a huge crowd in front of the Pyramid Stage. Jeff had on his black jeans and boots and a pale taupe shirt. He hadn't gotten around to dyeing his hair again.

They started strong, if a little restrained, with a lengthy version of "Dream Brother." I was always amazed at the different, instinctive ways they made their songs so elastic without making them overblown, or full of solos.

“Lover, You Should Have Come Over” was always a highlight, but today Jeff placed it early in the set. When he got to the line about the rain falling on a field of mourners, he added, “Hopefully not today!”

“So Real” began with a chorused guitar sound that felt like a tribute to the Cocteau Twins and ended with a scorching crescendo. “Last Goodbye,” introduced by Jeff as “another twisted love song,” was a powerful version with Mattie’s rimshots cracking like a pistol.

The most stunning moment of the show was “What Will You Say.” As I watched Jeff lean into that song on that cloudy afternoon, it felt like the moment he finally stepped out of his father’s shadow. When he went into the scream at the end of the song before his twelve-string guitar solo, it was like he was getting every demon out of his system. There are lines in that song that always gave me goose bumps. It’s some heavy shit. On that day, he gave the most powerful performance of it I’d ever seen. There were around a hundred thousand people in that field, most of whom hadn’t seen him before, yet it was like he was playing a small, intimate venue. The new, heavy iteration of “Eternal Life” got the crowd bouncing, and then Jeff went straight into “Kick Out The Jams,” announcing it as a “mellow Christmas ditty.” It was a raucous climax that demonstrated how much Jeff had moved on from *Grace*, whose title song closed the set. No “Hallelujah,” no “Lilac Wine,” no acoustic interlude to show off Jeff’s tender side, just an hour of intense music, thrilling enough to win over those who had never seen or even heard of him before. Jeff had altered a hundred thousand moods. And I had witnessed his music expanding before a huge crowd; songs from the coffee bars that had swelled in the clubs were now impacting a field full of people on the other side of the world. It made me feel, once again, that the planet was his for the taking.

On the Monday after Glastonbury, I took Jeff to Elvis Costello’s house in London for a rehearsal for Meltdown. Elvis had a baby grand in his living room, and they sat together behind it and rehearsed and just gabbed about music all afternoon—a two-man mutual appreciation society. As well as “Dido’s Lament,” Jeff was singing “Grace,” “Corpus Christi Carol,” and Nina Simone’s “The Other Woman.” I felt like I was watching history.

"It's not everyone who can just get up and sing something they take a liking to and make it their own," says Elvis Costello.[57] "Not many people who develop that natural instrument sing true to their heart and can be that curious about all different strains of music. 'Corpus Christi Carol' was a completely conceived interpretation. I'd never heard the piece before, and when I heard the original I realized it was even more amazing, what Jeff had done. It was very faithful, but he'd taken it into his own world. That's something my favorite classical musicians can do—be entirely themselves but use all that training and expertise to make the music more beautiful. Jeff could do that naturally. There are only a handful of people capable of that."

The show was a few days later and, although not quite a black-tie event, the atmosphere was very formal—the crowd was seemingly classical music fans having a daring night out. There were some priceless looks on their faces when this rumpled dude came out and started singing. It was so much fun watching their reaction that I hardly watched Jeff. But he sounded incredible. That kid in the Bath music store knew what he was talking about. I got chills.

Elvis Costello: "When he started singing 'Dido's Lament,' there were all these classical musicians who could not believe it. Here's a guy shuffling up onstage and singing a piece of music normally thought to be the property of certain types of a specifically developed voice, and he's just singing, not doing it like a party piece but doing something with it."

"That's an understatement," says cellist Philip Sheppard, who was in the orchestra. "I remember the silhouette of his frame as he bent almost double to wrench every ounce of meaning from a song written three hundred years ago. Better than any classical musician I've ever heard. It's probably the greatest musical experience of my life; it turned my world inside out...made me realize I was a musician who played through study rather than played through feel, an incredibly pivotal moment for me. I think about him nearly every day, which is quite strange really, because I only met him for about half an hour."[58]

[57] Interviewed by Jim Irvin in 1997.
[58] Quoted from his website, https://philipsheppard.com

I wish Jeff could have done more of that kind of thing. When you saw how he shone in those unique environments, there was definitely a conversation to be had about whether alternative rock was a big enough playground for him.

I really regret that we didn't manage to film the two shows at the Olympia in Paris, as they represented the absolute pinnacle of Jeff and his band. The crowd was vocal and animated, involved in every song. "I witnessed utter desire [among women] when he played," recalls Julie Borchard. "That was his star-making moment at the Olympia. He'd been doing some press and there was this alley by the side of the venue, and a gaggle of women were waiting at the end of this alley, and as he came around this corner in his sparkly jacket, a bit like the one he had on the cover of *Grace*—may have been the same one—they all went crazy. He's loving it but has to dart into the building. He didn't know what to do with that energy; it terrified him."

The band was skin-tight at that point. There was a magic to them—they all knew what they were doing and kept elevating one another to new heights; the music built and built. You could smell the sex for miles, just as Jeff had imagined. On the second night, during the encore, Jeff leaped from the stage and started crowd-surfing. The passionate French crowd roared with approval for twenty minutes when it was over.

"The walls of the venue were bleeding, it was so hot in there," says Julie. "It was ridiculous, and we looked at each other afterwards like, 'Why didn't we fight harder to get this filmed?'"

I'd been trying, believe me, but I'd hit a Donnie Ienner-shaped wall. For all his belief in Jeff, he would occasionally just clamp up the cash flow at the most inopportune moments, and it drove me nuts. This was one of those times. When I called to request the budget to film these shows, he flatly refused: "Jeff's already the most documented new artist ever," he said. Which I didn't believe was true at all. So I called up Virginie Auclair at Sony France, explained the problem, and she promised me the money. She saw the benefit of capturing a potentially great Buckley performance and knew that the French market, at least, was ready for a career-defining live recording. But then Donnie heard about it and, pissed that I'd gone behind his back, bawled out Sony France and ordered them not to film it.

Just another awesome moment lost forever. Jeff's career was full of them. But even he knew this night was special, the peak of this phase of his career. Abbo and I were talking backstage when Jeff appeared dripping with sweat after his crowd-surfing finale, his shirt literally ripped from his body by the audience, just a towel around his shoulders. He started to run up the spiral staircase that led to the dressing room, stopped halfway, and came back down to look at me.

"Attitude?" he asked, raising an eyebrow.

"Attitude. Now you have it." We laughed and Jeff swept back upstairs.

CHAPTER 8

A Bomb Goes Off

IN THE MID-1990s it became a fad to bring artist managers into executive positions at record companies. It made sense; good managers come with an ability to communicate with bands and record company staff alike, with organizational and planning skills and a seasoned bullshit detector. That's what you hope for, anyhow.

Now that Jeff was starting to blow up worldwide, I was getting some subtle and not-so-subtle approaches from record companies to see if I might bring my magic beans to their boardroom. My attorney, Elliot Groffman, called me one day and said that a certain label was very interested in talking to me about a particular role. It wasn't a solid offer, just an invitation to talk. But, as you know, if more than one person knows about something, word gets around.

One morning in August, shortly after we'd returned from Europe, Jeff turned up at the DE-EL office on Worldwide Plaza at about 9:30 a.m. This never happened. Jeff was never spotted in the office this close to breakfast.

"I've come to sort out my fan mail," he said. Another first. Becky and Jack, my assistants, would usually take care of any letters, requests for autographs, or whatever, hand interesting stuff to Jeff and toss the rest. When Becky arrived, she looked at me and, standing behind Jeff, mouthed: "What's *he* doing here?"

"Fan mail," I said, in a tone meaning, "What else could it possibly be?"

Lunchtime came and went, and Jeff was still dicking around with his correspondence. I liked to sit out on the balcony that looked onto the plaza's courtyard; it was sort of open and private at the same time, and I appreciated working in the fresh air. I'd sit out there pounding the phone or dictating letters. Around 4 p.m., Jeff finally went for a sandwich, and Becky said, "Why's Jeff been here all day, Dave?"

"Beats me," I said. "We'll find out eventually."

Sure enough, when Jeff returned, he came out onto the balcony with his sandwich and, as casually as he could, struck up a conversation.

"Dave, are you going to go and work for [such and such record company]?"

"What makes you think that, man?"

"Well, I'm hearing that you are."

"I haven't had any offers," I say. All true.

"Were you considering it?"

"Why, would you miss me?"

"Bastard."

"Don't worry, Jeff. I'm not going anywhere."

Jeff looked at me and said nothing. Then he picked up his bag, said, "Okay, guys, see you later!" to the others, gave a cheery wave, and left.

Jack, Becky, and I looked at each other and burst out laughing. I know Jeff hated any kind of confrontation and would go out of his way to avoid discussing difficult issues, but this was a record for him—six hours to get to the point. I was one of the only stable things in his life. I showed up for work every day, I wasn't stealing his money, and I was always trying to do right by him. I'd promised I wouldn't leave him, and I meant it. But he must have known that I was thinking about the baby and wondering about how I was going to provide for it. Great as Jeff was, I was making hardly any money from him. Perhaps he was worried that fatherhood would take me away from him.

For some time there had been pressure from on high to release "Hallelujah" as a single. Donnie Ienner was very keen on it. I thought it made sense, and the obvious slot would be Christmas. Jeff was pretty adamant that he didn't want it out, but we needed another single. Jeff decided on "So Real," a good song that didn't have a fly on a rat's ass's chance of getting on the radio. We reached a compromise: release "So Real" in late summer and then discuss "Hallelujah" again closer to Christmas.

But Donnie, mindful of the money spent on "Last Goodbye," insisted that the video budget be kept to a minimum. Sophie Muller was an experienced English video director who'd worked a lot with Annie Lennox and Sade, but also edgier acts like Hole, Come, Bjork, and The Jesus & Mary Chain. She agreed to shoot and edit everything herself, and the band would get plenty of input. We'd shoot it in Brooklyn, so there'd be no renting warehouses in Paris. It seemed ideal. However, at some point I went over the figures again and realized that we needed another five thousand dollars to bring it in. Sophie was on her way over from Europe when Missy Worth called and told me that Donnie was canceling the video, as he didn't want to spend the extra five thousand dollars.

"You're fucking kidding me," I said. "Okay, Missy, thanks for letting me know. I'll talk to Michele."

I called up Michele Anthony.

"Michele, Dave Lory. Look, Donnie is refusing to give us the extra five thousand bucks we need to bring in this video. The director's on a plane; it'll cost more than that to cancel the shoot. I've had it with this guy. I'm gonna call him, but I need your assurance we'll get the five thousand *dollars.*"

"That's fine, Dave. You've got it."

"Thank you, Michele. I appreciate it."

Then I called Donnie. There were all kinds of rumors floating around at the time that someone high up at Columbia was going to be ousted. Maybe he was feeling antsy and wanted to show he played hardball with budgets, but I didn't need it and I told him so.

"I'm not spending another penny on this thing, Dave. The costs on Buckley are way out of line, and I hold you responsible."

"And you're willing to throw a wrench into his career for the sake of five thousand bucks?"

"Uh-huh. The song's not a hit. We all know that."

"Donnie, if you don't give us the five thousand dollars for this video, I'll go straight down to the Village and find every credible artist that

Sony is looking to sign, and I'll tell them and their managers just what you do for Jeff Buckley, and you won't be able to sign anybody and you'll be finished at Sony."

"Dave, you're threatening me."

"I'm promising you, Donnie."

There was silence.

"All right. I'll do this for you, Dave."

"Now you're just sucking up to me," I said. "Don't do it for me; do it for Jeff. Do it because it's the right thing."

I put the phone down still angry. I hate the smell of burning bridges in the morning.[59]

Jeff didn't know any of this. There are things managers get involved in that if the artists knew about, it would drive them nuts.

As for the "So Real" video: Jeff and the band are in a Brooklyn diner playing busboys, waiters, and customers and then changing into gorilla suits, while Jeff, in a cheap brown two-piece suit, rides a bicycle. Jeff liked it. I couldn't make heads or tails of it and didn't think it was worth all the grief.

It may have had something to do with the 50 Most Beautiful People article, but Hollywood was sniffing around. In late August 1995, Jeff received an offer to appear in *The Mirror Has Two Faces*, produced, directed by, and starring Barbra Streisand. She wanted Jeff to play the part of Luke, a handsome teacher's assistant who was trying to pick up an older woman, another teacher at the college. The casting director sent over a script. It was one scene, about thirteen lines. We laughed about it, but Jeff would never have considered it. Not only did he not want to act, but he wasn't all that keen on having his music used in movies or on TV shows. Amazingly, we were always knocking back the kinds of offers most artists would jump at these days. NBC wanted to use "Eternal Life" in *Homicide*. They offered twenty thousand dollars for ninety seconds of the song. But we turned down all such requests.

We hadn't fully appreciated the demand for Jeff in Australia, although we knew "Last Goodbye" was getting heavy airplay on national

[59] There were consequences to my forcing Donnie's hand, but for legal reasons, I can't tell you about them.

Jeff and the band on the set of the video shoot for "So Real."

station, Triple J, and we knew *Grace* was selling well. When we booked the shows, we'd purposefully booked small venues, as we figured we wouldn't be able to do them again, and Jeff liked the intimate spaces. But by the time we arrived, *Grace* had practically gone gold and the demand was so strong that the promoter, Michael Chugg of Frontier Touring, had added more shows in each city we visited and suggested we book another tour immediately.

Dave Lory and Samantha Way in Sarasota, Florida, on vacation in summer 1995, prior to the tour in Australia.

Chuggy, as everybody called him, reminded me of Bill Graham, a loudmouth with a big heart, very hands-on at the gigs, picking up garbage, taking tickets, hosing down the crowd at sweltering summer festivals, drinking with the band after the show. He was famous for swearing like a drunken sailor, sometimes from the stage at rowdy factions of the crowd—a no-nonsense, working-class guy who always brought great energy with him. Although this was officially the end of the *Grace* world tour, once we saw the demand and had worked out that playing the kind of venues Chuggy was suggesting, with merchandise sales on top, would actually turn a substantial profit, it seemed foolish not to book a return visit. Jeff agreed it would be great for everyone to share in a payday after all the hard work. So Chuggy got to work booking new shows for February 1996.

We had a couple of days to acclimatize after the grueling flight. On Saturday evening, while I was resting, Jeff banged on the door of my room in a panic. "Dave, open up, open up quick. You've got to look at this." This wasn't like Jeff; he almost never did anything in a hurry or raised his voice. I thought his bed was full of poisonous spiders. He took me to his room. On the TV was some incomprehensible talk show with a guy standing next to a giant puppet ostrich that was being rude to all the guests. "Dave, we're booked onto this show," said Jeff, practically shaking with panic. "You've got to get me out of it!" Julie Borchard had given us videos of all the TV shows we'd been asked to appear on. I had demanded full shows, not just clips of bands' performances, because I needed to see the environment, the presenters, even the advertisements, to get the atmosphere of the show. I don't know whether it was deliberate, but she hadn't given us a video of *Hey, Hey, It's Saturday*. We asked around and were told it was really popular, the nation's highest-rated show, but this kind of Aussie irreverence really wasn't Jeff's style. We were due on in a week. I told Jeff I'd handle it, but I wanted to wait until after the gold record presentation that had been booked for Monday night after Jeff's show at the Metro, at the Hard Rock Cafe in Sydney. The show was phenomenal and made Jeff the talk of the town, as the entire Aussie music industry seemed to be present. I turned up at the Hard Rock Cafe to find Jeff doing tequila shots with the local chairman of Sony, Denis Handlin, and Chuggy. Denis came over and slapped me on the back.

"Amazing show, Dave. Incredible kid you got there." We shot the breeze for a while, then Denis said, "Oh, Jeff told me all about *Hey, Hey*. No worries; I'll sort it first thing in the morning." I was cross about Jeff's going directly to the chairman, but hey, when you're hot, you can get shit done. I went to get a drink and on the floor by the door I saw Jeff's bracelet. I was always finding this thing. It must have been six times already during the course of the *Grace* tours that I'd found it lying around and handed it back to Jeff. I'd found it on the street, in hotel lobbies, and in venues. Once I saw a cleaner sweeping it up and rescued it from the trash. No one else ever mentioned this thing going missing; it seemed to happen only when I was around, and it was only ever me who found it. I went over to return it to Jeff for the seventh time. He laughed when he saw me approaching with it.

"Dave! You seem to have that bracelet more than I do," he said. "You know what? It's yours. You were obviously meant to be together."

"No, man, I couldn't take it."

"Yes, you can. My gift to you. With love and gratitude."

I was touched. I put it on and wore it every day after that.

On the Street magazine Sydney cover.

The Music Network cover for the Australian tour.

Despite the sense of triumph in the air, there was something coming to a head during that tour that would pull the band apart. As the *Grace* shows had wound on, it was clear that harder drugs were being consumed on the road than previously. Matt Johnson had watched it unfold from his seat at the back, and it was making him uncomfortable. When he began playing with Jeff, he was green, wide-eyed, and went along with the regimen of beers, burgers, and blow, but over time he had realized that, especially as a drummer, he needed to look after his body and soul, and he had started practicing yoga, meditating, and had also become a vegetarian. Although he felt much better for it, he was beginning to detect murmurings that the others thought he'd become too prissy and serious. Once, while Matt was doing a yogic headstand in the hotel room they shared, Jeff squirted some kind of lotion into Matt's shorts and said, "Transcend this!" It was funny but disrespectful too. As he became increasingly spiritual in his outlook, Matt was turned off by the sex-'n'-drugs excesses of the road and increasingly unhappy with the band's decreasing ability to communicate, as drugs began to dominate in the band's offstage pastimes. "Imagine you're around a dinner table with three people that are fully on their cell phones," he says today. "It creates a dead zone. Not only do you not have access to that person, but it creates entropy. You're bringing down the potential of people to give of themselves.

"I think it started with Mickey. He's a Skidmore kid, from a well-to-do uptown family. I think he thought it was cool in an art-school way to start using drugs. Mickey was a gorgeous guy—tall, soft-spoken, beautiful deep voice. Girls loved him; he was a movie star—a really smart, well-educated kid. But when he took drugs, he was just a typical kid wasting it all on drugs. What Jeff should have done is fired him, but he didn't; he went off in that direction too. Michael was another intelligent guy, one of the most intellectually astute people I know. His involvement with drugs was very different from Mickey's. But he was definitely joining in.

"I know Dave and Gene really wanted to make sure they had drugs under control. Gene even got at me about smoking some pot. Drugs made Mickey a potential threat to the stability of the organism, and that might have been at the root of the anger that developed between those parties. [The others] would moan about Dave a lot. He was a Southerner like me. White, liberal New Yorkers are, in their own way, snobs. Northerners look down on Southerners all the time, and I felt that was happening."

At this point, Mattie felt he was not as culturally aware as his bandmates. He would listen to them discussing movies, books, and poetry he had no knowledge of, and would feel left out. With his musical lightness of touch on the drums, he was also becoming wary of Jeff's need to make the music louder and more extreme. The increase in volume had given Matt tinnitus. It was reaching the point where being onstage was becoming as painful as being offstage.

"You don't just switch off from gigs like this. You don't punch in, punch out, and then go home to the wife," he says. "You're living with these people all the time. So what they do has such an effect upon you. If I were in that band now, I'd look each one of them in the eye and say, 'You guys are the biggest bunch of fucking douchebags I've seen in my life' and then continue to play with them, laugh in their faces, and say, 'I love you, but you're an idiot.' Tell them what I'm thinking and not give two shits what they think of me. But at that time I was too young and too insecure."

I wasn't aware of the depth of Mattie's feelings at the time. I wish he'd come to me and said all this then, because I really valued him as a player and, like he said, I was aware that the other guys weren't team players. Mickey and I obviously weren't getting along. If I'd known he was getting high so often, I might have had a reason to fire him. The thing is, it wasn't apparently disrupting the work. Mickey was showing up for everything and doing a great job onstage. When the band was strong and Jeff was happy, I was too. But I should have looked more closely at Mattie's mood.

Matt mentioned to someone, Gene I think, that he was unhappy and thinking of leaving, but Gene never reported back to me. I think I'd have noticed if it was getting out of hand, though. I'm pretty good at spotting the signs. Years on the road with the Allman Brothers showed me exactly what heroin looks like and how users behave, and I wasn't seeing it here. Junkies have a way of covering their tracks. Smack addicts will often use someone else's hotel room to shoot up in, for example, so their own space is never a source of suspicion. I once found my toilet full of Gregg Allman's syringes. That was a red-letter day.

Gregg, who was both an alcoholic and a junkie, had his addictions down to a fine art. He was never late for gigs, always showed up for interviews, was courteous to journalists and cameramen, and behaved in a thoroughly professional manner, but once he was off-duty he could turn into a prize fuck-up. I once found him asleep standing up, his forehead stuck to the glass shelf of his fridge, where he'd gone looking for something to eat and nodded out.

Gregg was definitely getting high to forget. He was racked with guilt about the deaths of his brother Duane Allman and colleague Berry Oakley. He'd told me that he'd lied to Duane fifteen minutes before his fatal accident. He'd stolen Duane's cocaine but denied it when challenged. Duane had ridden off angry and crashed his bike. When Gregg went to counseling, the psychiatrist got him to a write a letter: "Sorry, brother, but I lied to you. I did steal your cocaine. And you rode off on your cherry-red Harley..." He wrote another to Berry, who'd died after a freakishly similar accident, same intersection, a year to the day after Duane's. Berry was thrown off his bike and got a concussion. Gregg wanted to take him to the hospital, but Berry said, "Let's go back to your house." Gregg put him in his bedroom, and Berry died of the concussion.[60]

It was hard for me to watch Gregg hurting himself, as I really cared for him, and to see his suffering and not be able to help him unless he wanted to help himself was too painful. All that and Dickey Betts's fondness for pulling knives on me were why I quit working with the Allmans. Co-manager Danny Goldberg puts it best. "All bands give you this much shit," he said, holding up one hand in a straight line level with his chin. "If the money's here"—hand above his eyebrow—"that's great, stick around. If the money's here"—hand level with his chest—"time to go."

There is no way I was witnessing that kind of drug use in Jeff's band. No one was freebasing or snorting speedballs. 911 was not being called every weekend. There was some dabbling. But I understand Mattie's feeling that, already somewhat at a loss around his colleagues, he was now excluded from the inner circle they'd constructed to do recreational drugs together. When you're feeling alienated on all fronts, it's hard to want to stick around.

Just as we were preparing to leave Australia on September 5, the French government detonated a nuclear device at Mururoa Atoll, about seven hundred fifty miles away from French-administered Tahiti. The effects were picked up by seismic monitoring stations in Australia, and there was international outrage about the blast's potential to damage and poison vast areas of the South Pacific. The French Defense Ministry said the bomb was merely the equivalent of twenty thousand tons of TNT—which, considering that Hiroshima was the equivalent of fifteen thousand, didn't sound particularly harmless. Australia immediately withdrew its ambassador from France, and the foreign minister declared, "This is not the action of a good international citizen."

When we saw the news, we were understandably shaken. Horrified that a nuclear device would need to be tested in the late '90s, Jeff was

[60] Gregg put a silver dollar in the caskets of people who died around the Allmans. He always carried one with him , a reference to the lyric of his song, "Midnight Rider.".

particularly upset, as France was our next destination.[61] He had been awarded a gold disc there too, and the presentation was to be a big deal. Jeff had previously received the Grand Prix International Du Disque, an occasional award given by a jury of producers, journalists, and industry professionals to only the most outstanding musicians, like Edith Piaf, Jacques Yves Montand, George Brassands, Bruce Springsteen, Bob Dylan, Joni Mitchell, Leonard Cohen, and Joan Baez. It was a sure sign of how highly Jeff was regarded in France.

When we landed, Sophie Zannettacci, who adored Jeff, had laid on a large formal dinner, as only the French can, with exquisite food and drink and a room full of interesting luminaries. She met us at the airport and told us about the event. "Sounds good," said Jeff, "but I want to go to a McDonald's now." I wasn't sure if he was just being a prick because of the atomic bomb test or just wanted a hamburger because he was homesick. He did attend the dinner, though.

The gold award itself was happening on a TV show, and Jeff was going to play live. Unusually, he had decided to wear a suit and tie. The lighting was dark and moody—blue and white light behind him, throwing his body into silhouette and revealing only his face. He spoke before starting his song:

"About two days ago, I woke up in Australia and I saw the bomb go off, and I felt sad that the French government had joined a long list of fools who insist on sending death sentences to the earth. This is for all the people who know the only good place for a nuclear bomb is in the garbage, dismantled. This is for Leonard, wherever you are, and this is for Nina Simone."

He sang a wobbly "Hallelujah," sounding distracted, his eyes closed for the entire song, his anger detectable in the slight disdain he brought to the performance. I watched on a monitor offstage thinking, "This is awkward." This was the biggest TV show in France, and it was live. I was nervous.

When Jeff came off, we adjourned to his dressing room. I stuck my head out to gauge the reaction and, sure enough, there were a lot of

[61] President Jacques Chirac said that there were seven or eight tests planned to assess the effectiveness of computer modeling tests—which, once verified, would mean they would never need to physically test again. At this site, one hundred seventy-six tests had occurred since 1966.

A French tour postcard.

people jabbering animatedly in French, all pointing toward us. Jeff had just dissed the French government on prime-time TV. I was wondering if we'd get out of there alive.

Later that fall, back in New York, it was time to seriously discuss the follow-up to *Grace*. I was practically getting daily calls from Donnie asking when we'd start recording, and I couldn't hold him off any longer. We arranged an afternoon meeting with Donnie and Steve Berkowitz to make definitive plans.

At the appointed hour, I went to Berkowitz's office and we waited for Jeff to show. An hour went by, and there was no sign of him. Berkowitz held off Donnie but then said he had other things to attend to and went off to do them. I thought, "I may as well wait and see what Jeff's excuse is."

Jeff finally showed up, three hours after the meeting had been due to start. He was wearing his fluffy black winter coat with a fedora shading his eyes. I looked at him and knew immediately that he was on smack. It was so obvious.

"Really?" I said.

Jeff grinned.

"You fucking idiot," I said. I was really pissed off. This was a whole new level of disrespect, especially as I had some explaining to do to a guy I'd been fighting with for months over Jeff's career, budgets, and requirements. And he'd been snorting heroin. This was a real kick in the pants. I snatched up my coat and strode past him. "Be at my office at 9 a.m. tomorrow," I said, and left.

Naturally, he showed up at 8:30 a.m. Overcompensating. Which annoyed me, because I wasn't ready. We left the office and went across the road from the plaza to a place called the Coffee Pot.

"Okay," I said, once we'd ordered breakfast. "What the fuck are you playing at? You show up three hours late. For Donnie? High as a kite? I'm not going to deal with an artist on drugs. I've been there and done that; that's why I left the Allman Brothers. I made it very clear to you when we began that I wasn't interested in that any longer. You didn't even smoke when I signed up, and that was a really good reason to work with you. You expect me in the office at ten every morning to work your career. What if I went out all night and got high and rolled in at two in the afternoon?"

He looked sheepish. "Are you going to drop me?"

"I'm thinking about it," I said. "You threw me under the bus there, and I'm not gonna tolerate that. I'd never do that to you."

"I'm sorry, Dave."

"And heroin?! Are you for *real*? You know what it did to your dad."

"I know, I know."

"Look, I don't care what an artist does on their free time. If you want to do that shit, that's your concern. But don't screw up at work. When it's work time, you have to have your shit together. I expect you to show up bright-eyed and bushy-tailed so we can put on a united front in Donnie's office and get what we need out of him for this next record."

"I'm sorry, Dave. I didn't want to be there yesterday. There's a lot of pressure on me right now. I need some more space to work, to develop my ideas."

"All right."

"I didn't want to put you on the spot. I just don't want to talk about the next record yet."

"Phone call, dude," I said. "Call me and I can call you in sick, but don't fucking do this to me. Or yourself."

"Sorry, man. But I did get to thinking last night. I got lots of ideas for this record. It'll be amazing. I promise you I'll make the best record ever. It's going to blow people's minds." He was looking at me for a reaction. I knew he was trying to work me. He was going to seduce me back on side.

"So you need space to work?"

"Yes, Mickey's parents have a place at Sag Harbor. We could go there over the winter and work."

"And take shitloads of drugs?"

Jeff laughed. "No, I swear we wouldn't. Smoke a little weed, maybe."

"Hmm."

"You know how hot this band is right now."

"Two fucking Ninas?"

"We're on another level."

"Yes. But Mattie's not happy. And now I know why."

"He'll come around. I promise you, Dave, if we can do this, all come together to work for a while and really flesh out these ideas I have, I think this could be one of the truly great records. I promise you, we'll do it."

He was starting to bounce around and get excited; he was talking himself into it. And working his charm on me.

"Donnie wants to take us to dinner," I said. "I think he wants to talk about 'Hallelujah' again."

"Okay," said Jeff, quiet again for a moment.

"Just show the fuck up this time. Huh?"

He laughed. "I promise."

We talked some more, and once he was certain he had talked me down, Jeff got up and bounced out of the Coffee Pot.

The meal with Donnie was hilarious. I'd been in agreement with him that "Hallelujah" could be a Christmas smash. He'd been talking about it ever since *Grace* was first released. I figured we could shoot a simple, well-lit solo performance, a bit like the TV slot Jeff had just done in France, without its costing the earth. Something classy like that could play around the world and really kick sales of *Grace* to another level. When the subject finally came up over dessert, Donnie said: "So, Jeff, you don't have to release 'Hallelujah' as a single just because your manager wants to."

Jeff was kicking me under the table; he knew I was sitting there freaking out.

Donnie went through this whole rigmarole of pretending he wasn't bothered by it being a single, almost like he was talking himself out of it, but all in the guise of him and Jeff getting one over on me.

When we got outside, I turned to Jeff and laughed.

"What the fuck was all that about?"

"Who knows?"

"Do you think I'll ever figure that guy out?" I said.

Jeff tapped the side of his nose. "It's about the music fucking business, stupid," he said.

I know I give the impression that Donnie and I never got along, but that's not true. We both had brash management styles and both wanted Jeff to be a success, but Jeff had a way of pitting people against each other, and he did it no better than with Donnie and me. Julie Borchard recalled that Donnie appreciated straight answers and wanted people to follow through on their promises. There were occasions when I bullshitted him—like pretending Michael Tighe was an experienced player—and that might have upset him, but I appreciated Donnie's commitment and passion regarding Jeff. He was always looking for new angles. "We have to huddle after every play" was one of his favorite sayings—checking that our plan, which was fine yesterday, was still valid today. My biggest beef with him was the way he seemed to manage people by making them fearful of losing their jobs. I tended to side with the people on the shop floor, and they could be infuriated by him. But overall, for a guy with a ton on his plate, he gave Jeff a lot of attention, and provided him with the freedom to be himself.

• • • • •

Sag Harbor is a leafy village in the Hamptons—population around two thousand—once a whaling port on the easternmost tip of Long Island, now known primarily for being quiet and expensive. Mick's parents' place there was empty out of season. For a pretty reasonable sum, the whole band could stay there, hang out, rehearse, write, and generally get into the headspace for making the new record.

The plan was to spend the whole winter there—apart from a few gigs over Christmas and New Year's, mostly solo things that Jeff wanted to do—away from the temptations of Manhattan and, hopefully, write some great songs. Mattie, though still feeling sidelined, agreed to attend and see how it went.

At first it mostly involved Jeff tinkering with his guitar pedals. Mattie quickly decided this was not where he wanted to be, in Mickey's domain, listening to Jeff fussing with sounds. So he went back to Manhattan. Mickey had some songs he wanted to work on, so they brought in another friend of his, Eric Eidel, to sit in on drums. Eric turned up and noticed the air in the house was heavy with pot smoke and incense. They jammed on Mick's songs, but nothing conclusive seemed to happen.

Sometime in January, Berkowitz invited himself up to hear the work in progress. Jeff had sounded enthusiastic on the phone, but what Berkowitz heard when he arrived was the kind of endless jam the band had always conjured in rehearsal, this time dominated by Jeff's guitar effects, almost emulating what Gary Lucas had done on the first album.

"The gist of it is, Jeff was really a composer. He needed to work on his pedals; he needed to work on the full sound. It wasn't just about sitting down and playing it acoustically," says Berkowitz. "What's going to be the *feel* of this? How do you explain *Sgt. Pepper* to anybody before you make it? How could you explain *A Night at the Opera* by Queen without understanding how you're going to stack the vocals and the dynamics of the thing?"

That's Berkowitz with hindsight. When he returned from Sag Harbor, he was pretty worried. "Dave, they've got nothing," he reported. The rent may have been reasonable, but we were spending a bunch on hiring instruments, mics, and recording equipment. To be three months and twenty five thousand dollars in, with only meandering twenty-minute jams to show for it, we were getting anxious.

My first child was due, and suddenly the whole question of where my living was coming from had been thrown into sharp focus. The baby was coming at the end of January, so I flew out to London in December to stay with Sam in Barnes and wait for the birth. Sam woke me up on the night of January 25—she'd been out for the night working with Alice In Chains, as you do, nine months gone—and said, "My water broke!" and drove herself to the hospital because I didn't trust myself driving on the wrong side of the road. I called in to see if I was needed, but was told it was too soon. Labor went on for two whole days. After the first day, I went home and watched the Super Bowl on late-night TV. Unable to sleep, I went in at dawn, and one of the midwives who had been there the previous day said, "I'm leaving here by 7:30 a.m. and goddammit, I'm going to deliver this kid." Finally, Charlotte Amber Way-Lory popped out. The midwife cut the cord and handed her to me, and I quickly counted all her fingers and toes just to make sure everything was all right. She was perfect. But now the realities of being a parent kicked in.

None of my acts were poised to generate any money. The second Australian tour, the final *Grace* shows, would turn a decent profit. It was an unashamed victory lap. But that would be it for Jeff for a while. I was also managing singer Greg Garing, who was bluegrass one minute, rock 'n' roll the next—a tough sell whose first album hadn't exactly caught fire and who was finding it hard to focus in the studio. Abbo and I were collaborating on managing a Swedish singer called Sophie Zelmani, who was really promising, but it was early in her career. And I'd taken on Katell Keineg, whom Jeff had met while playing Sin-é. Katell was a Welsh singer who had relocated to Dublin and wrote beautiful, limpid songs with dream-like lyrics. It was easy to fall in love with her, musically and personally, and I agreed to work with her when she told me about the nightmare she was having with Elektra Records. Her excellent debut album had sold zip, and now she was preparing her second. As it turned out, it would be over a year before we were ready to release it.

So I'll admit I was nervous about money. But I was also nervous about money on Jeff's behalf. In February, aware that the wheels were starting to wobble, I wrote an eight-page letter to him about the state of the union and what we needed to achieve in 1996. I pointed out that, with all our pre-production money spent on Sag Harbor, the band couldn't remain on retainers without eating into Jeff's own money. We couldn't go to Sony for any more unless we had a recording and producer budget settled. Jeff was liable to make ten thousand dollars from the Australian tour, but the cost of keeping the band on retainers for three months would be twelve thousand dollars and change plus payroll taxes and so on. The letter went on:

> *If you record in June, we would probably not have a record done (i.e., recording, bio, pictures, video, marketing plans setup worldwide, etc.) until well into the fall of this year. That would mean a January 1997 release at the very best.*
>
> *The bottom line, Jeff, is there is not enough demand for you and the band without a new record. For the New Year's Eve show at Mercury Lounge it took a week to sell out two hundred fifty tickets. This in your biggest market in the US but because there is no new material, sales were slow. If you and the band elect not to take the above advice and continue to tour, even if the four of you went out in a van by yourselves, the band would not make nearly the retainer money they currently make. You would maybe make one hundred to two hundred dollars a week each tops. So this will not take care of keeping the band afloat financially.*

Everyone around him needed a new record to happen from a financial point of view. I'm pretty sure that never even entered Jeff's mind, the responsibility of looking after the team he'd built around himself. If anything, he was missing the freedom of the Sin-é days—just showing up somewhere with a guitar and blowing people away, making enough to live in his sparse apartment and to buy some takeout and a few CDs.

I reminded him of our original three-stage plan. His contact with Sony guaranteed the release of three albums. Album one: set up a broad fan base around the world so that he could tour whenever he liked and not need to go to Sony for tour support. I was proud to say we had achieved that goal. Album two: get as close as possible to recouping on record sales and break new markets so that he would start to see a healthy revenue. Album three: secure his career so he could record or perform live whenever he wanted, and pursue any extended musical venture (new band, change of genre, whatever he was feeling), effectively giving him total control for the future. I wanted to remind him, while he was starting to feel anxious about Columbia, that our plan was designed to effectively free him from the label over time, and that he should try not to be impatient. (Simultaneous with urging Jeff back into the studio, I was pointing out to Columbia that Michael Jackson, Springsteen,

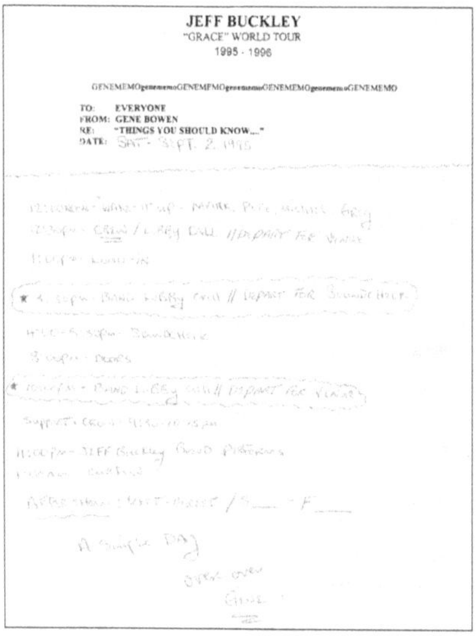
JEFF BUCKLEY
"GRACE" WORLD TOUR
1995 - 1996

TO: EVERYONE
FROM: GENE BOWEN
RE: "THINGS YOU SHOULD KNOW..."
DATE: SAT - SEPT. 2, 1995

A day sheet. Tour manager Gene Bowen would slide these under the hotel door of the band and crew each night, so everyone knew what was happening the following day.

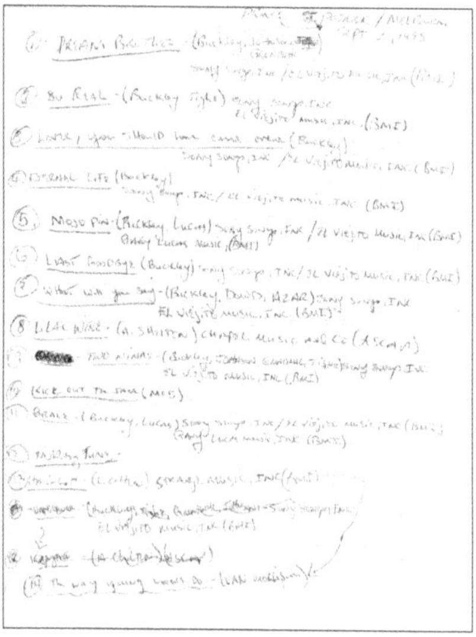

The Melbourne set list that would be sent in to collect show royalties from BMI.

whoever, had needed to disappear for a few years between albums to create demand. I knew Jeff wasn't at their level, but I knew that creativity couldn't be rushed and artists needed time to decompress, particularly after the kind of tour Jeff had just completed.)

I pointed out to him that a lot of personnel changes had taken place at Sony while we doing other things, changes that required me to revisit various territories and make sure the new members of staff were up to speed. You can never rest on your laurels with record companies because staff turnover can be ridiculously high.

The last four pages were a detailed schedule for March 1996 through September 1997, covering rehearsing, recording, marketing planning, recording B-sides, doing photo shoots, creating album artwork, writing a new press biography, designing posters, drawing up a worldwide marketing plan, shooting videos and a new EPK, sending out promos, conducting interviews, booking trade ads, doing long-lead promotion, releasing the album in January 1997, rehearsing, doing a US tour, a European tour, a Pacific Rim tour, a second US tour, a second European tour, booking a third US tour...

It makes my head spin just to look at all that again, plus, as I said in the letter, I was writing it at 4 a.m. while waiting for Charlotte—who was suffering from colic—to finally stop screaming and get to sleep. You can sense my desperation to get the second record underway sooner rather than later.[62]

The letter was faxed to Gene to hand to Jeff when the band arrived at the Doubletree Ritz-Carlton in Sydney. I would call to discuss it later. Yet the plan I'd meticulously mapped out wouldn't kick in for another whole year. We were about to make a bunch of time-consuming and costly false starts.

This final tour was dubbed The Hard Luck Tour. I can't say that things went according to plan right from the start. Even the flight from New York to LA was not without incident. A flight attendant took a shine to Jeff and plied him with free drinks. Leah Reid, who was working from LA by this point, went to hang out with the band at the airport—you could do that then—and was surprised to see Jeff de-planing completely hammered. Gene was annoyed but dealt with it calmly. But when they got on the plane to Australia, Jeff threw up all over the seat in front of him. The prospect of the smell of vomit in his nostrils for the next twenty-four hours did not please Mattie at all. "We'd just got on the plane for this long, long flight, and I smelt vomit and realized he'd thrown up all over the back of the seat, and that was a deciding moment for me: I don't wanna be working with someone who's doing this. It's not even about professionalism; it's about common human decency. It was just foolishness. There were many small things that served as triggers to leaving. But they were quite subtle. Malaise, a general feeling of unease—Jeff seemed somehow unstable and perhaps self-destructive."

Mattie also began feeling that Jeff was picking on him. "There was one time, one of the last gigs, maybe after I'd said I was thinking of quitting, where Jeff introduced me as, 'He has Jesus hair and he's loyal like a dog.' It was subtly degrading. It wasn't something I could wield back at

[62] The letter ended: "By the way, some nights 'Hallelujah' does not work...so I need a new record for Sam's and my sanity (just kidding)."

him; he was using a forum I didn't have. I felt beaten up by it. In many ways Jeff knew me better than I knew myself. That's the tricky thing about relationships past a certain point. When you're intimate with somebody, you can only really know yourself through them. If there's some kind of malice in the eyes through which you know yourself, if there's something unresolved, that can be painful."

An extra incentive for Jeff on this tour was that The Dambuilders and The Grifters would be supporting him. Joan Wasser's presence helped diffuse the tension that had grown around the band, to some extent, but it didn't help when Matt came in from a late night out to find that Jeff and Joan, in their enthusiasm for one another, had destroyed both the beds in the room he was sharing with them. There was a blazing row.

I flew from London for the Sydney show and there, standing by himself in front of the venue, was Matt. He told me definitively that he was leaving the band, and about everything that had been going on. I had no idea it had gotten that bad. I wondered how I could have been so blind and why Gene had never said anything. Merri told me once that, when I came out on the road, it was like Dad showing up and that they'd all be on their best behavior until I left again.

"What was I afraid of?" says Matt today. "Afraid of losing this gig—'How do I head into the fear?' I quit. 'Boom, I'm doing it.' That's the most primal thing I could do—the best way I could deal with my fear of failure and the fact that I didn't want to be part of this, to be around those people anymore. Jeff didn't try to dissuade me. He was surprised, he might have felt hurt, but he was nowhere near as hurt as I was."

Unfortunately, the tension—and the long layoff between gigs—was visible onstage. Some of the shows were stiff, didn't flow too well. Some of the reviews were less than ecstatic. Two new songs, "Moodswing Whiskey" and "I Woke Up in a Strange Place," were coming along, though obviously threw the crowd a little, but as for "Edna Frau," one of Mickey's songs that he sang himself, it was nothing short of terrible. People in the crowd, who were putting their fingers in their ears, accosted me and asked what was going on.

"What's that dirge doing in the set, Jeff? No one has come to hear Mick sing," I said, after once particularly excruciating rendition.

"It's the next phase of the band, Dave."

The Australian Hard Luck Tour book cover.

"You're not still clinging on to that Two Ninas shit, are you? They've come to see Jeff Buckley. You've spent two years building up that name and getting people to fever pitch. You'd be crazy to throw it away now."

As Mattie said, there was something self-destructive in Jeff's behavior. I've witnessed it many times in rising musicians—a fear of success, of being subsumed by the public and its regard for you. The natural reaction is to smash up the thing you've built until it's a little less attractive, less people are interested in it, and you can manage their expectations. I'm not sure Jeff was ever 100 percent serious about the Two Ninas idea, but it was a useful tool. He could use it to allow the band some autonomy and input and then step out of it, if necessary, as a solo artist. I understood the logic, but I knew Columbia would never buy it. I also knew that Jeff would want to pull away from the singer-songwriter thing sooner or later. He was capable of too much to stay in one lane for his whole career.

Occasionally on that tour, the band was at its very best. The *Grace* songs were growing more intense, and the crowds' reactions grew to match. A clutch of shows at the Palais in Melbourne were recorded by Triple J radio for a live broadcast and a potential live album. Jeff took a keen interest in this and stayed behind after the band flew home to help Mark Naficy mix it in a Melbourne studio.[63] One of those gigs was also notable for the presence of Jimmy Page by the mixing desk, clearly transported by the music. Both Page and Robert Plant had stood watching Jeff in the wings at a festival in Bern, Switzerland, earlier in the year and had been vocal at every opportunity about their love for *Grace*. Backstage after the Palais show, Page asked Jeff if he would support them on the upcoming Page & Plant tour. Reluctantly, we turned them down, as it would clash with our recording plans. Nonetheless, it was a major moment for Jeff, getting the wholehearted approval of the man who'd first made him want to play guitar, whose music had provided one of his abiding childhood memories: lying in the dark in his stepfather's van listening to the majestic *Physical Graffiti* and feeling a universe open up before him.

The band's last show was at a vast pub called Selina's, on Coogee Beach in Sydney. It held two thousand people—which, considering this was the fourth Sydney show on this tour, was quite something. But the atmosphere was pretty tense. After a ferocious version of "Eternal Life," Jeff introduced Mattie and said: "Matt decided that this will be the last show he plays with us. It's been two fucking years of outstanding service and musical inspiration...I want you to wish him a fond farewell." They went into "What Will You Say" with tears in their eyes.

It was a curious ending. Jeff went up alone for the encore and sang "All Flowers in Time" the song he'd written with Elizabeth Fraser—as far as I'm aware, the only time he ever sang it in public. Maybe it was a tribute to Mattie. The band returned for "Vancouver" and a particularly unhinged "Kanga-Roo." Jeff told the crowd to "go and get drunk," and Mattie jumped offstage and left the venue alone to walk along the beach, visibly upset. He opted to stay in Australia for a few weeks after we'd left, to decompress and assess what he wanted to do next.

---

[63] The album as Jeff oversaw it was never issued, although five tracks from the Palais shows are on the posthumous *Mystery White Boy* album.

The *Grace* campaign and the band that had waged it around the world were now undeniably over. Band, crew, and management were burnt out. That long plane ride home felt even longer than usual. Before we left, Jeff was telling me how he wanted changes. He meant he wanted to get off Columbia. I had no idea how he thought that would work. I reminded him of the plan. Told him to be patient. I still wanted to know what we were going to do about following up *Grace*.

CHAPTER 9

"My Sweetheart the Drunk"

EARLY IN 1996, JEFF RAN into his friend Lenny Kaye at Electric Lady Studios in Greenwich Village. Apart from being a brilliant music writer and the compiler of *Nuggets*, the album that defined garage rock, Lenny is a fine guitarist and producer and has been the trusted musical sidekick of Patti Smith since her earliest recordings. Jeff and Lenny would hang out, drink, and listen to doo-wop records together, and Lenny knew that Jeff was a huge fan of Patti's music. Lenny and Patti were back at Electric Lady, the site of their very first sessions, making *Gone Again*, an album born out of the death of her beloved husband, Fred "Sonic" Smith, whose band, The MC5, originated "Kick Out the Jams," that Jeff loved to play live. *Gone Again* was also inspired by Patti's brother, Todd; photographer Robert Mapplethorpe; pianist Richard Sohl; and Kurt Cobain, all of whom had passed away since Patti's previous record in 1988.

Jeff was invited to put a harmony vocal on the title song. Then to the long, sad "Fireflies" he added one of his exotic musical devices, a Turkish bowed instrument called an esraj, which provided a haunting drone. He also added acoustic guitar on another track (which didn't make the album), "Wander I Go," on which he played alongside Tom Verlaine, former leader of Television, the pioneering New York band that emerged at the same time as The Patti Smith Group.[64] Verlaine's striking, iconoclastic guitar on the title track of Television's *Marquee Moon* was a key text for Jeff, and he was thrilled to meet the man behind it.

It planted a seed in Jeff's mind. Verlaine could be just the guy he was looking for to produce the next record: a brilliant guitar player, a punk rock pioneer with at least one stone-cold-classic album, cool, experienced, but enough of a maverick to not do the obvious. The more he thought about it, the better the idea seemed. It was a punt, a thought from left field—the same twisted logic he'd used to select the members of his band.

Viewed from another angle, Verlaine hadn't had his name on anything significant in years, had never produced anything you could call a hit, and had a reputation for being headstrong and perverse. We discussed all kinds of hit producers whose work Jeff admired, from Steve Lillywhite and Butch Vig to Brian Eno, and I lobbied for the return of Andy Wallace, but Jeff wasn't interested.

Steve Berkowitz was taken aback. "Jeff and I did not see eye to eye on [Verlaine], though I did not try to dissuade him; that was not my job. My job was to ask the questions. When Jeff mentioned Verlaine, I said, 'Oh, what a great idea, Tom and all his sounds and ability to play guitar and create sonic structures—he'll be great on the record,' and Jeff said, 'No, I want him to produce it.' And I said, 'Based on what? What Television did is not what you do.' I had only respect for Tom, but I didn't understand how he'd be the producer for Jeff.

"Before they went to Sag Harbor, Jeff had sent me cassettes, one of them called *Globulous* and the other *Son of Globulous*. I don't know what that meant, but it was him playing solo and telling jokes, recorded gospel radio shows, and some of the beginnings of the songs that would have been on *My Sweetheart the Drunk*. My point is that the guy was actually a composer; he wasn't a singer-songwriter. He needed to work out the entire symphony and that takes a long time, especially with all the choices and the musicality that he had. You don't just come up with what you think and write it down."

---

64 "Wander I Go" was later added to a Patti Smith compilation album, *Land 1975–2002*.

I agree, but we hadn't worked that out then; we wanted songs that were ready to cut. There was the new material they'd tried live in Australia and one or two other demos that Jeff had made, but he seemed about to go into recording his second album with even less material than he had when starting *Grace*. Jeff had declared that his days of doing cover versions were over; he wanted it to be all original material, so that option wasn't available. There was one other problem: no Matt Johnson. No songs, no drummer, and a producer without any hits didn't feel like a great way to start, but I'd seen Jeff pull greatness out of an empty bag before, so...

I made the budget as tight as I could, with Verlaine being paid a flat fee. I figured on enough time and money to get down four songs and see how they went. Berkowitz booked Verlaine's chosen venue, Sorcerer Studios in New York, from June 15, 1996 and we held our breath.

Verlaine thought he was going to hear four songs that were ready to roll and simply record a band who had rehearsed the material, but the band couldn't play together. Verlaine became exasperated at the lack of direction he was being given by Jeff about how he wanted it to sound, and the producer's irritation affected the band's performances. It was quickly apparent that Eric Eidel wasn't the guy to replace Matt Johnson. Somehow they managed to get down versions of "Sky Is a Landfill," a song that Jeff had been tinkering with for a while; "Vancouver," the instrumental they'd been playing on tour for about a year, now with a wistful topline added; and Jeff's ballad, "Morning Theft." Then Jeff did a solo turn for "You and I."

The results weren't disastrous but fell some way south of the magic of *Grace* and had nowhere near the explosive power Jeff had been talking about. It had been suggested that we might release this session as an interim EP, but it was obvious it wasn't up to snuff, merely a step on the way somewhere, destination still undecided. The conclusion was that the band should go away and work on the material and do some more with Verlaine later in the year.

I was disappointed. I thought we'd have something ready for Christmas, but this was going to take time. Jeff seemed despondent too. He became quiet and insular around this time, looking like some refugee from *Crime & Punishment*—long coat, long hair, and a goatee—and not being his usual upbeat self. He'd call up with some paranoid thought about someone at Sony or one of the team and have to be talked down. Then he told me he'd started a new regime of getting up around 7 a.m. each day and running in Central Park. He'd work on songs after his run and then the band would rehearse in the afternoons. It seemed to work, because by the end of July he had a list of sixteen songs proposed for the next sessions. The new titles included "Skyblue Skin," "Demon John," "Murder Suicide Meteor Slave," "Haven't You Heard," and "Ever Since Then."[65]

In September, Berkowitz and Jeff went to look at Easley-McCain Studios in Memphis, which had been talked up by his friends Dave and Tammy Shouse of The Grifters. Jeff admired their album *Crappin' You Negative*, which had been recorded there, as had stuff by The Breeders and Sonic Youth. They enthused to Jeff about the relaxed atmosphere and the cheap but comprehensive facilities.

The reconnaissance mission went well, and Jeff decided that this was where the next sessions with Verlaine would take place. Though the studio was inexpensive compared to New York prices, there'd be the added costs of putting the band and producer in hotels for several weeks, so the budget started to climb. Berkowitz wanted to hear some of this new material before committing, so we booked Sony Studios in September to run through everything that Jeff had prepared. But Jeff's habit of keeping everyone in the dark about new material meant that the band struggled to keep up, especially poor Eric, who still wasn't working out and was, like many of us, clashing with Mick by this point, who seemed to spend the time he wasn't being standoffish being dissatisfied with everything. The atmosphere was not conducive to good work, and the sessions barely gave Berkowitz a chance to assess the material.

The plan to de-camp to Memphis was put on hold while we solved the drummer problem. Jeff was starting to have doubts about the band

[65] There's a bootleg, easily available online, called *Rarities From NYC*, which pulls together demos from different times and sources. One particularly interesting track is called "River of Dope." The recording is Jeff singing quietly to himself and tapping to keep time, almost like a voice memo, and it's a well-written gospel- blues about the temptations of drugs; particularly poignant as the central metaphor is a river, one that recurs, chillingly, in so many of Jeff's songs. Maybe his earlier declaration that he would keep the blues for his own private consumption stopped him from taking this promising sketch any further.

as a whole. On October 1, he wrote in his journal that he was "going to lay off the band." He wanted to keep Michael, who was still a good friend and ally, but "Mickey—I can't work with that anymore...His songs? I can't sing 'em. His bass playing is *really good* when he's happy—but for him it's about control, not music, not flow. I can't sit alongside that...I need a heavy man on the bass [and] the drums in my life. Eric is not right. I am not right. I need to go away."[66]

Leaving New York was suddenly very appealing. The Lower East Side was changing. It was full of fans, for one thing, so it had become less pleasant for Jeff to hang out in his usual haunts, as word had gotten around where to find him. Sin-é had shut down, so Jeff drifted uptown to West 51st Street, where two of his friends had opened the Daydream Cafe. He spent his thirtieth birthday on November 17 there with Joan. They had planned to see Soundgarden play, but the show was canceled, so they went to the Daydream and danced to the jukebox instead.

Considering his misgivings about Mickey by this point, it was odd that Jeff would listen to yet another staffing suggestion from him, but once again, Parker Kindred was someone Mick knew who was looking for a gig and, after a series of auditions, he was asked to join the band. I was mortified. As a former drummer, I took pride in my meter. Parker was apparently listening to what we used to call the "Jell-o metronome," some weird shifting sense of time that drove me nuts. His main influences were jazz drummers. But he was a nice guy and brought a more cheerful, outgoing atmosphere into the room with him, so that was a start. Jeff seemed to be happy with his bandmates again.

All our plans were nearly thwarted in late October when Jeff was out driving with Inger Lorre after recording some demos for her and was spotted chugging a beer in the car by a cop, who then pulled them over and busted Jeff for possession of enough marijuana to get a mouse high. An hour late for the court hearing, Jeff was lectured by the judge but, after pleading guilty, was let off as long as he wasn't arrested again within six months.

---

[66] Quoted in David Browne, *Dream Brother: The Lives and Music of Jeff and Tim Buckley* (New York: HarperCollins, 2001), 295.

The Memphis session was finally booked for February 1997. Jeff decided he wanted to get a feel for the songs in his own head before laying them onto tape, so we hastily booked a short tour, rather like the first shows Jeff and I had done together, but this time with Jack Bookbinder or Gene Bowen accompanying him. The tour was to be called On the Road...in a Car, With a Guitar and a Couple of People, but has become known as the Phantom Tour because it was booked under a series of silly band pseudonyms: A Puppet Show Named Julio, Possessed by Elves, Smackrobiotic, Topless America, Father Demo and the Crackrobats. Actually, the sets had just two or three new songs each night, but those gigs helped Jeff remind himself what he was best at. Looking back, I feel for him. He didn't react to pressure well at the best of times and this must have been a testing period, trying to hold on to his self-belief while being questioned from all sides—management, band, label, fans—about what he was brewing: "What have you got for us, Jeff?!"

Arriving in Memphis on February 11, Jeff and the band checked into the Claridge Hotel. Easley-McCain was in a quiet cul-de-sac in southeast Memphis. It was a mellow place. The lobby was decorated with folk art, and its owner, Doug Easley, who'd run a studio with his name on it since the early '70s, was an easygoing soul who believed in the musical mystique of his home city and kept his studio proudly old-school and non-digital.

Once tape was rolling, however, things weren't that much better than in New York. Verlaine was used to getting something useful down within a few takes, but theses tunes obviously needed more work on the arrangements. Parker and Mick weren't locking as a rhythm section, and everything sounded oddly uninspired. Worse, somehow, than being completely shit, it just sounded okay. Out of nowhere, Jeff plucked one gem, "Everybody Here Wants You," which had the potential to groove like a Smokey Robinson song, and which everyone agreed was one of the best things to emerge from these sessions. Verlaine's instruction to Parker to hit the snare as hard as he could meant it turned out exactly as asked—heavy-handed—but Jeff's vocal was exquisite, emotional without being as refined as the *Grace* performances, and his harmony embellishments were gorgeous. Mick played brilliantly too. When I first heard this song, I thought it was a massive hit in the making, but only

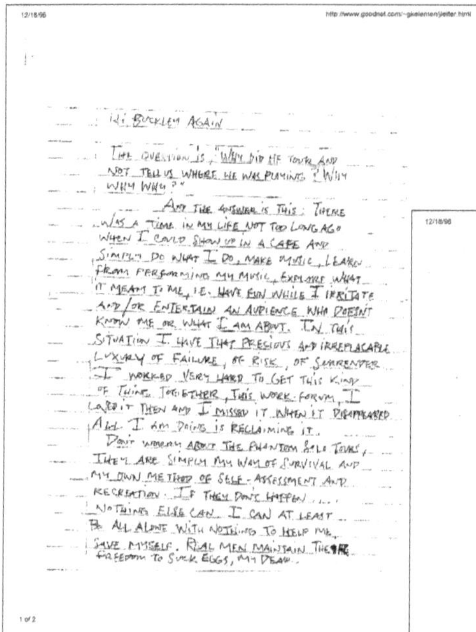

12/18/96 http://www.goodnet.com/~gkeleman/jletter.html

HI BUCKLEY AGAIN

THE QUESTION IS, "WHY DID HE TOUR AND NOT TELL US WHERE HE WAS PLAYING? WHY WHY WHY?"

AND THE ANSWER IS THIS: THERE WAS A TIME IN MY LIFE NOT TOO LONG AGO WHEN I COULD SHOW UP IN A CAFE AND SIMPLY DO WHAT I DO, MAKE MUSIC, LEARN FROM PERFORMING MY MUSIC, EXPLORE WHAT IT MEANT TO ME, I.E. HAVE FUN WHILE I IRRITATE AND/OR ENTERTAIN AN AUDIENCE WHO DOESN'T KNOW ME OR WHAT I AM ABOUT. IN THIS SITUATION I HAVE THAT PRECIOUS AND IRREPLACABLE LUXURY OF FAILURE, OF RISK, OF SURRENDER. I WORKED VERY HARD TO GET THIS KIND OF THING TOGETHER, THIS WORK FORUM, I LOVED IT THEN AND I MISSED IT WHEN IT DISAPPEARED. ALL I AM DOING IS RECLAIMING IT.

DON'T WORRY ABOUT THE PHANTOM SOLO TOURS, THEY ARE SIMPLY MY WAY OF SURVIVAL AND MY OWN METHOD OF SELF-ASSESSMENT AND RECREATION. IF THEY DON'T HAPPEN ... NOTHING ELSE CAN. I CAN AT LEAST BE ALL ALONE WITH NOTHING TO HELP ME SAVE MYSELF. REAL MEN MAINTAIN THE FREEDOM TO SUCK EGGS, MY DEAR.

1 of 2

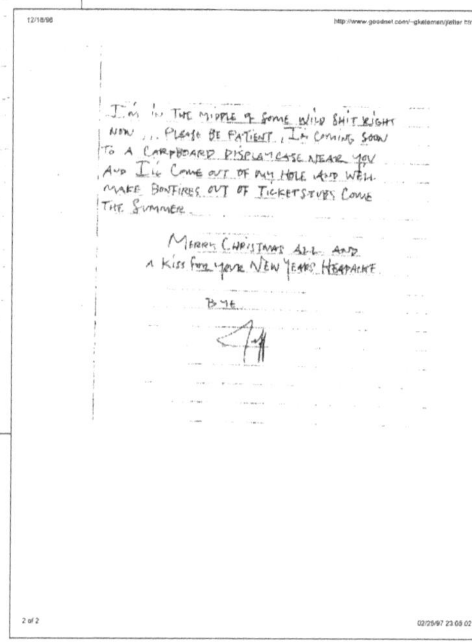

12/18/96 http://www.goodnet.com/~gkeleman/jletter.html

I'M IN THE MIDDLE OF SOME WILD SHIT RIGHT NOW ... PLEASE BE PATIENT, I'M COMING SOON TO A CARDBOARD DISPLAY CASE NEAR YOU AND I'LL COME OUT OF MY HOLE AND WE'LL MAKE BONFIRES OUT OF TICKET STUBS COME THE SUMMER.

MERRY CHRISTMAS ALL AND A KISS FOR YOUR NEW YEARS HEADACHE

BYE

Jeff

2 of 2 02/25/97 23:08:02

A letter from Jeff to his fan club about his "Phantom" solo tour in 1996.

in the making. There was still a way to go on it, and that was the general feel of these recordings: a kind of flatness that was the complete opposite of what Jeff usually delivered.

"Nightmares by the Sea," with its spongy Nirvana-like guitar riff and sinewy tune, came close to being great. "Witches' Rave" was good but the chorus line—"I can't help from looking outside for a guarantee"—though I knew what he was driving at, seemed a bit obscure. What surprised me the most was how mellow all the songs sounded. The guitars were very restrained, with none of the "scary" stuff Jeff had been promising. Yet as I hear everything now, I can't help thinking there was a lovely album taking shape. Maybe a simpler, gentler record was being born while we were expecting the opposite. Kept tight and minimal, something like "New Year's Prayer" could have been the centerpiece to a quietly mesmerizing record.

In late March, Berkowitz and I went to Memphis to hear what was happening, and Jeff, obviously nervous about being judged, didn't show up.

Steve Berkowitz: "We arrange to go to Easley Studios and they'll play us everything they've done: 'Be there at noon.' And I'm there at noon, and one and two and three—Verlaine and Parker and the other guys are there—and we're all waiting hours for Jeff, and eventually Verlaine says, 'Well, I may as well play you the stuff.' And so we're listening, and Jeff walks in and, 'Oh my god!' It's like we've been caught! 'Oh, you played the tapes?' And he's kinda pissed off, in an emotional state for one reason or another. Furious at me. 'But I'm the A&R guy. They're playing me the tapes; that's what I'm supposed to be here for. It's not my fault you're four hours late for a session.' He's *very* emotional. I put my arm around him and say, 'Let's go for a walk.' And we go for a walk and there's lots of tears, and I say, 'You're not ready; the songs aren't done yet, right? You're rushing faster than you want to go? Let's not do that.'"

There was another issue. Jeff was anxious about "Yard of Blonde Girls," a song written by Audrey Clarke, Lori Kramer, and Inger Lorre. It was the only cover he was cutting, and it had turned out pretty good. It had a bunch of hooks; it was obviously catchy. Jeff, in his newly paranoid manner, was concerned that we might seize on it and declare it was the first single—run back to Columbia with it, cackling gleefully. He'd asked Verlaine not to play it to us. But while we were waiting for him to show up, Berkowitz had spotted it on one of the tape logs and asked to hear it. It was playing when Jeff arrived.

I had a long talk with Jeff myself. I told him we were shutting down the session. He and Verlaine could tidy up what they'd done, but the band would be flying back to New York. This was the first time I had not backed Jeff unconditionally; he wanted to carry on, and I knew there wasn't any point. I also tried to pump him up emotionally and to take the pressure off him. "Do what you do; write the record and we can begin again whenever the songs are ready, no problem. One thing, you should call Mattie and ask him to play on the record. It would make things so much easier."

Berkowitz said he'd call Donnie and tell him we weren't ready, but not to worry.

"Jeff was coming to the point of realizing that he was kind of ahead of himself; he wasn't really finished," recalls Berkowitz. "He didn't like the end result, saw that maybe Tom actually wasn't the right choice, but he couldn't say that because he was very loyal or stubborn or he'd spent the money and didn't want to admit it was not ready. I wasn't holding him responsible for any of the decisions—no one had done anything wrong. It was a process for him, and I wanted him to get as creative as the first time and have all the bells and whistles go off in his head, because that's what we needed to get to."

I got back to the Peabody Hotel in time to see their daily ritual: at 5 p.m. on the dot, a bunch of ducks would waddle through the lobby and out the back doors, while tourists snapped pictures. All that and Elvis too. Memphis is one hell of a town.

In the days when he and Verlaine were alone in the studio, Jeff worked on "Opened Once," and also got The Grifters in to re-play some backing tracks. Verlaine thought Jeff was better without his band. Jeff confided in him about his experiments with heroin the previous year and told him it had scared him. At the Grid Iron coffeeshop near the Claridge Hotel on their last morning together, Verlaine said, "You're not happy with any of this, are you?" meaning the recordings they'd made. Jeff absolved Verlaine of any blame and added, "I know what I have to do now." Verlaine said that if Jeff was unhappy with the tapes, he should erase them, in case Sony had other ideas.[67]

Jeff had made up his mind that he was going to stay in Memphis to finish his writing. The Shouses knew a local landlord who had somewhere to rent, a little house at 91 North Rembert Street. Jeff went to see it. It was basic, a front room and bedroom divided by a kitchen and a small bathroom, and there was barely any furniture, but it was cheap and there was a phone to connect to the outside world if he so chose. Jeff decided this would be his new home until the album was done.

He had a small green velvet sofa, a single bed, and a couple of chairs, and a milk crate to stand his boombox on. He'd discovered Saigon Le,

[67] Browne, *Dream Brother*, 316

a Vietnamese place nearby that he could get takeout from. He had a bicycle. He was pretty much set. He started to go regularly to a nondescript looking basement bar, Barristers, to play solo, just as he had at Sin-é. He booked himself in for Mondays, their quietest night of the week, and he'd show up and sing whatever took his fancy, just as he always had, including whatever songs he was working on during the day. He liked that almost no one knew who he was, although word started to get around that the guy on Monday night was really good, and Barristers began to fill with new fans. Occasionally, an existing fan who'd heard Jeff was in town would drop by and be taken aback by the casual way these shows went down, but that was the way Jeff liked it.

The work started to flow. Joan would visit each month for a few days, and she watched Jeff relaxing into the place. He'd asked his landlady if he could let the grass grow in the front yard. In waist-high grass he could lie down and think, day or night, and on her visits Joan would join him there. He'd also discovered the attic space above the little house and had set some Santeria candles—little human-shaped candles that you find in Caribbean religious stores—up there for when he would meditate or write.

His only recording equipment was a temperamental secondhand Tascam four-track tape machine that he'd picked up in the local Tandy. He was monitoring everything on headphones until Joan pointed out that he should probably buy some secondhand speakers too. He rigged a pair up and played Joan his demos, delighted at the sounds filling the room, at last hearing his new work in a space that wasn't just his head.

The house was just a few streets away from the Memphis Zoo, which became a regular haunt for Jeff. Tammy Shouse recalls his becoming fixated on the butterfly house. He thought it wasn't being kept properly, so he insisted on applying for the job of butterfly keeper. "Jeff took a shower and got all spruced up. He put on his vintage suit, and he was all shiny and went in to put in his application. He wanted a normal-guy life."[68]

Jeff was facing a curious situation. Away from the touring life and the craziness of Manhattan, he appeared to sober up and relax, but now

[68] Charlie Moss, "I'm Only Here for This Moment," *Mojo*, June 2, 2017.

that there was nothing to do but create, his mind started to race. Tammy Shouse described how Memphis allowed Jeff to slow down physically but speed up mentally: "On the one hand he was *more* erratic, but in another way grounded."[69] That frantic mind that was teeming with all the music he'd ever heard and all the music he'd never make was churning out ideas for the new record, some of them decidedly strange.

Tapes started to arrive in New York for me, Berkowitz, and the members of the band: Jeff and his four-track, just a voice and guitars, sometimes drumming on boxes. Some of the songs were odd compared to the elegance of the *Grace* material, but there was an intensity to them that had been missing from all the earlier sessions.

"I found out after he died that he would make different versions of the songs for different people," says Berkowitz, "because Parker and I compared what each other had been sent and thought, 'That's funny, he sent the deeper, darker, heavier stuff to the record company guy and the prettier stuff to the drummer.' He's brought these songs further along, he's got his pedals together, he's writing a big *Sgt. Pepper*–sized record, albeit in this very limited, early hip-hop style of production, and it could either stay like that or he could take it all Roy Thomas Baker, or make it an *Abbey Road*-style record with Andy, just like last time but now he's ready to develop to deliver the songs and the ideas."

In early May, Jeff returned briefly to New York to see to some business and pick up some of his stuff. He had arranged for Inger Lorre, distraught because her father had just died, to sublet his apartment on East 12th Street where, the previous Christmas, he'd painted the main wall a vivid lime green. Luckily, Inger didn't seem to mind. Having handed her the key, he called me and said he wanted to come over to Worldwide Plaza and bring me some stuff. Half an hour later, Angel called up.

"Mr. Buckley here to see you, Mr. Lory. He has many boxes with him. I will keep them in the storeroom."

The doorbell rang and Jeff was there, grinning away. He came in and gave Sam and me a hug—I don't know if he noticed the black rings of fatigue around our eyes—and then went straight to where Charlotte was playing and cooed over her for a while.

---

[69] Browne, *Dream Brother*, 326.

"Angel said you brought some boxes," I said.

"It's all the tapes and video from the last two years," he said. I'd held these before but had given them to him when the tour ended in case he wanted to review any of them. "I'd like you to look after them all while I'm in Memphis."

"Sure."

"Make sure Sony never gets hold of them."

"You got it," I said, wondering exactly what he meant by that.

"Wow, Charlotte sure looks like Sam now, doesn't she? Hasn't she gotten big?"

"Big enough to keep two adults on full alert 24/7," I said.

Jeff laughed as he bounced Charlotte up and down. She chuckled and looked like putty in his hands, like every other woman. I wonder now if he felt at all envious about the attention she was getting from me and Sam.

"So, man, it's great that Andy can do it, isn't it?" I said. We had finally convinced Jeff that Andy Wallace would be the best producer for the album. Luckily he was available.

"Yeah, the songs are all there. I just have to do my own thing to them."

"I still think you should get Mattie on the album," I said. "Parker's style isn't right for you. When Mattie left, all the groove went with him."

"Maybe you're right. I could always overdub the drums myself, if necessary."

"Yeah, but that's a bitch. You need a solid track down for everyone to play to. Give Mattie a call."

"I already did. He's gone underground; I haven't heard back yet."

"Well, if he calls, let me know straight away. I'll happily fly him down, and I can deal with Parker if you don't want to. And if Mickey kicks off about it, I can fire him too. You could definitely play all the bass parts."

"Yeah, sure."

"Has Andy seen the studio yet?"

"He's coming to have a look next week," he said.

"It's going to be a cool record, you know that," I said. "I loved the tapes. The songs are sounding great. There are hits! And hooks!"

We laughed. He'd written to his mailing list about how the new album would be stuffed with hooks. It was kind of a running gag, as it was completely counter to what he usually thought about.

"You know, Dave, I've been thinking. I'm not scared of being popular anymore." We'd discussed this a lot, the idea that there's pop music, ephemeral stuff designed solely to sell records, and then there's popular music: Miles Davis, Bob Dylan, Bruce Springsteen, The Clash, Nirvana—music with integrity that people buy because it moves them, not because it ticks boxes. That's where Jeff belonged, and I thought he should embrace that kind of popularity, not resist it.

"Well, that's good news," I said. "Ain't no shame in being good at your job!"

We shot the breeze a little more and then he hugged us both goodbye.

"Take care, dude," I said. "I'm off with Katell soon, and I'll see you when I get back. Call me anytime. Enjoy the sessions."

He walked out of the apartment. I never saw him again.

Once Jeff had got back to Memphis, Andy Wallace went down to check out the studio, and hung out with him for three or four days. "We spent a lot of time talking," he says. "I don't remember hearing what he'd done with Tom Verlaine at that point. He said the chemistry wasn't right. I don't think his intention was to throw out the material, but to record it again from the ground up. We went to the bar he was playing in to keep his chops up, Barristers, so I heard some of the songs there, and during our private conversations he took his guitar out and played a couple of things. I liked the songs, and I still really do. 'Everybody Here Wants You' is one of my all-time favorites. I didn't need to be sold on doing another record with him. He could have played me 'Happy Birthday' and I would have made a record with him.

"I went and saw Easley studios. It was a funky place—not a dump but down-home and clearly not a corporate environment, and I liked that. And a little on the dry side, acoustically, which I like. Jeff was enthusiastic about working there. I don't believe he got back in touch with me in the hope that we could make *Grace 2*. He wanted it to be different, to move on."

The band would fly in on May 29 and Andy would return a few weeks later to start on pre-production. We had spent a ton of cash already, so we decided that instead of hotels, the band should stay at North Rembert Street. Back in Sag Harbor, there had been endless complaints from the neighbors about noise, so I drew up budgets including a sum for soundproofing material to line the attic or wherever they'd be playing in the house. In the end, though, we decided that a constantly available rehearsal space would be best, somewhere the band could go anytime, day or night.

Before the band arrived, Gene Bowen had to pick up their gear from our storage place and make the fifteen-hour drive from New York. He had hired his friend, Keith Foti, a twenty-three-year-old hairdresser from New York who was also an aspiring musician, to help him haul the gear, set it up at the studio, and run errands while in Memphis. Foti had done something similar a few months earlier and had met Jeff then. He was short and stocky with bright blue punky hair and a wide face, with a young man's energy and enthusiasm. His modest luggage included his own boombox—a cheap little RCA double cassette player—and an acoustic guitar. Gene had brought some linens and found a company that would deliver rental mattresses on Thursday evening, just before the band's flight touched down.

I was flying to Dublin for the launch of Katell Keineg's second album, *Jet*. She had worked hard on the record, and it was vital that the launch went smoothly to give Elektra the kick-start they obviously needed to give her a chance at success. They'd screwed up the first album, and I'd been trying to get to the bottom of the problem in the months I'd been working with her. At Sony, as soon as the button was pressed, everyone knew their job and got on with it. The setup at Elektra's parent company, Warner Brothers, seemed more haphazard, much less tightly structured, so there was more onus on me to map out a route through the company and make sure we had all the vital people on our side. Hopefully, by the time Katell was underway, Jeff's album would be done and I could focus on whatever he needed.

I was pleased that Gene Bowen was taking care of things. However, perhaps because I was overseas, Gene didn't keep me fully abreast of some strange stuff that was starting to occur. Jeff had just been for his interview at the butterfly house, which was weird in itself, and now was starting to fixate on a rusting car hulk with no wheels that he'd seen next to a local garage, saying it could sit in the front yard and that his stepfather, Ron, could fix it up. This may be because it was on the hood of this car that Jeff had sat and proposed to Joan Wasser a few weeks earlier. The garage owner told him repeatedly it wasn't for sale, but Jeff didn't seem to hear him. Similarly, he kept talking about buying the house he was renting. He'd even contacted Victor, his accountant, about these purchases, and Victor was concerned when he heard from the owners that neither item was for sale. Thinking about it now, I find these attempts by Jeff to settle somewhere totally heartbreaking.

One evening Gene came back to the house at midnight to find Jeff lying in a cold bath, so absorbed in writing in his journal that he had chewed through his pen, and red ink was trickling down his chin into the bathwater like blood. Gene's first survey of the scene, before he realized what he was looking at, had startled him. Jeff didn't seem to care.

Jeff had spent a lot of time on the phone in the past couple of weeks. Many of his friends would later mention these unexpected, long, strange calls on which Jeff would sing to them for ages or ramble on semi-coherently. Chris Dowd called him once, and Jeff didn't recognize his voice. He'd been going to friends' houses in Memphis and, once they'd gone to bed, sitting up by himself all night watching TV and returning home without any sleep.

The day before the band was due to arrive, Jeff and Foti locked themselves out of the rehearsal studio. While they waited for Gene to come and pick them up, Jeff started screaming incoherently and clambering up the chain-link fencing—Foti thought he might have been scream-singing a song—until people came out of doorways telling him to shut up.

The next morning, Jeff wandered aimlessly around the Piggly Wiggly supermarket piling up goods and placing them in front of Foti, before putting them all back on the shelves again and keeping only a bag of dog biscuits. Individually, these eccentric moments weren't cause for concern, but taken together they do look like something was happening to Jeff. Gene apparently asked Tammy Shouse if she knew of a local psychologist Jeff could visit. But he didn't tell me about it.

On the morning of May 29, before his abortive shopping spree at the Piggly Wiggly, Jeff called Joan excitedly to tell her that he had realized he had manic-depressive tendencies.[70] If his mood swings had become so pronounced that he was starting to see a pattern, this would suggest those last weeks had been a strain on him. Joan said he sounded peaceful that morning, having finally come to a conclusion about himself.

At around 7:30 p.m., Jeff and Foti hatched a plan to go back to the rehearsal studio and fool around on the two drum sets they'd put up. Foti also had his guitar with him and fancied playing his new friend some of his work in progress.

Jeff appeared in his standard baggy black pants, some cheap black boots he'd bought at Kmart with Joan, and a white T-shirt with long black sleeves that had "Altamont" written on the front and the image of two crossed rifles.[71] Although it had been a muggy spring day, Jeff also took a jacket with him. Foti was wearing blue-and-green wave-patterned pants that offset his blue hair. Gene couldn't go with them because he was waiting for the mattresses he'd ordered, and after that he would be picking up the band from the airport. Gene told them to make sure they were back around 9:30 p.m., when he would be getting back with the others. He asked if they knew where they were going. "Yeah, sure," said Jeff, and they took Foti's cassette player and guitar, went out the door, and drove off in the yellow Ryder rental van Gene had driven down in.

Despite having been to the rehearsal studio at 2263 Young Avenue in Midtown the day before, neither occupant of the van could have been paying much attention to the route there, roughly an eight-minute drive from North Rembert Street. Although they were having a good time singing along to Foti's boombox, they soon realized they weren't seeing the red brick studio building anywhere. Once they'd decided they were lost, they found a payphone and tried to call Gene, but he had already left for the airport. Jeff knew that the owner of Barristers could give them directions to the studio. There was no answer when they called, so he suggested they drive to the bar—which he did know how to get to—although it was some way uptown. When they got there and banged on the anonymous black steel door, it was obvious the place was closed.

70 Browne, *Dream Brother*, 330.

71 Altamont, a speedway track near San Francisco, was the site of a disastrous free show staged by the Rolling Stones at which Hells Angels, hired as security staff, beat a member of the audience to death. But it is also a clothing brand known for its surf wear.

However, someone had thrown out a semi-circular diner's booth upholstered in orange Naugahyde, which Jeff thought would be a perfect addition to his paltry furnishings at home—somewhere for the band to sit, at least. He and Foti hauled it into the rental van. Jeff suggested going for ribs. Foti wasn't hungry but said he'd accompany Jeff somewhere. It was nearly 9 p.m. by this point; the best idea would have been: "Fuck it. Let's go home, order some takeout, unload this booth, and wait for the guys." But Jeff had another idea: "Why don't we go to the river?"[72]

The "river" was actually a small, slack water harbor created in 1960 when the long Wolf River's entrance to the Mississippi was dammed and re-routed. The resulting dog leg off the main Mississippi was called Wolf River Harbor, an inlet with a marina between the Memphis mainland and Mud Island,[73] the site of an amphitheater—a venue I'd been to many times with bands over the years—and the Mud Island River Park, a popular tourist destination accessible by a monorail, and then, farther up the island, its own district, Harbor Town.

When they parked at the Tennessee Welcome Center, a tourist information office just off Riverside Drive, it was just after 9 p.m. The sunlight was almost gone; the murky stretch of water under the monorail bridge didn't look particularly picturesque. Foti, carrying his guitar and the boombox, assumed they were going to chill out, play some songs, maybe throw some stones in the water before heading home. But Jeff was now in a gleeful mood. He pranced down the slope from the road, keys and chain jangling in his pocket. Halfway down, he just shed his jacket and then, turning to face Foti, walked backward into the water until it was up to his knees.

"What are you doing?" Foti asked. Jeff crouched down in the water and started doing the backstroke.[74] Foti thought it was weird but had already pegged Jeff as impulsive in the short time he had known him, so he didn't question it any further.[75] He had thought about playing Jeff one

[72] In an interview with Kevin Birsch in *The Black Book* in 1998, Parker Kindred said: "Foti had those aqua pants on, kind of trippy, kind of waving. I can just imagine Jeff looking at those pants and going, 'I want to go for a swim.'"

[73] Actually not an island but a peninsula.

[74] Joan Wasser told Charlie Moss of *Mojo* magazine that it was she who had taught Jeff to do the backstroke, and that otherwise he could barely swim.

[75] Jeff had actually swum in the harbor before. He'd told friends it was "refreshing."

of his songs on the guitar, but this didn't feel like the right moment, so he switched on the cassette player while they chatted and then, still floating on his back, Jeff started singing along to the music.

The marina was where houseboats, yachts, dinghies, and other craft would dock for Mud Island. The locals were aware that this was not a prime spot for swimming—indeed it was illegal, although there were no warning signs placed there at the time. Apart from the water traffic, it was extremely weedy and muddy, had a tendency to smell bad, and was deceptively active with undercurrents. In other words, this apparently calm stretch of water was dirty, unpredictable, and dangerous.

Jeff had been in the water a few minutes when a couple of small boats approached. Foti called to him to get out of the water. Instead of coming in to avoid the vessels, Jeff swam farther toward Mud Island, singing along to Led Zeppelin's "Whole Lotta Love," his voice reflecting off the monorail bridge as he swam under it.

Shortly after the first boats passed, a larger vessel, possibly a tugboat, approached from the opposite direction. Foti called to Jeff to look out, saw the boat pass, then realized that the wash from the tugboat was threatening to reach his boombox. He turned around to move it and then, when he turned back, could no longer hear or see Jeff in the water. It was almost dark, and the shadow from the bridge made the area he'd last seen Jeff look even darker; it was hard to focus on the water. There was no sign of anyone in there. Foti called out. No answer. He shouted again, "Jeff, Jeff!" thinking maybe Jeff was playing a trick and would stick his head up above the water in a moment, laughing. Gordon Archibald, a worker at the marina, later told the Memphis police that he and another man, Randy Dupont, were walking by the marina at about this time when they both heard a single cry of "help," but didn't investigate because they thought it was some kids playing around.

After several minutes, Foti realized Jeff wasn't going to reappear, and he ran to the Welcome Center. There was a light on. Foti banged on the door until a member of the night staff answered and led him to a phone. It was around 9:30 p.m. when Foti called 911 and then, about half an hour later, got hold of Gene, who was just getting back to the house, as the band's flight had been slightly delayed. A Coast Guard search team was at the harbor by 10 p.m. Witness Archibald immediately helped the search with his workboat.

Memphis police sergeant Mary Johnson took a statement from Keith Foti, who told her that neither he nor Jeff had been drinking. Foti informed her that he'd been a member of Narcotics Anonymous for two years. She had this information corroborated by Gene Bowen, who said he had "been with the victim all day Wednesday until midnight and all day Thursday with no drinking or drugs taken."

As I write this, I keep thinking of him sitting in the rental van on that afternoon, going back to the house from the Piggly Wiggly with Foti, munching on a bag of dog biscuits. That pathetic image haunts me. There's something about it that is pure Jeff, carefree and screwy. What was he thinking that day, having called the woman he'd proposed to on the hood of that rusted, abandoned car with no wheels, and told her he was a manic-depressive? We all knew his mood swings, his ADHD ability to parrot entire albums, his extreme reactions to criticism or interference from figures of authority, his obsession with death and dying. I subsequently saw the manic way he wrote about his life in his diaries. I know Jeff had been seeing an analyst when he first came to New York, a Jamaican woman who died not long before he went to Memphis, so he was seeking help of some sort. I doubt he could have seen her much while he was touring. Was he on the brink of mental illness? The clues were in front of us: the eccentric episodes in the days before his death point to a mind that, if not actually unwell, certainly had the capacity to go wrong, sooner or later. I wonder if any kind of diagnosis would have saved him that day. Who knows? If only he'd had the presence of mind to ask a stranger for directions to the studio, pull into a gas station and buy a map, give up and go home—anything would have been better then what he did. Would an awareness that your mind was apt to run away with itself make you more careful, or make no difference? Making the record gave him a focus, but it also might have marked a return of the kind of pressure that upset him.

Every life—and every tragic death—is full of "what-ifs." I've been over Jeff's death thousands of times in my mind, wondering if we could have—should have—done anything differently. Of course we could have, but none of us could have predicted the one last risky, no-parachute move Jeff made that day, walking backward into forever, his mind full of music, lying back as if he were in the long grass in front of his new home.

CHAPTER 10

"Missing"

Friday, May 30, 1997

A PHONE IS RINGING. It isn't mine. Hotel phone. It's not my second wake-up call, so I ignore it. But I didn't order a wake-up call. So someone is calling me in the middle of the night. Where am I? Dublin. Is it Katell? It can't be. I saw her go to bed; she was fine. Is it Samantha—has something happened at home? It's still ringing. I'd better answer the fucking thing. I can hear rain. What time is it? Five fifty-eight a.m. I've been asleep for only four hours. This had better be good.

"Uh-huh."

"Dave?"

It's Jack...Someone's in jail or the hospital. Great.

"Dave, I'm at Kristen's. Gene has called me. He says it's urgent. He needs to talk to you. I'm gonna put Kristen's phone up to my phone. Okay, Gene, I've got Dave."

I can just about hear Gene. He's agitated, shouting so that I can hear him from five thousand miles away. There's a weird noise in the background that I can't make out, like motors running.

"Dave! It's Jeff. He's gone missing."

"What do you mean, 'He's gone missing?'" I work it out. One a.m. in Memphis. The band had flown in that evening. They were due to start rehearsing straight away. Jeff was late for the session. Really annoying, but he's always pulling that shit. He's just being Jeff. He wants to know everyone has missed him. He'll show up.

"He was swimming in the Mississippi. Two tugboats came along, and he went underwater. We can't find him."

Something has punched me in my stomach with all its force. I drop the phone.

"Dave? Dave?"

I pick up the phone again. "Shit, Gene, is this real? Am I having a bad dream?"

"It's real, Dave. There are helicopters shining searchlights on the river. There's a team dragging the water."

Helicopters. That was the sound I couldn't identify.

My brain doesn't know what to ask, but my mouth comes up with something.

"When did he go into the water?"

"Around nine o'clock," says Gene, his voice breaking. "Four hours ago."

"He's not coming out, is he?"

We share a silence. Into it rushes a sound like someone pounding on my hotel room door. It's blood racing around my head. I try not to pass out.

"Okay. Give me a minute, Gene," I say. "I'll call you back when I've worked out what to do, but call in the meantime if there's any development. And tell everyone there to say nothing. No press."

"Okay."

I put the phone down. It's like I've let go of a life raft at sea. Is my lung about to give out again? My guts are being tugged by something. Bereavement. My soul is being yanked, a slow-motion pulse of panic and confusion. How can this be? I am not prepared for this. What the fuck am I supposed to do?

These days you can at least research a situation online, but back then it wasn't an easy question to answer. No one had written a manual for managers dealing with the premature death of their rock star. I reel at the thought. I stare at the wall. There is a pattern in the wallpaper like an embossed ribbon. I look at it for what feels like an hour but is probably only thirty seconds, and I wonder what kind of machine embossed a string of ribbon and a little bow onto a thick sheet of paper. Would they use a metal drum with something etched into it? How far apart are those bows? They'd need a drum about six feet in diameter. And do they print the color at the same time as they do the embossing? How the fuck do they do that? I bet that's one loud factory...I jump as the imagined roar is sucked away to a dead silence. I look around me, shocked at how tranquil it is in this room, in this hotel, considering what has just happened. Shocked at how alone I am. Why aren't alarms ringing? Why aren't people hammering on the door? Is anyone coming to help me?

There is a soft click and a humming sound. The mini-bar has come on. It is the only sound in the world until I start to hear Jeff singing. The fear subsides and I get a rush of what I can only describe as privilege, a feeling of pride that I've known him. I think about the first playback of *Grace*, when we knew we were about to release something really special, knowing I was one of only a dozen people in the world who knew how incredible this record was. That was a major high. This is the opposite. I am one of only a dozen people in the world who know that Jeff Buckley, my artist, my friend, is missing. Presumed dead. On my watch. It is an overwhelming thought. My knees buckle and I sit heavily on the bed.

There is a bottle of Jack Daniel's on the bedside cabinet, and a dirty glass from my last nightcap. I pour a couple of shots and sink them in quick succession. I don't know where to start. Who do I tell? Who do I not tell? I have to think of some kind of strategy, an order of events. I stare at the wall some more and hope it will come to me. I notice cobwebs in the upper corner of the room.

Fuck, what has he done? Was he drunk? Was he high? Did he do it on purpose? Who else knows? Gene, Jack, the band...no one is going to tell the press, but the Memphis police will put out some kind of statement, sooner or later, if they're dragging the river. Will they say who Jeff was, or will it just be, "A white thirty-year-old male walked into the Wolf River this evening..." We don't want people who were close to him hearing this on the news before they hear it from us. What will the press say? What will the music press say? "Wow, it's just like his dad." Oh, Christ. Should I wake up Sam and tell her? She'll be heartbroken. She loves Jeff. I love Jeff. No, she and Charlotte need to rest. And what am I going to say to Katell? She'll fall apart, and it's the start of her tour and her album launch tonight. She loves Jeff. I loved Jeff. She needs me here. Shall I get on a plane to Memphis first? Do planes go to Memphis from Dublin at six in the morning? Can I get back in time for her show?

Nothing is connecting. The bed is stationary and the world is trying to revolve around it, all my questions coming in and zooming past at hundreds of miles per hour. Nothing makes sense; nothing is being answered. But then, slowly, statements start to align and pop out of that tornado of thought, like ripped-up road signs calmly detaching themselves from the twister and replacing themselves in the ground. A route starts to form before me.

I can't be in the air today. It is Friday. I need to be on the phone to Sony, to all our contacts, to everyone involved in the album, to the media. I have to be available before the weekend. I have to help Katell get through this, through tonight, but I can't do both, so I need to call someone to come and take care of her. The logical call is Sam, and also maybe Abbo, who know Katell well. Abbo and Sam between them can take care of business and promotional duties. If necessary, Sam can field calls about Jeff for me too.

Then I can fly to Memphis on Saturday. But while I'm in the air we'll probably need some kind of press release. And we need to set the agenda, dial back any speculation. We want to quell any sensationalism and comparisons with Tim, which Jeff would have hated.

I get a sudden pang of joy. What if he'd just walked out of the river, onto the other side, downstream somewhere, wandered dripping wet into a bar, and a girl said: "You need to get out of those wet things..."

I realize the fantasy is futile. He was about to cut his record, for Christ's sake. He'd been buzzing about it; he was hyped up, excited. Shit, that's what he was on: adrenaline. He was excited enough to walk fully clothed into a muddy river. Why would he ever think he wouldn't come out of it again? He's Jeff. Walking away from things and jumping into things is what he does. He never packs a parachute, a life jacket, or a guardian angel.

I call Katell. It is still early; I've woken her up.

I tell her the news as calmly as I can. Jeff is missing in the Mississippi River, and everyone is doing everything they can to find him...but even her just-conscious mind knows what this really means. She howls with pain, drops the phone, and I hear her screaming, "Nooooooo" and sobbing in the background. Because we are still connected, I can't hang up. So while she sobs, I run down to a payphone in the hotel lobby, call the house where her band is staying, tell them what has happened, and ask that they get over immediately to Katell's house, check that she's okay, put the phone back on the hook, and stay with her until I call.

My next calls are to Samantha and Abbo. I expect Sam to be shaken and emotional, but she detects the steel in my voice and she is rock solid, practical, going straight into business mode. Abbo is the same. They both agree to fly out to Dublin on the next possible plane from London. I ask Abbo to keep an eye on Sam too, as I know the news will impact her sooner or later. Katell needs as much support as possible, and I know she loves both of them. I don't feel like the emotionally reassuring presence she needs right now. I can feel myself becoming numb. Something else is kicking in. I have to protect my artist. We have to find him.

Next I call Howard Wuelfing, our publicist. I wake him at around 2:30 a.m., New York time, and ask him to go into the office and prepare a press statement. We need to issue something immediately. God bless him, he agrees. We are so lucky to have him on the team. Jeff and I trust him totally.

While I wait for Howard to get into Columbia from New Jersey, I call George Stein, Steve Berkowitz, Andy Wallace, the marketing people, agents and publishers, all the people heavily involved in Jeff's career who need to hear the news from me first. Nowadays you probably couldn't hold it back; someone would have tweeted about it from the riverbank.

I tell each of them, rather than request, what I need them to do. I tell George to be on the first flight to Memphis to handle all the legal stuff. I need Berkowitz on the ground in Memphis more than anyone else, because of his loyalty to Jeff and his management experience, to make sure no one does anything stupid before I get there on Saturday. To everyone's credit, they simply take it in and do what they have to do without question. I have to do it this way because time is critical, and I'm so thankful all of them are stepping up. I appreciate all of them and their unquestioning support.

More and more road signs are placing themselves in front of me. I feel like some kind of general planning for battle. I call the office and speak to Jack. He is a great organizer, so he works out the sequence of events that needs to unfold in New York and Memphis. One of the first things we have to do is move Inger Lorre from Jeff's apartment into a hotel so that we can secure all of Jeff's belongings. Though we trust Inger, we know there'll be vultures who'll come to pay their respects and help themselves to souvenirs, and we especially want to get all of Jeff's music into the office.[76] I ask Jack to book my flight to Memphis, the first flight out on Saturday morning with no return trip, and Samantha to Dublin from London. Then I ask him to brief our staff that when calls start coming in on Friday morning, they should just take messages and use the words: "We cannot comment at this time. I will have Dave call you back when he can." That is an absolute.

Finally, I ask him to call Mary, Jeff's mom, and have her meet me in Memphis. Jack is the only person who has ever talked to Mary when she's called the office. I met her once in LA, but Jeff had told me not to communicate with her or send her tour books, itineraries, or anything else related to him, and I kept my word. Now I have to deal with her, as she is the next of kin. Jeff hadn't made a will.

I am flooded with adrenaline. I've not even had a coffee yet. So I give myself a few minutes to have breakfast. Even though I have no appetite, I know I have to eat something. As soon as I put the phone down on room service, it rings again. It is Katell. She is in a bad way, asking question after question that I have no answers for. She keeps sobbing, "Please go and find him, Dave." It breaks my heart. I assure her I will, but I can't leave until tomorrow, as there is so much to organize first. I tell her I'll be at the show tonight, and that Samantha and Abbo are flying out to be with her.

"Dave, I don't want to do the show. Cancel the show. And the tour."

"You've worked so hard for this, Katell. We can't cancel. All the Elektra people will be arriving this afternoon; everything's in place to launch your record. The show has to go on. Try and rest and get yourself

[76] Actually, there were reports of Inger, already grief stricken from the recent loss of her father, tearfully handing out Jeff's clothes to passers-by on the street.

into show mode. The band will do everything they can to help you. I've got to go now."

As soon as I hang up, the phone rings again.

It's Howard. He is in place at Columbia and ready to draft a statement. We decide to state simply that Jeff is missing. But we don't want any Elvis sightings or conspiracy theories. Howard's boss, Larry Jenkins, will open a hotline to the Memphis police so that he hears of any developments before the local media. A lot of people will be hearing about Jeff for the first time with this news; we don't want their first impression of him tainted by his father's fate. This was just an awful accident, unrelated to drugs or alcohol, according to Gene's statement to the Memphis police. Although neither of us knows for certain what Jeff had been up to that day, we tell the press that, whatever the truth, we will let them have it as soon as we know it, as long as they don't run any rumors or compare this to Tim Buckley's death from a drug overdose. These are contacts Howard, Larry, and I have spent many years cultivating; we cannot lie to them when the facts do emerge, so we roll the dice for Jeff.

Howard is to tell everyone on the Columbia team that it is a flat "no comment," whoever asks. Management must be in control of any information that goes public. I won't be attributed; I will be "an official spokesperson." This is all about Jeff; no one else's name needs to get in the way. I have to protect my guy at all costs.

Something at the back of my mind won't stop screaming, "Why Jeff, why? How could you do this?" I feel like a parent feels watching his or her child run across a busy street without looking: horror, dismay, guilt, anger, and that recurring thought, "All those times we talked about crossing the street! Were you even listening?"

I get word that Sam and Abbo have landed in Dublin and are on their way to the hotel. I grab a quick shower and then rush down to the lobby to meet them. I am so relieved to see people I love. So happy they are safe. As soon as I see them, the tears start to come. It is the first chance I've had to consider what is really happening. In the middle of the hotel lobby, I hold my wife and weep.

• • • • •

We all go to Katell's apartment.

She is still in her robe, and her eyes are puffy from six hours of tears. She doesn't want to do the show. She is overcome with grief. It doesn't help that her single is called "One Hell of a Life." It is being played on Irish radio, and she will have to perform it tonight. As gently as we can, we speak about the importance of the show. We cannot give Elektra any reason to get cold feet at this late stage. This is her shot. We tell her Jeff would have wanted her to perform. Gradually, she realizes what she has to do. By that time she is due at her sound check, so we all go together. It's nice to be able to focus on some music, but I'm not focusing much; my mind is still thousands of miles away in Memphis.

Samantha is the only person with a mobile phone, so that becomes our hotline. It is around 10 a.m. in New York by now, and more calls start coming in as Sony employees get to their desks. Everyone is amazing, asking what they can do to help, pulling in one direction. I am stunned by all the messages of support I receive from staff around the world who have been touched by Jeff's music or have met and worked with him for a few days, or even just a few hours. They are all worried, upset, and incredulous. One of the sweetest calls is from Denis Handlin of Sony Australia, who is worried about me and my family; he even offers to fly us out for a vacation once we get through it. It is comforting but strange to have so much emotion directed toward me, but I suspect if I didn't hear this, I would crumble completely. I am still in the eye of the tornado; if I let my concentration slip for even a second, I feel as if I'll be swept away. My head is spinning again. One thing is clear: the longer we go on without any news, the less chance there is of finding Jeff alive. I'm still clutching on to some hope.

• • • • •

With a whole lot of Irish and some British media in attendance, Katell's performance is nervy, distracted, obviously below par. The band sounds great, but Katell, usually funny, talkative, and engaging onstage, is on the brink of tears all the way through her set. Abbo and I gently explain the situation to as many journalists as we can. (It seemed to work; they mostly wrote about how gutsy she had been and how good the album was.) After the show, I let myself go off-duty and throw back a few JDs. I need to escape this awful day, and booze is my way of doing it.

Samantha has to assist me back to the hotel. As I weave toward the front desk, I summon enough smarts to ask them to block all calls to my room unless they are from Gene Bowen or Jack Bookbinder. I need a few hours' sleep before flying to Memphis, but despite my deep exhaustion after the longest day of my life, I can't sleep. I finally pass out with the assistance of Mr. Daniels.

I pay for it the following morning, however. Dublin to Memphis with a jackhammer hangover is not recommended. My flight is at 6 a.m. I watch all the passengers buzzing around me and crave their normality. None of them realize what I am dealing with. The newsstands are full of Jeff's disappearance. The TV news shows Bono stopping U2's show at Meadowlands with a version of "Hallelujah." The huge crowd pays silent tribute. It is beautiful, but it doesn't make things any easier.

When I finally arrive in Memphis, I pick up a local paper and see that the Elvis sightings have already begun. The story, on the front page, is full of "Is he or isn't he?" speculation, implying that this might be some elaborate stunt. I need to nip this shit in the bud. I call Howard in New York and we discuss making an official announcement that Jeff is dead. It has been over thirty hours since he went into the water, and the chances of him being found alive are impossibly small. It is easier to do it now, in the comparative quiet of the weekend, when we aren't dealing with a busy Monday-morning news cycle. Howard drafts the release while I make my way to the hotel.

When I arrive, George, Gene, Berkowitz, and Jeff's mother, Mary are waiting for me. I tell them what we are doing and ask Mary to give me a quotation. No one else on the team will be quoted. Dated Monday, June 2, the release is issued with the headline "Jeff Buckley Still Missing as Search Continues; Family and Friends Believe He Has Drowned."

> *Jeff Buckley is still missing after swimming in a Memphis, Tennessee, marina at approximately 9 p.m. last Thursday. An extensive search of the area began at 10 p.m. that night and has continued, with Memphis authorities utilizing boats, horse and foot patrols, helicopters, and scuba divers in an attempt to locate Jeff. While Jeff is still officially listed as missing, his family, close friends, and advisors believe that he has drowned. He was thirty years old.*

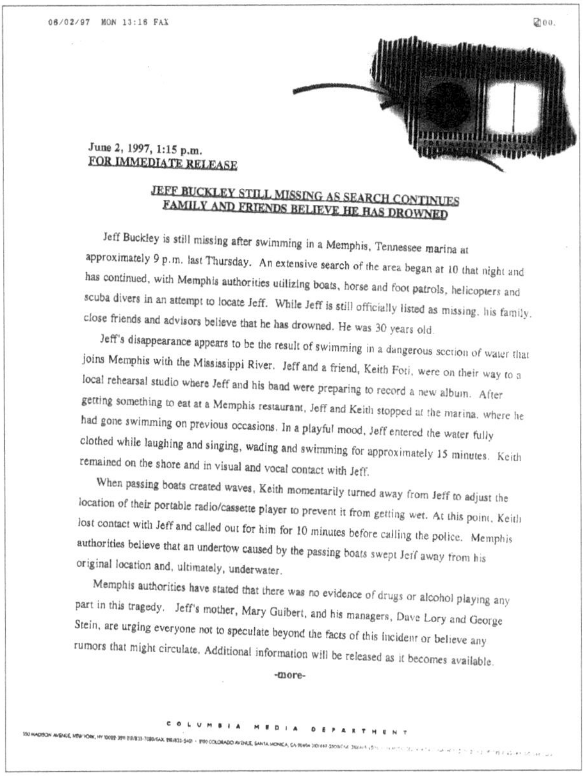

06/02/97 MON 13:16 FAX

June 2, 1997, 1:15 p.m.
FOR IMMEDIATE RELEASE

JEFF BUCKLEY STILL MISSING AS SEARCH CONTINUES
FAMILY AND FRIENDS BELIEVE HE HAS DROWNED

Jeff Buckley is still missing after swimming in a Memphis, Tennessee marina at approximately 9 p.m. last Thursday. An extensive search of the area began at 10 that night and has continued, with Memphis authorities utilizing boats, horse and foot patrols, helicopters and scuba divers in an attempt to locate Jeff. While Jeff is still officially listed as missing, his family, close friends and advisors believe that he has drowned. He was 30 years old.

Jeff's disappearance appears to be the result of swimming in a dangerous section of water that joins Memphis with the Mississippi River. Jeff and a friend, Keith Foti, were on their way to a local rehearsal studio where Jeff and his band were preparing to record a new album. After getting something to eat at a Memphis restaurant, Jeff and Keith stopped at the marina, where he had gone swimming on previous occasions. In a playful mood, Jeff entered the water fully clothed while laughing and singing, wading and swimming for approximately 15 minutes. Keith remained on the shore and in visual and vocal contact with Jeff.

When passing boats created waves, Keith momentarily turned away from Jeff to adjust the location of their portable radio/cassette player to prevent it from getting wet. At this point, Keith lost contact with Jeff and called out for him for 10 minutes before calling the police. Memphis authorities believe that an undertow caused by the passing boats swept Jeff away from his original location and, ultimately, underwater.

Memphis authorities have stated that there was no evidence of drugs or alcohol playing any part in this tragedy. Jeff's mother, Mary Guibert, and his managers, Dave Lory and George Stein, are urging everyone not to speculate beyond the facts of this incident or believe any rumors that might circulate. Additional information will be released as it becomes available.

-more-

COLUMBIA MEDIA DEPARTMENT

Press releases announcing Jeff's disappearance and presumed death.

There follows a short description of the events at the river. It ends with an appeal not to spread rumors and a quotation from Mary.

> *Memphis authorities have stated that there was no evidence of drugs or alcohol playing any part in this tragedy. Jeff's mother, Mary Guibert, and his managers, Dave Lory and George Stein, are urging everyone not to speculate beyond the facts of this incident or to believe any rumors that might circulate. Additional information will be released as it becomes available.*
>
> *According to Mary Guibert, "It has become apparent to me that my son will not be walking out of the river. It is now time to make plans to celebrate a life that was golden. I ask people who cared about Jeff to please be honorable and faithful to his memory, to send their best wishes to Jeff and to all of us who are mourning his passing."*
>
> *A memorial service is being planned, and appropriate details will be released in the next few weeks.*

We have to speak to the band and make arrangements for them to leave Jeff's house, as the press are camped outside and we definitely don't want them being hounded by the media. They are not happy. They want to stay here and grieve for their friend, but we tell them it is better for everybody, including themselves, if they are kept away from any press and crazy fans.[77]

My next onerous task is to meet with the police and the National Guard to discuss what might happen when Jeff is discovered. They have stations all along the banks of the river with white blankets ready to cover the body, if found. They have also set up a press area to keep the paparazzi in one location. They are really well organized. We have to make arrangements for an autopsy, the taking of DNA samples to protect his estate from any future paternity disputes, his cremation, and on and on. It is terrible, shitty stuff, calmly turning someone who has been such a huge presence into a logistical puzzle, something to be photographed, dissected, transported, and disposed of. I can feel my blood starting to run colder.

My good friend Danny Goldberg and his brilliant colleague Janet Billig keep me sane. They managed Nirvana together. They know what to do. They have been here. Danny is always "family first"; he calls me immediately when he hears of Jeff's disappearance to make sure my family and I are okay, and he calls every day for weeks to check that we are fine. He puts me on to Janet, who tells me about the DNA tests, and all kinds of things I would never have thought of. Danny tells me I am now "part of a club you never want to belong to. There are only a few of us, people who had to find out what to do when their rock star dies young and unexpectedly." He says I will get the call one day from another manager going through this. (I get that call just a few months later when Michael Hutchence from INXS commits suicide.)

I call Samantha and Abbo, and they say Katell is feeling a little better and they are keeping her in good spirits. They are flying to London on Sunday to begin the UK segment of the tour, and I am going to join them once we have found Jeff.

When Sunday morning comes, I realize it has been only two full days, but it feels like two years. All of us are pretty beaten up, and I am

[77] In fact, the band stayed in the house until Jeff's body was finally found, six days later.

starting to flag. Steve Berkowitz and I have breakfast together. He has already been down to the river, and Keith Foti has explained to him what happened. I am due to meet Foti and do the same after breakfast. I have to go to the bathroom. When I come back, Berkowitz says with a hopeful look, "Did you check your voicemail?"

We are both hoping, vainly, that Jeff has left a message saying he screwed up, that somehow he made it across the river, then went out that night and came back to find all the attention with the police, the helicopters, and he doesn't know what to do. It would be one of us he'd call, laughing, to confess to.

After breakfast, I go with Foti down to Wolf River Harbor, where Jeff had waded into the water. Foti goes through what happened yet one more time...

I feel sorry for him. He is still in shock and really worried about getting blamed, but we all know there was nothing more he could have done. I try to reassure him. I ask to be left alone for a minute, and he goes back to the car. I stand by the murky water and try to imagine looking at it as night falls and wanting to walk into it. I can't imagine anything I'd rather do less. I grew up next to the Missouri River. One day you could walk out and it would be five feet deep before dropping to thirty feet deep, and then the next day you could walk all the way with the water waist high. People who know the Mississippi and the Missouri know that they have terrible undercurrents that can quickly drag you under and that it's not uncommon even for the best of swimmers to get into trouble. No one who was brought up here would ever dream of going into this water.

"Jeff, you stupid fucking..." Tears begin to gush down my cheeks. I'm not sobbing; I just have water pouring out of me, as if something inside is trying to get to the river, to join it and escape.

Was he showing off to Foti? Trying to look cool to the new kid? Was it some kind of challenge to himself? A cry for attention, mistimed because there was nobody there who knew how to get him to stop? He'd been acting pretty strange these past few weeks; did he have no idea what he was doing? Did he zone off and forget he wasn't lying in the long grass in his front yard? Did he get caught in some weeds? Did he hit a freakish undertow? Christ, how long was he struggling out there?

Why wasn't I here? Why did he have to leave like this? Why couldn't he remember the way to the fucking studio?

I ask Jeff all these questions—out loud but into my chest, staring at the stones on the shoreline. I keep going round and round all the stuff I need to ask him.

"Man, that record was going to be good, really good. The songs were starting to sound great. Everyone was stoked about it. Why didn't you hang around? Why did you let everyone down? What the fuck were you thinking?"

And then I sense him, or at least I sense someone listening, someone interested in what I have to say. I look out at the water, half expecting Jeff to rise out of it, hair stuck to his head, his wickedest little boy grin on his face, his T-shirt soaking wet and Mississippi River mud slopping out of his boots.

"Dave! Did you miss me?"

I pick up the biggest stones on the shore and start hurling them into the water with all the fury that's rising in me. "How dare you leave me with this shit!" I shout, so loud I pull a muscle in my throat. I throw stones at the water as hard as I can. "Why, why, why?" ricochets around my head, and I start to heave with sobs. I feel like I am throwing everything we've done together into the river after him. "Here you are! Have it! Take this shit back! Vancouver! 'So Real'! *Grace*! 'Kanga Roo'! Olympia! Attitude! Fuck you! Here's your fucking parachute! You promised me you knew how to cross the road. We said we'd see this out together. I gave you my word. I told you I never take my hands off the wheel! What gave you the right to go and leave me stranded?!"

The irony isn't lost on me. Jeff, who grew up fearing rejection and people walking out on him, has shoved it back in all our faces. I cry for me and I cry for him. I cry for everyone who loved him. Everything I've bottled up these past few days drains into the river. The efficient robot I've been for the past seventy-two hours has turned back to aching flesh.

Foti is quietly listening to the radio when I get back to the car. I don't know whether he has heard me shouting.

"Okay, I'm done here," I say. Foti says nothing.

Back at the house we discuss what has to happen next. We decide that Gene will stay in Memphis until Jeff is found. Mary, Berkowitz,

George, and I will return to New York the next day, Monday, where George will take care of estate matters and Berkowitz and I will attend the idiotic marketing meeting at Sony that Donnie has scheduled, then I'll head back to London to be with Katell. She's alive; there is nothing more I can do in Memphis for Jeff. Gene will handle the final things here: identifying the body, packing up the studio and Jeff's belongings, and bringing his ashes to New York. We all feel awful. These meetings are the worst I've ever sat through, putting an end to the affairs of my client and friend. This is a bad dream.

• • • • •

I feel like shit the next morning on my way from the airport to 550 Madison Avenue, to sit in Sony president Donnie Ienner's office with Steve Berkowitz, Sony Music Entertainment chairman Tommy Mottola, and Sony Executive Vice President Michele Anthony.

I'll admit that by this point I have absolutely no faith in Columbia to do the right thing by Jeff. Before the meeting, I go around as many desks as I can to thank and support those who are in pieces over Jeff's death. Outside Donnie's office I see a copy of that week's *Billboard*, the trade publication. Someone has taken out a page ad with a photo of Jeff, the dates of his birth and death, and a line saying how much Columbia loved him. It is a photo that people there knew Jeff hated, and it makes me angry.

I walk into Donnie's office with a tightly clenched jaw. My resolve lasts about four seconds. I yell about why they'd called a meeting, why they'd chosen a picture Jeff hated, and why they think we can discuss future releases before we've even found his body. Donnie looks at me like I'm a kid having a tantrum. Or maybe he's seeing his raging style reflected back at him.

I shout for the better part of thirty minutes. It probably isn't the best strategy for getting Columbia on my side, but I don't care anymore.

Finally, Tommy Mottola speaks up. Tommy is the guy who discovered, developed, and married Mariah Carey, and two days before this meeting it was announced that their marriage was over. I expect he doesn't want to be in this room either, but he lays a steadying hand on the meeting and it sighs with relief.

Ad design for *Billboard* magazine.

After I leave Sony, I head over to my apartment to take a shower and re-pack for my trip back to the UK. I appreciate the quiet of the empty rooms. It is around 1 p.m. I never drink when I work, but as far as I am concerned, work is over for the day unless I suddenly get a call from Memphis. I am burnt out. So I pour myself two fingers of Jack Daniel's. Giving the pain the finger.

Without even thinking about it, because it's what I do when I come home, I go over to the answering machine and hit the playback button. The first few messages are nothing—the dry cleaner, a friend of Sam's—and then there's Jeff speaking: "Hi, Samantha and Charlotte. Hope you are both okay. Play the music, play it loud; love, Jeff." The timer has it at about fifteen minutes before he went out that evening. This may have been the last call he made.

And then there are all the messages from people calling to see what I know or see how I am. They go from, "Dave, I heard a rumor," to people just crying and screaming. From quizzical to hysterical. It is awful, crazy, the saddest parade you ever heard go by.

I pack my suitcase in a daze then go down to the Mercury Lounge, where my good friend Theresa books the bands. I walk into the bar and order a drink. Theresa sees me come in and runs up to me in tears. She gives me the biggest hug and tells the bartender my drink is on the house; in fact, she tells him to give me the biggest bottle of Jack they have. I tell her I am on my way to London and have some time to kill before heading to the airport. That big bottle of Jack whiles away the hours just fine, obliterating as much of the pain as possible. Then I'm standing in the airport, uncertain how I got there.

A day after landing in London, I am returning to the Royal Garden Hotel. It's Wednesday evening. "Mr. Lory?" says a girl at the front desk when I go to collect my key.

"Yeah?"

"I have a message for you."

She hands me a note. I unfold it.

"We found him. Call me. Gene."

CHAPTER 11

Last Goodbye

"Not all of me is dust
Within my song, safe from the worm,
My spirit will survive."
—Alexander Pushkin

JEFF'S BODY WAS FOUND AT 4:40 p.m. on June 4, 1997, near the mouth of Wolf River Harbor, at about the point where Beale Street meets Riverside Drive. Two workers on the American Queen, a riverboat leaving Beale Street Landing for a cruise to St. Louis, said a passenger saw what looked like a body in the water, and they had maneuvered it to the side of the harbor and called the police. At 7:19 p.m., Gene identified the body at the forensic medical center. The swollen face was practically unrecognizable, but the clothes were Jeff's and the gold beaded earring he wore in his navel was present.[78] His watch was still working. DNA samples were taken, as we had requested. Jeff's medical and dental records and recent x-rays were sent in to be conclusively matched with the body, so that no one could ever claim this was not Jeff Buckley.

[78] Gene told me that when he lifted the shirt to look at the navel ring, a ladybug flew out. The ladybug is a Native American symbol of peace.

It turned out there was a faint trace of alcohol, the equivalent of less than half a can of beer, found in his blood. There were no traces of any narcotics in his system.

Mary Guibert had asked that the body be cremated. Gene drove back to New York with the urn of ashes beside him in the Ryder rental van. He took it to a little wake at George's apartment, where the band gathered. I have no idea whether I attended that or not. I was so shattered by Jeff's death that I blanked out on much of what happened in the weeks following. That marketing meeting with Donnie about posthumous releases. I totally recall that being just days after Jeff disappeared, which is why I was so angry about it, and why I wrote it that way. But when I spoke to Steve Berkowitz recently, he said that, according to his diary, it was scheduled for two weeks later. There were two memorial services. They felt like a week apart, and I thought I went to one and not the other. In fact, they were a day apart and I attended both. When you lose someone you love, you inevitably walk around in a daze. When that person is someone you manage and you have to attend meetings and make decisions and tidy up a trail of loose ends, that daze is not helpful.

Because Jeff had wanted so little to do with his mother while he was alive, if there was any interaction between my office and Mary it was usually handled by Jack Bookbinder, who'd become the second-in-command at DE-EL Entertainment, after being with me for nine years. In the first forty-eight hours after Jeff's disappearance—when, admittedly, we were all confused—Mary had no idea who I was and assumed Jack was Jeff's manager. Actually, I had met her fleetingly before, at a gig in LA, when Jeff introduced us. When we met again, I was in efficient robot mode and informed her about the press release, told her that we needed a quotation from her and that we were assuming Jeff was dead. There were intakes of breath in the room. She was silent, but then dictated her dignified statement.

But the next few weeks were made more stressful by Mary, who was staying in Jeff's apartment, constantly getting on the phone demanding that stuff happen immediately, and managing to trample over things her son and I had carefully put in place. Somehow, she and I had to plan the memorial services together. But her requests became so bizarre—we'd made a list of artists who might like to appear, and she insisted I get

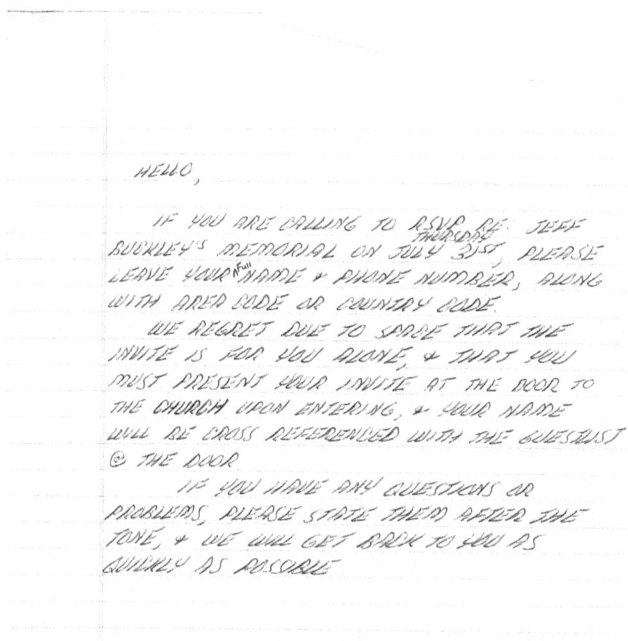

HELLO,

IF YOU ARE CALLING TO RSVP RE: JEFF BUCKLEY'S MEMORIAL ON THURSDAY JULY 31ST, PLEASE LEAVE YOUR FULL NAME + PHONE NUMBER, ALONG WITH AREA CODE OR COUNTRY CODE.

WE REGRET DUE TO SPACE THAT THE INVITE IS FOR YOU ALONE, + THAT YOU MUST PRESENT YOUR INVITE AT THE DOOR TO THE CHURCH UPON ENTERING, + YOUR NAME WILL BE CROSS REFERENCED WITH THE GUESTLIST @ THE DOOR.

IF YOU HAVE ANY QUESTIONS OR PROBLEMS, PLEASE STATE THEM AFTER THE TONE, + WE WILL GET BACK TO YOU AS QUICKLY AS POSSIBLE

Note written by Dave Lory on the plane from Memphis.

instant answers about their availability, and tell them they had to wear white suits and that she had to have approval of their lyrics; she ordered one thousand kazoos for people to use at the service, things that had nothing to do with Jeff's taste or personality as I understood it—that I decided to turn everything regarding the service over to Gene Bowen. It felt like Mom was trying to make up for lost time, and I didn't need to be part of it.

None of us wanted to make hasty decisions about the unreleased material. Steve Berkowitz and I listened to and logged everything, made copies of the cassette multi-tracks, and Andy Wallace mixed the Verlaine sessions. It wasn't until we'd done all these things that we could properly judge what material deserved to be made public, if any. But Mary was increasingly impatient.

Having called me regularly to check that I was okay, Danny Goldberg, who was now in charge of Mercury Records, said, after a few weeks, "I've had an idea that'll take your mind off all this." He flew me down to his summer place in Malibu and there he asked me to be the new VP of

International at Mercury. I accepted the job on the understanding that I would still be overseeing Jeff's affairs. We were still assessing his tapes when I started work at Mercury, later in the summer.

I was at my desk there when I was forwarded a fax from Mary's attorney. It said: "Effective immediately, you are no longer managing Jeff Buckley's affairs" and it asked for all further requests and business to be forwarded to Mary Guibert care of this guy. George Stein and Steve Berkowitz each received similar communications.

At first, I was furious. Then I felt a wave of relief. "At last, I don't have to think about him every single day. I don't have to fight for him anymore." (I was wrong about that.) But then I had a pang of panic. "What the hell is going to happen now? Mary has no idea what Jeff wanted to do." Of course, I had the utmost sympathy for her; losing the father of your child and then that child, both under tragic circumstances, is not something I'd wish on anyone. I didn't question her qualifications for taking on her son's estate, but I did wonder if she was getting the right advice, or was in the right frame of mind, so soon after her son's death, to assess the best path for his legacy. To completely sweep aside the people who had most to do with the career she was now going to steer seemed, at the very least, foolhardy.

After a few months, George and I became aware that Mary was making deals with Sony for forthcoming releases. Veteran A&R man Don DeVito had been hired to take over the project. Mary was taking advances from Sony and not paying me and George our commission. Our contract stated we were to be paid, in perpetuity, on anything Jeff wrote or recorded during the time we managed him and she wasn't honoring this. So we sued.

. . . . .

Samantha Way-Lory

I was absolutely stunned by the news of Jeff's disappearance. It was weird; I was immediately angry that he'd gone swimming. So annoyed. I was shell-shocked but I didn't see it as final. I just assumed, or hoped, that this was some awful mistake and he was going to turn up at some point. I do remember thinking, "How could you do something so stupid?"

I was trying to be supportive to Dave, when he called to tell me the news, but as soon as I put the phone down, I started bawling. I was very upset. I've no recollection of how I got to Dublin.

Somehow we got through the next weeks.

We all went out to Randall's Island in New York City to see Katell play at one point, and Mary was there. It was the first time I'd met her. She was full on, saying things like, "Charlotte is like the grandchild I never had." It was just peculiar. For someone who had just lost their son, she was so vital and free-spirited. I didn't see any grieving or tears or anything. She had just immersed herself in this role, and she was living it. I knew she and Jeff weren't that close, but this was someone who had just lost her son...so upbeat about everything, so busy in the land of the living and almost enjoying the attention. But I gave her the benefit of the doubt. You go through a tragedy like that, you can't possibly judge anyone unless you walk in their shoes.

We had all Jeff's belongings in our apartment for a while, and that was pretty depressing, seeing his furry coat hanging up in our wardrobe, before it was all sent to Mary. Dave was worn out and distressed by the whole thing. Mary wanted control, and that was that. It was all about her and what she wanted to do. It didn't matter who Dave or George was, or whoever. She stuck with Dave's assistant Jack Bookbinder and Gene Bowen. Shortly after Jeff had died, Dave was asked to go over to Mercury Records to run international there, so he was pretty wrapped up in his new job, but he really wasn't pleased about Jack and Gene. He understood why they needed to go with Mary, but he still felt betrayed.

Jeff Buckley has had a huge impact upon my life; he is responsible for a lot of things. Without him I wouldn't have had my daughters. It's rather nice that someone can have that big an effect upon you, to allow fate to play such a big part in your life. When I first met Dave, I knew he would be a big part of my life, as if I'd already known him for a very long time, and Jeff too. I'd love to have seen where his music would have gone. He would have been a long-term artist who went off on so many different tangents. I just so wish he was still around to fulfill all the promise that he had. The possibilities were endless.

Leah Reid

I'd stopped working at Columbia; I'd been working at Virgin Records for several months. I was at home. The phone rang; it was a former co-worker of mine at Columbia. He woke me up and said, "Leah, hi, I know you and I have never really seen eye to eye on things, but I wanted to call you up to let you know that Jeff Buckley's dead." I sat up and was like, "What?!" He basically told me what had happened, and I said, "So, he's *missing*..." and he goes, "Well, yeah." "So they just haven't found him." "Well, yeah." And I'm like, "Thank you for calling. Goodbye."

I thought, "This isn't happening; he's just missing." Because Jeff *would* go missing. And then I got to work, and my call list was already this long from all these people who had called me. And people were like, "Why are you here?" because they had heard. Then I couldn't do any work and somebody just told me I should go home. And I remember being in a full daze that day; I had no idea what was going on. I can't recall who else I spoke to. I think I talked to Gene at one point and realized that it might be more than just Jeff going on a walkabout.

It was about the time of the Tibetan Freedom Fest, which was in New York, and I felt that was where I needed to be, and my boss was like, "Absolutely, whatever you need. Go." So I went to New York, and I remember still being in a daze, and I got the news for sure on MTV or something, That's how I found out it was real. Anyone who knows Jeff can't be surprised at the way it happened. It was a very Jeff thing to do. Every single one of us who had spent time with him had been there when he'd done something stupid like that. He just lived for the moment, and I'm sure at that moment I might have done that too. What a beautiful moment that must have been, up until the point that it wasn't.

The private funeral was in a church in Orange County two weeks after he died. It was family. Steve Berkowitz and I were the only business-people, I think. Then there was the more public memorial in New York sometime later.

Mary spoke at the memorial. Rebecca did too; she read something and told a story of when they first met. Elvis Costello sang. Steve spoke and played "Opened Once," and that was supposed to be the only time that song was ever played, which I thought was a beautiful thing.

Every person who was lucky enough to have spent time with Jeff Buckley was a fortunate person. Those of us that he chose to spend more time with were even more fortunate. I'm glad that his musical legacy of *Grace* is still available for all to appreciate. People now say of artists, "He's the next Jeff Buckley," which is ironic, because we didn't have anyone to compare him to. I'd be curious to know what music he'd be making at this age. I wish he was still around.

Chris Dowd

My grandmother had just died. I'd flown to Arkansas from London, because I was living there at the time; I was in my first year or two of marriage, and Jeff was down in Memphis. He wanted me to come, and we were going to track "What Will You Say" for the album, and I was just like, "Dude!" My grandma had died, my uncle was sick with pancreatic cancer, my wife was pregnant, and while I was at my grandma's funeral she had complications with the pregnancy and had to be induced—all this horrible shit was happening to me, and Jeff got that and he didn't want to say to me, "Well, let me tell you about my record." He was sensitive to what was going on with me, but he wanted me to come and see him. He was very freaked out, because he had no idea how he was going to follow Grace, and it scared him. He was very frustrated. I think he had an idea what he wanted the record to be like, but when you're creating something it's such a no-man's-land.

I was kind of strapped after all these flights, and because he had done so much to help me after leaving Fishbone, I didn't want to impose myself by having him see me like this, and coming to Memphis, it just felt weird. "I can't Jeff. I love you, but right now I can't."

We spoke the day he died, the weirdest conversation I ever had with him. I just called him up, and he didn't recognize my voice. I was like, "Hey, man," and he was, "Who?" and I was really super excited because I'd just signed a new publishing deal and got my shit semi-together financially, and I was going to India and it was a trip we always said we would do together, and he didn't recognize my voice. So I said, "Dude, this is me,

Les Inrockuptibles cover, June 1997.

your best friend," and he was like, "No, my brother." I'm like, "Okay, your brother. What the fuck is going on? Are you okay?"

When you're on that edge, man—you're writing, you're so spiritually open—it puts you on the edge emotionally, because it's all coming up: your first kiss, falling down, shit your parents told you, every girl you ever loved, every lie you ever told. It's all pouring out of you at once, and it makes you very between two worlds. If you're an artist and you're worth anything, you're an amazing chef or you paint or you write, you'll go crazy to get that shit out. And there's a level at which you drive everybody else crazy, people who are around you, and you get weird. Does that make you suicidal and want to jump into the fucking Mississippi River? No. Does it make you stupid and susceptible to doing some dumb shit? Abso-fucking-lutely. My shit was to drink tequila till I passed out. Everybody's got something.

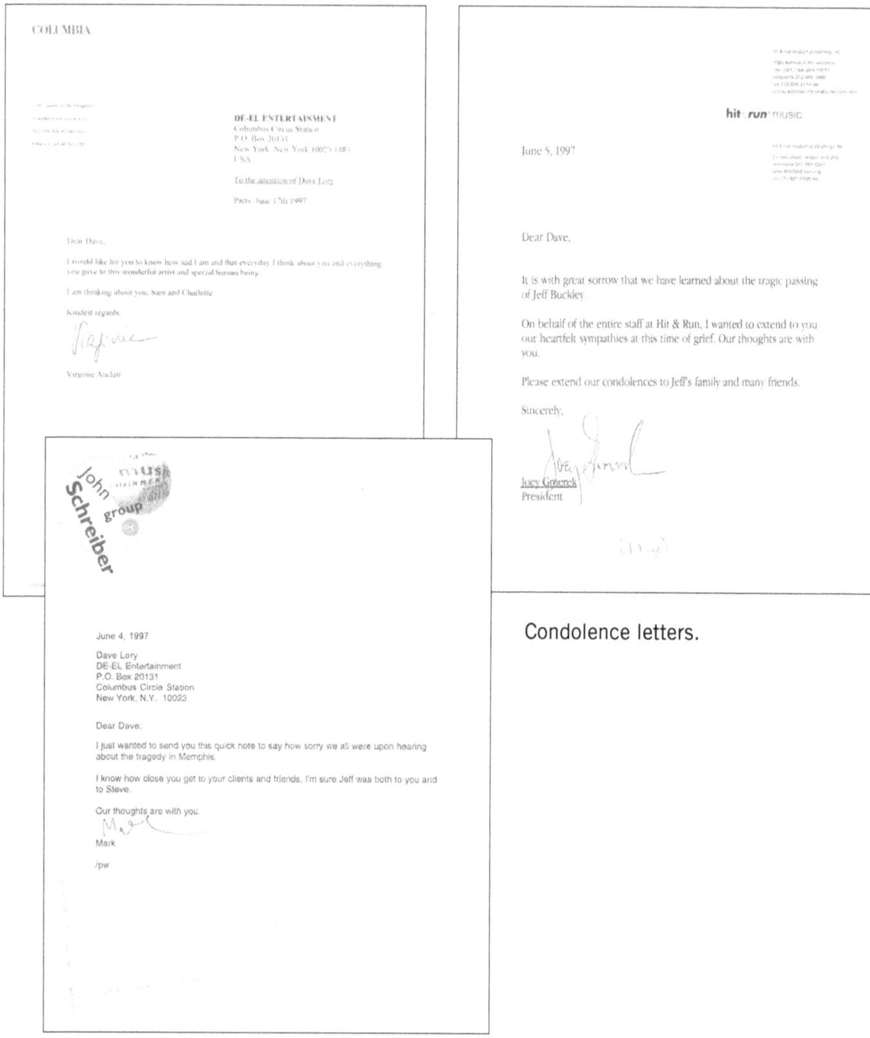

COLUMBIA

DE-EL ENTERTAINMENT
Columbus Circus Station
P.O. Box 20131
New York, New York 10023 1483
USA

To the attention of Dave Lory

Paris June 17th 1997

Dear Dave,

I would like for you to know how sad I am and that everyday I think about you and everything you gave to this wonderful artist and special human being.

I am thinking about you, Sam and Charlotte

Kindest regards,

Virginie Auclair

hit & run music

June 5, 1997

Dear Dave,

It is with great sorrow that we have learned about the tragic passing of Jeff Buckley.

On behalf of the entire staff at Hit & Run, I wanted to extend to you our heartfelt sympathies at this time of grief. Our thoughts are with you.

Please extend our condolences to Jeff's family and many friends.

Sincerely,

Joey Gmerek
President

John Schreiber group

June 4, 1997

Dave Lory
DE-EL Entertainment
P.O. Box 20131
Columbus Circle Station
New York, N.Y. 10023

Dear Dave:

I just wanted to send you this quick note to say how sorry we all were upon hearing about the tragedy in Memphis.

I know how close you get to your clients and friends. I'm sure Jeff was both to you and to Steve.

Our thoughts are with you.

Mark

/pw

Condolence letters.

Jeff did not kill himself; he was not that dude. He loved himself too fucking much, trust me. He really did. Were we young and careless? Absolutely.

Jeff had cleared all the bad shit out and dealt with everything and felt good, I'm telling you. My life is littered with Layne Staleys and Chris Cornells and Chester Benningtons. Music's a fucking blood sport.

Steve Berkowitz

I was home when Dave called me at night and told me that Jeff was in the river, and my old Panasonic answering machine malfunctioned and recorded the entire conversation, and I have it somewhere. Dave is shaking and his voice is cracking. I guess Gene had told him what had happened, and I'm in complete denial. "Come on, he just swam across. He's fucking around—wait, he'll come back."

My diary for May 29, 1997, has a heart with a line through it, a broken heart, and it says "Jeff Buckley vanishes."

I called Donnie Ienner at eleven or twelve at night. Next morning, I took a 6 a.m. flight to Memphis, found a taxi driver at the airport in an old 1963 Cadillac, and he took me out to Mud Island. And it was horrible. Like I was at the River Styx. I'm in Memphis at the Wolf River by this pyramid down in that space behind the Elvis statue, and there's steam coming off the fricking pyramid and they're dragging the river looking for my friend. It was horrible.

Later, I met with Keith Foti and got him to show me where they were and what had happened the day before, and I picked up some stones from exactly where Jeff had gone into the water.

Jeff was happy; there's no doubt about it. He had got to the point where now he knew he'd get to make this record and all his guys were going to be there. He was happy, and he went into the river and he was silly. Excited. Happy. It was dusk. It's deceptively wider than you think; people die there every year because they think they can swim to the island and it looks like it's fifty yards to the island and it's three hundred yards and there's a terrible undertow.

The guy went into the water happy but made a terrible mistake, and I miss him every day, as a person, as a friend, and also miss his tremendous ability and the idea of what he was going to make and going to become.

Jeff was a seeker, and he wanted to go beyond. He wanted to make a statement and make beautiful music, or scary stuff or emotional stuff. He wanted to find out the essence of what he was as an artist: "Am I any good? Can I summon it, and what the fuck's it going to mean?" In a way, like Miles, he wanted to keep going and feel free. "When did this music get made? What does it mean to me? What's it going to mean to anybody else? Is it different, is it new, is it interesting? Is it *badass*?"

Bud Snyder

It was just too surreal. I had gone with Gregg Allman to do a gig in Japan and, prior to leaving, I got all these photographs from Merri Cyr that she took at Criteria. She'd sent me these beautiful ten-by-eights, which I opened just before I left. I flew straight from Japan to Miami to do a gig with Jimmy Herring, Derek Trucks, and that whole band. We just do the one show, and afterwards me and Jimmy Herring are hanging out and I told him I'd just been to Japan, and he said, "I love Japan," and I said, "Yeah, I had a really great time there when I went with Jeff Buckley." And he looks at me and goes, "You know Jeff?" And he started telling me stories about when Jeff was at GIT. Jimmy had been a student there, and he did so well that they made him a teacher, and Jeff fell for Jimmy and would go over to Jimmy's house on a Friday and stay until Sunday, which was cool except Jimmy was married with a couple of kids. And his wife, who was a sweetheart, eventually had to say, "Jeff, this is the only time we get to see Jimmy!" Anyhow, Jimmy was saying to me how much he loved Jeff and next time I see him say hi, and to give Jeff his phone number. And I flew home from that, walked in the door, saw those pictures still out on my dining room table, where I had left them before flying to Japan, and the phone rang and it was Dave, telling me the news. It totally freaked me out. I felt the same way I felt when I was contacted and told that my son had died. Exactly the same way.

People who come to my studio are often influenced by the blues; they know about my relationship with the Allman Brothers and all of that. But what's been happening in the last year and a half is, I'm working with a whole new generation of musicians, and they'll do something and I'll hear Jeff in it. I can pick 'em out within an hour of meeting them, and I'll say, "So Jeff Buckley was an influence on your music," and they'll look at me and say, "You know Jeff Buckley?" and I'll point over to the picture of me and Jeff at Criteria—which I've put up in all my studios since he died—and they'll go, "Oh my god, you worked with him?" And now that word's starting to spread, I'm getting an amazing amount of work because of my relationship with Jeff. He's been a mammoth influence. All the college kids here in Sarasota, they're all Jeff Buckley fans.

Steve Abbott

I was last with him in the pub the night before he went to Memphis. We got hammered in Tom & Jerry's on Elizabeth Street, and I remember it clearly because there was a horse drinking Guinness from a bucket on the bar. You know, New York. And Jeff just started singing, a capella, playing drums on the table, all the horse songs he knew—"Horse With No Name," "Mustang Sally," and so on, a repertoire of about fifteen songs about horses, one after the other. And we proceeded to get hammered and sing along to the jukebox, and the last thing he said to me was, "I'm gonna make big, big changes when I get back. Big changes are going to happen; I'm really gonna do it this time." I read into those comments that he wanted to take the commercial pressure off and might need a different team around him. I don't think that would mean losing Dave, as he truly loved him, but he was kicking against the system that he had unwittingly fallen into. For Jeff, it was about making the music, and he derived the same pleasure from performing cover versions as he did his own songs. He wanted out of the rat race.

I do think, however, it was a case of "the sun is always brighter." I told him that Sony was not necessarily the enemy, but he wanted to be everything to everyone musically. It was hard on him going out on the Lower East Side and being surrounded by lesser musicians who wouldn't allow him into their club of coolness because he was signed to a major label. He was a dreamer; he almost hoped the deal would fall apart. He was determined to change something; he just wasn't happy.

But there was never any doubt in my mind about whether it might have been suicide. He just wasn't in that frame of mind. There was something selfish about him, but never that selfish. He knew there were a lot of people who wanted him to remain on the planet. I know he was looking forward to going to Memphis and recording.

Dave, Gene Bowen, and Jack Bookbinder were very tight and very, very protective of Jeff, and he realized that. The key to Dave's relationship with Jeff was that he was a constant. Jeff knew Dave was looking out for him, and Jeff didn't have many people looking out for him. Dave was a father figure to Jeff, without a doubt. George was a lawyer—a friend, but a lawyer. I was perhaps more the stepbrother, the fellow music fan. Dave was a music fan too, but in more of a business sense. Jeff and I were fans of wider, more obscure music. It was all part of a continual searching.

Dave was very good at figuring out the financial support, going on the road with the band. He'd been on the road a lot, and the road is where you can piss tons of money away, and the record company is happy to lend it to you 'cuz you're selling their record for them.

Dave and I went out and got hammered after Jeff's funeral. It was cathartic. We knew the memorial had been run in a way Jeff wouldn't have wanted...it was great, all the tributes and everything, but the subtext and the party afterwards—I suppose it was supposed to be a wake, but it was more like a party. They were giving away [guitar picks] with Jeff's name on them. In a way, it was sweet; a mum had lost her son and you can't be critical of it, but...

Dave and I locked up after that. People found out over the years that I had worked with Jeff Buckley, but it wasn't something I wore on my sleeve. If I heard someone listening to his music, I never said, "Oh, I used to be friends with this guy."

I met Dave again about four years ago in New York, and we had lunch and swapped stories about him, because we hadn't even talked to each other, and this jigsaw was being put together. I knew a big chunk of the story, and Dave knew a bigger chunk of the story, but knew him in a different manner. I knew how many pints he could drink before he had to go for a pee, or what the first song was he would put on the jukebox.[79] Dave could tell you other stuff, different details about Jeff. Our stories, when put into one, made for a pretty complete picture of someone that, despite all of our years working in and around music, probably will

[79] Abbo: "He was good for four pints of Guinness before he started getting silly. Around six and he was over for the night. During that time he would plug the jukebox with dimes and even picking the records became a performance for anyone in his presence: Vienna Boys Choir's 'Joy to the World' (which he sang along to note-perfect in the same key), Creedence Clearwater Revival's 'Lodi,' Van Morrison's 'Fair Play,' *James Brown Live at the Apollo* (the whole album), Mahalia Jackson's 'Satisfied Mind.'"

never have an equal for either of us in terms of raw talent and promise. That Buckley guy still is, simply, irreplaceable.

Reggie Griffith

One time we were in Detroit, on our way to Toronto, and got talking to this guy on the street who was a ticket taker at the Motown museum, and we spent the afternoon there. They'd play these hits and Jeff would sing along, not just Marvin Gaye's parts but Tammi Tyrell's parts too! Jeff said to me, "Wouldn't it have been cool to have been a fly on the wall and hear Trouble Man getting made?" He'd sing "Mercy Mercy Me" all the time.

When we got to Toronto, he bought all these Nusrat Fateh Ali Khan CDs, and we danced to them for about forty minutes in the middle of Toronto. Just out on the street. I was cool with that; I could do that.

Jeff carried himself as a character who was very soft-spoken. Even when he got excited, he wasn't boisterous. But he could be a fuck too. He was just some guy. It was the first touring job I'd had, but it turned out he was no different than Prince, Booker T. Jones, Kesha, other people I've worked with—they're all just people.

There was always a sense that Jeff had assembled this team of amateurs who were trying to be professionals. And I was part of that too. All of us—the band, everyone—were green, and he's going, "So who's gonna take care of me?" That was a frustration; he felt he was carrying people. With all due respect to everybody involved, they put it on him; everybody was thinking, "We're gonna ride this horse...this guy will be our golden goose." There was a sense of desperation behind it. I knew Jeff recognized that.

I got a Prince gig through a production manager. I was living at Paisley Park for a while and doing front of house there. It was during the time that he had stopped using his name. Once, when I was on a hiatus from Prince, I went to see Jeff on 12th Street and tell him what it was like, and I really got a sense from him of "I'm being expected to do this; I'm being expected to do that"—being everybody's golden goose.

When I went to the funeral in New York, I was with Katell, and I walked in and Mick came over and said, "Why are you here?!" and I felt like, "Wow, you've got issues."

Sara Silver

By the time we got to the end of the first record, I think he'd sold about one hundred fifty thousand albums across Europe, and we'd reached a tipping point where we knew he was destined to be successful, in the terms of that era. The whole machinery of success was turning. It was all about the next record. We were all talking about how things were going to move forward.

Then Dave called me with the news of his disappearance. It was a shockwave of monumental proportions. There was a lot of backtracking over the details of months gone by, and now something terrible had happened on the back of clowning about. It was the "disappearance but nothing confirmed" which was horrific, such a lonely act.

I couldn't stop thinking about him wading into the water; incredible sadness, the magnitude of who it was going to hit and affect—Dave, Sam, Jeff's family, everybody. It was absolutely, profoundly shocking.

As far as I remember, when we got the call that they'd found his body, everyone in the office just went home. You were at work, this is your job, not something personal, but we couldn't take it any other way. And I also thought, "Stupid boy!" I got angry. He had so much that he wanted to give; his lifetime as an artist had barely begun.

It was terrible, the marketing machinery that kicked in after his death. Someone has to look after the heritage, sure, but the whole thing [when Mary took charge] was just ridiculous, like watching a bad movie, so predictable and yet so tragic. The people who had nurtured this young artist should be the ones who participate in discussions afterwards, come together and try and do the right thing. Look at what happened to Prince. Every time somebody dies, you think, "What's going to happen now?" I didn't have the appetite to deal with what was going to happen. I didn't have any say in what happened in Europe after that. I had nothing further to do with it. I have never listened to the record again, and I change radio channels whenever "Hallelujah" comes on.

Merri Cyr

This guy from Sony called me, Steve Sussman, and told me Jeff was missing. I tried to leave a message on Jeff's answering machine. My first thought was that Jeff was fucking with people and had taken off. But I had this weird feeling. I rode my bike over to this girl I knew; she had this witch store and did tarot readings. I asked her, "Is he alive?" And she did a reading—I hate this; it sounds so corny—but the death card was right on top of the pack, and she just said, "He's dead." That was my affirmation. I rode this big old clunky red bike around Williamsburg, crying.

I went to the memorial at St. Ann's and hung up a bunch of pictures there. Mary looked like she was having a blast; she was finally in control of everything.

I took photos. I couldn't help it. That's what I did with Jeff, how we worked together. It seemed right that I should take photos at the last performance. But he wasn't there. It was just his mother. I threw those rolls of film in the garbage.

The best thing about Jeff was watching him perform live, by himself. There were things he could do that he couldn't do when he was with the band. Just watching him alone, tearing up different songs. There was that one day when I saw an in-store, a radio show, and a live show. That was freaking amazing; he played the same song three totally different ways in three sets in the same day, and every one was really good.

I remember talking to Jeff when Kurt Cobain died, and he said, "Do you think I'm similar to him? Is my music similar?" And at that time I didn't want him to be relating to Kurt Cobain that much, who'd just blown his head off, you know, so I said, "No, I think you're a lot different than him." But they were similar in some respects. Cobain was nihilistic in an overt way, but Jeff's self-annihilation in his music was just filtered through this terribly romanticized veil. Jeff was presenting things in more of a controlled way.

Jeff was a different idea. He admired the garage band sensibility, Shudder to Think and all that, but he wasn't like that. He definitely wanted to be famous, but he had a lot of integrity; he wanted to be famous for his music. Stars today are branded; they're known for everything: singer, actor, model, perfume. Jeff was nothing like that. He'd say, "Why do I have to waste my fucking time doing that stuff?" about a fashion ad or something. He was only interested in making music. He turned down a lot of things. Every relationship he ever had, he undertook somehow with the music in mind. He'd make trouble so that he could write a song about it.

His life was Oedipal, losing and regaining the kingdom; he was living out a mythological existence. Because he was a control freak, he was going to be in control of that myth, and I think I was engaged as part of that mythologizing. As much as I wanted to kill him half the time, I did love him very much. I never met anybody else like him before or since. He collaborated in the photography. He always said yes. He wanted to participate in making good art. He was my muse; he volunteered for the job, and I said yes. I tried as hard as I could to make art out of him.

He said to me once, "We're together doing this now, but you don't own me." That experience was right in the moment, and there was no obligation before or afterwards. People didn't know what just happened to them...you were the center of the universe and then he's gone and he never calls you again. "What did I do?" I've had people ask me that. I found out after he died that other people seemed to know a different guy than I did.

In tarot there's a symbol for a magician; he's holding up a wand and electricity is coming from the sky down through his body, and it's something akin to being a conduit as opposed to being in control of energy. Jeff was the conduit for this energy, and then it would come out into this audience. I don't think that's how he saw it, but that's how I saw him, as a conduit to an energy greater than himself. He felt he was the creator of whatever it was that was coming through him, more conjurer than conduit. But I definitely felt some kind of divine energy coming down as well, because it was bigger than him.

Andy Wallace

Jeff was careless—he was definitely the kind of guy who'd ride a motorcycle without a helmet—but I didn't feel he was ever flirting with self-destruction. I never thought, "It figures" regarding Jeff's death. If you want to talk out-of-control recklessness, there was Shannon Hoon from Blind Melon. That was an occasion where I couldn't say I was shocked, but with Jeff I didn't see that coming at all. He wasn't reckless when he was with me. I was there to interact with him for a specific purpose, and I had the ability to keep him focused and keep him working.

He was never a problem in the studio. He never showed up drunk or so out of it he wasn't able to perform. He liked to drink but didn't let it intrude, and I was shocked when I heard he'd been taking drugs toward the end of his life. I didn't have any contact with him between finishing making *Grace* and when I turned up in Memphis. I didn't see any of that in Memphis; he seemed very sober to me there. Jeff felt Dave had his back out there on the road. Jeff had a tendency to get a little distracted, showing up late for things and what have you, and Dave could reel him in and keep him on point.

Steve Berkowitz got me on board to do *Sketches for My Sweetheart the Drunk*. I don't know when he was removed from the project, but I do know that there was an altercation, and Mary butted heads with both Steve and Dave. I guess it happened after I'd finished mixing.

When I finally heard the material from the Verlaine sessions, I was surprised how good the production was. Based on what Jeff had said about them, I'd not expected those recordings to be as good as they were. I'd had the impression, without having heard them, that they [would be sloppy] or incomplete. But they were well done; there weren't missing parts, verses without lyrics, that sort of thing. They were good recordings which, for whatever reason, didn't result in what Jeff wanted to hear. Maybe if you know *Grace*, those songs are a little bit harder to get cozy with, darker and not as beautiful, but still [made for] a cool album, so ultimately I felt they should be released. Because I loved the songs, I felt cheated. I would have loved to have produced those songs from the ground up.

There's a line in one of the *Sweetheart* songs—is it "Morning Theft"?—that goes, "I miss my beautiful friend," and whenever I hear it I feel the same. I miss my beautiful friend.

Matt Johnson

I was visiting my family home in Texas, and I heard the news twenty-four hours after he died. My mum had a guest over both nights, and I went and told them about it and this woman said, "Don't you remember what you talked about last night at around this time?" I'd been staring at the river near my parents' house for about an hour, watching the water and sitting thinking about how music and water relate to each other, how the way it moves is like sitting in a musical space, and I came in and told my mom and her friend about it. And so the following night when I heard the news about Jeff, she reminded me: "Isn't it interesting that at the exact time he went missing, you were sitting here telling us all that stuff about the river?"

I drove up to Memphis to be with Gene and Parker and Joan and the others. We hung out there and Jeff's mom came. I was there a couple of days. At one point, Michael and I went up into the attic and we came across this little shrine up there, all these Santeria [items]—little human-shaped candles that you find in Caribbean religious stores. It felt like the attic was a place where he was exploring solitude.

There's that photograph of him going to purchase a car on the day he died, and the look on his face was quite remote, and I knew that look. I think he had a lot of reasons to feel alienated and dissociated: the experience of touring over the last few years without a consistent home, [plus] he'd left New York, he was living in a new city, he was being made into a media figure, he was becoming famous, he had been using drugs, he had the constant shadow of his father—all might have contributed to some instability of his psyche, an element of overall subversion of his mental health.

He had a Dada side to him; he valued absurdity and obscurity, trying to search for inspiration from randomness and meaninglessness. If you add all that, you can imagine seeing a topsy-turvy world where it's kind of easy to fall into a degree of insanity. For someone who was so sensitive and so aware, it's almost inevitable that he would encounter mental struggles.

Jeff was a pattern interrupt, somebody who broke the mold. If he had a mission, it seemed to do with having a very clear sense of the potential of reaching people and having an emotional or spiritual experience in a room, in a musical situation. He had insight into what's possible in music, what music can catalyze. He was intoxicated with that.

Jeff made me. The experience of playing with him was like basic training and then activity in a theater of war. There were so many things I had to wake up about to be a musician that is worth playing with. In order to play with him, I had to confront my deficiencies on a daily basis, and that was extremely painful and there was no escaping from it. Jeff showed me how to get better; he showed me what is worth getting better at.

My respect for Jeff is of the highest order. I feel like he's family, part of my psyche. I love him and I carry my memories of him with me at all times.

• • • • •

The lawsuit between me and George, Mary, and Sony dragged on for years. My job with Mercury turned into a job with Danny Goldberg's new label, Artemis, in 1999. My career was on a roll, things were great at home, but I couldn't get the whole issue of Jeff and his legacy out of my head. Such a major piece of unfinished business—on so many levels—will play on you, give you that feeling that you've left your house without closing the door, twenty-four hours a day. It was affecting my health. And Sam, of course, was in a similar state of mind. She had been close to Jeff too.

In the summer of 1999, while we were visiting Sam's family in England, somebody suggested she see a local woman who had a reputation as a psychic. Sam was open-minded about that kind of thing, enjoyed it, and was happy to try anything that might help make sense of what we were feeling. I was open to anything to get rid of the emotional tug-of-war I was dealing with regarding Jeff and his legacy, but I believed all psychics were charlatans. We pulled up to this unremarkable suburban house near Sam's childhood home in Colchester, Essex, and this woman invited us in and offered us tea and cookies. I was still dubious, so Sam went and sat with her on her own.

An hour later, she came out and said that the psychic had summoned up my dad, Robert, and he was saying how pleased he was to see us married. This woman had no foreknowledge of us at all, as far as I'm aware, but I know a little bit about how these "cold readings" work. A magician friend once told me all about mind-reading acts and how so-called psychics will manipulate customers into giving away information, and then let their gullibility fill in all the blanks, believing the psychic has a gift. It's mental conjuring, a different kind of suspension of disbelief. So when Sam came out and said my dad had been on the line, I didn't know whether to laugh or be angry. But I was intrigued to see this woman's act, so I went in and sat with her. She asked me if I had anything belonging to a deceased person. I was wearing Jeff's bracelet, the one I had rescued so often that he eventually gave it to me. She held it for a few moments and said, unbidden: "I'm seeing someone with the initials JB." I was shocked. Could she have known who I was? I don't think so. It got weirder.

"There's a lot of water. Was his death something to do with water?"

"Yes," I said.

"He drowned, didn't he? He was a young man and he drowned."

"Yes," I said. I was purposefully trying to give nothing else away.

"Well, there's something he'd like to tell you," she said. "He didn't mean to do it, but he didn't fight it."

I felt sick. She started to talk about things only Jeff and I knew, like certain conversations or events during our time together. She mentioned parachutes and "attitude" and asked if my lung was okay. I sat there saying as little as possible but feeling very peculiar.

"And he also says he's happy, everything's fine, he's in a good place, and he doesn't blame you for anything, and he wants you to move on."

I came out of there reeling. I was told subsequently that psychics almost always say this last sentence. It's what all grieving people need to hear. It was definitely what I needed to hear.

When we got back to the US, I decided to settle the lawsuit. I just wanted this bad dream to end. I was going to agree to give up my right to a percentage of Jeff's income in perpetuity. But I was making a six-figure salary and was in a good state financially; I didn't need lawyers bugging me any longer. I wanted to get on with my life.

We were in George Stein's conference room with all our attorneys present when I announced I was going to settle. George went nuts. He stood up and said, "I broke Jeff Buckley, and I am getting paid in perpetuity!" He also said that I'd got something out of working with Jeff—meaning my new career with Mercury and Artemis—and he'd got nothing. I got angry and told George that he did not "break Jeff Buckley." Jeff Buckley broke Jeff Buckley. And George certainly wasn't the one who had traveled with him worldwide dealing with all the Columbia affiliates and the media. That was the last time George and I ever spoke. I have no idea if he ever settled or not. He didn't answer a request to be interviewed for this book.

I finally sent all the boxes of Jeff's effects—the papers, the journals, and clothes—to Mary and hand-delivered all the live tapes, audio, and video to Sony. I was paid something like ninety thousand dollars by Jeff's estate as a settlement and had to pay eighty thousand dollars to my attorneys. I painted my house and called it a day.

Late one evening, just days after delivering everything back to Sony, I was hailing a cab back to Worldwide Plaza when I noticed that Jeff's bracelet was missing from my wrist. It made sense. I felt something leave me. I decided to walk home, as tears began streaming down my face.

As I walked through the city Jeff had loved, I thought about all that we had been through together and all that changed since he left us: my new job, my new family, the friendships that had strengthened, or fallen apart, the deep pain and intense joys. And, finally freed from the weight of my time with Jeff, I pondered why we had put ourselves through it all. A warm autumn rain started to fall on me, and I realized I already knew the answer. I heard Jeff saying it one last time: "It's about the music, stupid."

Jeff Buckley

Interview for Grace EPK, February 1994

I was captured by music at a really early age. I was really captured by it, everything about it. It was my mother. It was my father. It was my plaything. It was the best thing in my life. That had no face or name or body. And I wanted to be able to transmit that sort of feeling, that's all...

What do I want from the music? I want to get away from this whole thing. I just want to leave. I want to go someplace completely else. I want to forget what my name is.

Music is endless. And even though I've heard a whole bunch of music from so many different places and fallen in love countless times with all kinds of music, there is still something; somewhere there's just a vibe that's completely mine and whoever's playing with me. I guess it's called freedom. Some other place. Like where you dream.

Acknowledgments

I'D LIKE TO THANK some people without whom this book would not have happened:

To my parents, Robert and Emerita Lory. Both of you were so supportive when I made the decision not to attend college and become a full-time musician. May you rest in peace. Also to my brothers, Mike and Chris, and my sister, Jennifer, thanks for enduring the loud days of my playing the drums at home and driving you all crazy.

My wife, Samantha, the most important person in my life. You have put up with a lot of my crap over the years, and raised our beautiful daughters mostly by yourself while I was traveling the world during the "glory" days of the music business. Our daughters have become incredible young women thanks to you. You are the glue in my life, and I wouldn't be the same without you. All my love, and thank you from the bottom of my heart.

To Charlotte and Lily, my greatest joy. I can claim I got at least two things right in my life, having you as my daughters. May all your dreams come true. I love you both very much.

To all the Sony and Columbia personnel worldwide for their hard work and support—you know who you are; especially Tommy Mottola, Michele Anthony, Donnie Ienner, Missy Worth (my rock), Steve Berkowitz (without you, none of the music would have come out the way it did; thanks for making it happen and your daily guidance), Leah Reid (our quarterback who made everything come together), Julie Borchard (thanks for the world), Richard Ogden, Sara Silver (Europe was a piece of cake with you on board), Howard Wuelfing and Larry Jenkins (having you with me during the disappearance meant the world, thanks), Tom Corson, Paul Rappaport, Jon Cohen, Tom Aaron, John Ingrassia, Richard Rowe, Kerry McCarthey, Kip Krones, David Bower, Denis Handlin, Greg Johnson, Ed St. John, Virginie Auclair, Sophie Zannettacci, Greg Linn, Geordie Gillespie, Lee Rolontz, and all the others, too many to list. I enjoyed the ride with all of you.

Thanks to our booking agents, Emma Banks and Don Muller, and all the promoters worldwide, especially Michael Chugg, who allowed Jeff to take his music to the world.

Abbo, Linda, Frank, and Jacqui at Big Cat records for breaking Jeff in the UK and Europe. Without you, Jeff would not have had the career he had overseas.

Thanks to Merri Cyr for the photos. Good luck on your photo book on Jeff due out in 2019.

The team at Worldwide Entertainment, Becky Yeagle, Jack Bookbinder, and Gene Bowen for your hard work over many years together.

Personally, I'd be nowhere without the following mentors:

Richard Broderick, who ran the music business program at New York University, and was a father to me after mine passed away.

Danny Goldberg, who showed me the utmost respect when we managed the Allman Brothers Band together, taught me that artists always come first, and offered me some great jobs. I loved being senior vice president of stuff at Artemis Records.

My deepest thanks to Janet Billig, for her support after Jeff's disappearance. Without your experience in dealing with Kurt Cobain, I'd never have known what to do during that hideous time.

Tom Silverman for hiring me to work the New Music Seminar—a special time in the New York music scene that will never happen again. Thanks for letting me be a part of it.

Linda Moran! I was fortunate enough to have you call me one of your boys. Your advice and tough love, wisdom, and insight showed me things I could never have learned on my own. You and Michael were also there when things were tough. All my love to you both for your support throughout the years.

To Jim Irvin, my co-author. Your hard work, dedication, research, interviews, and musical knowledge made the events and timeline as real and as truthful as possible. It was a joy working with you on this, and now our friendship has grown much more as a result. It was a tough couple of years writing this book with me beating cancer, my mother going into a home, and your father passing away, but we saw it through! Deepest thanks from one music lifer to another!

To Simon Green, my agent at CAA. You told me at the beginning of this journey that I was not the manager any longer; you were, and I was now the artist. You remained steady and positive until we finally got the deal. I could not have made this journey without you, thank you a thousandfold! Also Rob Light, the head of CAA and an industry friend for decades. I will never forget your call with me and when I talked to you about the possibility of writing this book, you told me, "I want to read that book."

Thank you, Professor David Philp, Doctor Marcone, Rachel Miller, and the students at William Patterson University for your marketing efforts, along with Maggie Poulas, my publicist at Mixtape Media and Bernard Doherty at LD Communications, in making this book a success.

Last, but not least, I want to thank my publisher, Anthony Ziccardi, and Billie Brownell, Devon Brown, Madeline Sturgeon, and the staff at Post Hill Press for your encouragement, excitement, passion, and direction with this book. Thanks for believing in me.

Special thanks to all who participated in the interviews in this book. Together, we were privileged to work with and witness one of the most magical and talented artists of all time, and I am so glad to have been there with each and every one of you.

—Dave Lory

I DEDICATE MY WORK in this book to my parents, with much love. My father, Larry Irvin, died in the summer before it was completed. His support and approval were always so important to me. Dad, I miss you more than I can say. To my mum, Jo Irvin, your love and support, and your voracious appetite for books and writing, have always inspired me. Thank you.

My love and deepest gratitude go out to my partner, Sally. Thank you so much for providing the time and space to let this project happen and for your encouragement, insight and valuable input along the way. Love also to my beautiful son, Baxter, for being a constant joy. I loved having you hang out in the room while I was writing. No, really!

I'd like to reiterate Dave's sincere thanks to everyone who took part in the interviews for the book. I enjoyed meeting and talking to you all and hope you enjoy the result. To Anthony Ziccardi, Billie Brownell, and all at Post Hill Press and especially to Simon Green at CAA, thank you for your encouragement, enthusiasm, and understanding. Thank you, Elena Vega, for your excellent editing.

Special thanks to: Martin Aston, for permission to reprint the historic first interview with Jeff Buckley; Steve Cummins, for permission to use the interview with Michael Murphy; my former *Mojo* colleague, Barney Hoskyns, for steering me toward this project in the first place; and Danny Eccleston for some typically insightful comments on the first draft.

Finally, but crucially, I must thank Dave Lory for being such a source of energy, insight, commitment against the odds, and far too many salty anecdotes than we could use. Dave, you are a true original. Thank you for trusting me as your conduit for this story, which I know means so much to you, for answering my endless, ridiculously picky questions, and for your warm hospitality in New Jersey.

It has been an honor and a blast.

—*Jim Irvin*

The authors would like to thank the following people who purchased the book in advance through Pledge Music: Dominic Pandiscia, Debra, Jared, David Bradley, Paige, Edward Kaulfers, Scott, Donna Breault, Mark Dunn, Dale Black, Jill Partin, Lewis Stark, Pamela Henning, Mark Potter, Gary Trotter, Paul Lory, Joe Rubalcaba, Curt Sauter, Lisa L. Arnold, Coco, Brandon Ratten, Aidan Thompson, Bart, Wilfred Bekker, Trent Nielsen, Tatsuhiko Inokuchi, and Sutjahjo Ngaserin.

About the Authors

Dave Lory has worked in entertainment for over 35 years. Starting as a drummer and tour-manager, he rose to becoming a respected artist manager, record executive, and event producer working in rock, country, and rap. Apart from Jeff Buckley, Lory helped guide the careers of the Allman Brothers, Courtney Love, and Duncan Sheik. As an executive at Mercury and Artemis Records, he worked with Bon Jovi, KISS, Shania Twain, Def Jam, and Warren Zevon. His event productions include the New Music Seminar and the Songwriters Hall of Fame Awards. He was a founding member of the Music Managers' Forum and has lectured in music business at William Patterson University and New York University.

Jim Irvin, born and raised in west London, began his career in music as singer in UK indie band Furniture throughout the 1980s. In 1990, he switched to music journalism and became the founding features editor of *MOJO* magazine in 1994, where he first met, reviewed, and wrote about Jeff Buckley. He wrote acclaimed pieces on Radiohead, Talk Talk, and Sandy Denny, edited *The MOJO Collection*, a compendium of classic albums, and commissioned *MOJO*'s own book imprint. Although he continues to contribute to various publications, Jim returned to full-time songwriting in 2001 and has collaborated with artists including Lana Del Rey, Lissie, David Guetta, Gavin DeGraw, Anne-Marie, and Nothing But Thieves.

www.ingramcontent.com/pod-product-compliance
Lightning Source LLC
LaVergne TN
LVHW021540220826
846316LV00043B/1091